AF538474

Between Amateur and Aesthete

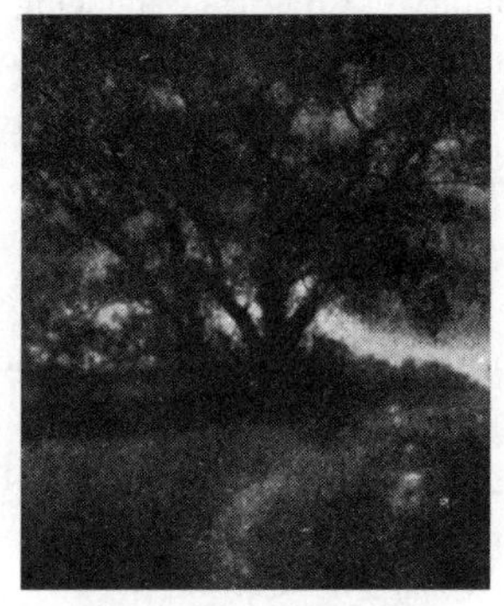

Between Amateur and Aesthete:

The Legitimization of Photography as Art in America, 1880–1900

PAUL SPENCER STERNBERGER

University of New Mexico Press ▲ Albuquerque

First edition
Library of Congress Cataloging-in-Publication Data
Sternberger, Paul Spencer, 1966–
Between amateur and aesthete: the legitimization of photography as art in America, 1880–1900 /
Paul Spencer Sternberger.—1st ed.
p. cm.
Includes bibliographical references (p.) and index.
ISBN 0-8263-2151-8 (cloth: alk. paper)
1. Photography, Artistic—Philosophy. 2. Landscape photography—United States—History—19th century. 3. Art and photography—United States. I. Title.
TR642 .S83 2001
770'.973'09034—dc21

Contents

List of Illustrations

Acknowledgments

Over the course of this study I have been fortunate in receiving support from a number of institutions, including a Smithsonian Predoctoral Fellowship at the National Museum of American Art, a Samuel H. Kress Foundation Dissertation Fellowship in Art History, a Mrs. Giles Whiting Foundation Fellowship, Henry Luce Traveling Fellowships, and Columbia University President's Fellowships. I would like to convey special thanks to the Library Company of Philadelphia, not only for an Andrew J. Mellon Foundation Research Fellowship in American History and Culture but also for their generous and liberal reproduction policies. The vast majority of the illustrations from nineteenth-century photographic journals used to illustrate this book were reproduced from volumes in their collection.

Barbara Novak has been a nurturing mentor from the beginning of my time at Columbia University, and I attribute to her scholarly enthusiasm my choice to investigate American art. Her staunch advocacy of her students earns her our unflinching fidelity. Like Professor Novak, Johanna Drucker has never hesitated to provide encouragement and advice, both scholarly and practical. Her remarkable dedication to her students serves as a model for me in my own teaching career. I would also like to express my sincere gratitude to Annette Blaugrund, Ella Foshay, and Jonathan Crary for their insightful suggestions in the later stages of this study.

I dedicate this study to the memory of my father, and to my mother, who finally learned to stop asking when I was going to finish my book. Finally, I wish to express my deepest appreciation and love to my wife, Joan Cummins, whose patient editing is but one of many invaluable ways she has helped me get through this project.

Introduction

Rather would I die, than to give up my faith in the ability of photography to produce works of art.

—Edward Livingston Wilson, "The Dignity of Photographic Art"

This book focuses on radical changes in the practice and theory of photography and discussions of its status as art. The two critical decades of these changes, 1880–1900, are framed by two of the most crucial moments in the history of the medium: the introduction of the amateur camera and the institutionalization of art photography.[1] The investigation historicizes debate over photography's claim to artistic legitimacy, studying the strategies employed by American writers and photographers in their attempts to elevate photography to the status of the traditional arts. It examines the contemporary journals in which photographers theorized artistic practice and the photographic pictures they took to be validations of the medium's claim to a position among the fine arts.

Faced with the condemnation of photography as inherently inartistic because of its apparently mechanical and chemical nature, a burgeoning class of amateur photographers strove to construct a place for photography among the pantheon of the traditional arts. The establishment of this artistic space for photography is not the natural, linear evolution that many historical paradigms suggest but rather an intricate, divergent, often passionately conflicting barrage of strategies. Photographers and writers drew upon sanctioned artistic traditions, both denying and exploiting the unique characteristics of the photographic medium, and ultimately, they restructured photographic practice and the institutional establishments associated with photography.

While the theories addressed in this study were often applied to photography in general, and I will sometimes refer to portraiture and genre photography, the primary focus of this study is on landscape photography, a focus motivated by several factors. Unlike portraiture which, when pursued professionally in America, was subject to a strong influence of patrons' concepts of fashion and egotism, landscape photography afforded many photographers more opportunity to assert their own agency. The compositional conventions drawn from the traditional arts were especially applicable to landscape, as were impressionist and naturalistic theories. In addition, many of the progressive foreign models in which American photographers found inspiration, such as the English Brotherhood of the Linked Ring, predominantly pursued landscape photography. Finally, because this study centers on America, landscape photography is especially meaningful, for it allows me to place legitimizing strategies within the context of American culture in general and within a larger American landscape tradition as well.

The primary sources of texts and images examined for this project are the major, yet understudied, American photographic journals of the late nineteenth century, among them the *American Amateur Photographer*, the *American Journal of Photography*, *Anthony's Photographic Bulletin*, the *Philadelphia Photographer*, *Photographic Mosaics*, *Photographic Times*, and *Wilson's Photographic Magazine*. For the most part, I do not rely on *Camera Notes* and *Camera Work*, which are already well studied and in fact do not give a sense of the full range of legitimizing strategies wielded in the 1880s and 1890s. The other journals present texts that were disseminated widely and the images that received broad reproduction, especially as the half-tone process enabled the inclusion of more and more illustrations. These publications reached the majority of serious American photographers, both amateur and professional. Over the course of the 1880s and 1890s, the journals became the forum for discourses on photography as art, and the body of literature on art photography increased yearly, providing the art-minded American photographer with an ever-growing variety of devices to incorporate in the quest for photography as art. By the end of the 1880s, the legitimization of photography became an increasingly popular topic in the photographic literature.

The Denial of Photography as Art

The denial of photography's claims to art status came from a number of camps, but whatever the source, it most often centered upon photography's apparent creative distance from the hand of the operator. This rejection of photography as a fine art was especially irksome to photographers when it came from artists in the accepted arts. The painter William Hart's comment that "the imitative faculty . . . is an important element in the artist, but one that is of small value compared to the creative faculty," was a point frequently used to malign photography, which was often considered a mere imitator.[2] The most infamous artist-critic to deny photography a place among the fine arts is the Philadelphia-born graphic artist Joseph Pennell. Pennell argued vehemently in the late 1890s that photography was not an art and that it had not even made any contributions to the established arts.[3] The photographic medium was accused of being too deeply based in optics and chemistry to allow the plasticity necessary for the creative investment that critics believed was the fundamental basis of art.[4]

Art-minded photographers faced a vexing paradox: their medium seemed indexical, relating directly to the object, but art critics demanded the iconic, an object translated by the artist.[5] For the art photographer, the supposed transparency of the photographic record was quite troublesome, for this apparently objective record seemed more akin to the production of the scientist than to that of the artist. Photography's adherence to the laws of optics and chemistry appeared incongruous with art, creating a troubling relationship that was the subject of much debate.[6] Bridled with a process of representation that did indeed seem more distanced from the hand of the artist than other traditional media and facing recurrent criticism that photography was too scientifically transparent to allow artistic production, champions of artistic photography sought to identify the means by which the photographer's creative intellect was reflected in the picture-making process.

Within my investigation of the struggle to legitimize photography as art, I will at several points fall back on three significant voices of dissent. These denials are the most telling, for they come from within photography's own ranks, and they underscore the pervasiveness and persuasiveness of the resistance to photography's claims to art status.

Some of the most promising proponents of art photography are precisely those who end up being the most adamant in denying photography's claim to art status. Three gifted photographers who had mastered the technical and aesthetic sides of their medium nonetheless concluded that photography could never be a fine art. Each affirmed strategies of legitimization only to turn and voice dissent, and each illuminated the strategies employed to legitimize photography as art in a particular way. The first is John Moran, brother of Thomas Moran, the famous American landscape painter. John Moran was a highly skilled photographer, well trained in the traditions of art. In the 1860s, he enthusiastically embraced photography as an artistic medium, and he presented early examples of concepts of artistic infusion and compositional convention. But over the course of years of practice, Moran slowly came to the conclusion that photography could not offer the artist a means of creative expression, and he eschewed photography in favor of painting. The second voice of dissent is William James Stillman's, an accomplished painter, a remarkable photographer, and a prolific writer who remained unwilling to admit photography to the realm of the fine arts.[7] An American who studied with Ruskin and traveled extensively, Stillman was an eloquent photographer who combined technical mastery with a highly artistic eye. Stillman was a staunch supporter of fidelity to characteristics he believed were inherent to the photographic medium, and he also produced some of the most bilious responses to photographers' claims to artist status. The final photographer is the oft-studied Englishman Peter Henry Emerson. Through his naturalistic photography, Emerson offered theories on photography's art capacity based on goals grounded in positivist perceptual science. Emerson abruptly denounced photography's ability to produce art when he found the medium was not as plastic as he believed. Despite his recantation of naturalistic photography, both Emerson's theory and the formal effects of his photographs inspired countless photographers on both sides of the Atlantic.

Strategies of Legitimization

The first chapter of this study examines a legitimizing strategy that appeals to traditional art through compositional tropes. Faced with recurrent criticism that photography did not merit the title "art" because of its dependence on seemingly unmediated chemical and optical processes, its reputation for objectivity, and its supposed distance from the hand of the artist, many American writers attempted to elevate the medium into the realm of the arts by drawing upon established discourses of painting. A simple record, a view, was not sufficient to art; rather, the artist must be able somehow to integrate into the photographic record some device that denotes art. Photographers looked to texts describing painting's compositional conventions by theorists such as Eugène Véron and John Burnet and used them as a foundation on which they modeled formulaic principles for photographic practice. Because it adhered to these rules of art, photographers argued, their medium deserved admission to the realm of high art. They underscored these formal features as evidence of the infusion of thought in the picture-making process, diminishing the importance of handiwork and finding primacy in the process of conception. Often these formal devices were seen as the means by which the photographer could embrace abstract ideals associated with the rhetoric of art such as beauty, truth, and nature. Americans also looked to the work of contemporary English photographers such as Henry Peach Robinson, who wrote volumes on "artistic" composition, drawing from established standards of pictorial representation.

Chapter 2 focuses on what I term the "antiphotographic," one of the predominant stylistic conventions of artistic landscape photography to emerge from the nineteenth century and the style of art photography appropriated by Alfred Stieglitz and his associates. On one level, the motivation of this style, which was later labeled "pictorialism," was the desire for effects of traditional graphic media. Soft focus, deep shadows, and richly textured tones were offered as proof of photography's ability to overcome its reputation as the producer of objective records devoid of human creativity. The purposeful subversion of characteristics associated with photography was a means by which art-minded photographers could assert their independence from the sort of photography that increasingly pervaded American life, a type that a turn-of-the-century observer described as "of the commercial and everyday character of such a vulgar-we had almost said brutal-character that an anecdote of the most searching kind was necessary."[8] In addition to this sort of differentiation from the blatantly commercial, the antiphotographic was also motivated by desires to appeal to subjective perceptual experience, allying itself with the naturalistic theories of Peter Henry Emerson and impressionism. This alliance with naturalism and impressionism created intriguing combinations of positivist science and romantic subjectivity. The appeal to perceptual experience at times posited photography as a means to reproduce empirically raw human perception. At other times, positivism coalesced with romantic bids to emotion, knowledge, and memory.

While pictorialism is generally accepted as the triumph of purely artistic photography, I will show in chapter 3 that the movement met resolute resistance from a variety of sources, including professional photographers, leading amateurs, and the popular press. Through the lens of the subsequent construction of the history of photography, these factions seem conservative and reactionary in their searing condemnations of the conventions of the antiphotographic. However, the values expressed in the writing and photographs of critics offer insights into notions about art photography prior to the entrenchment of pictorialism. The resistance to pictorialism and the celebration of a "pure photography" free from pictorialist affectation were an amalgam of traditional artistic theories and characteristics unique to the photographic medium, such as very broad ranges of tone and remarkably sharp detail. Both photographers and critics created a specific forum in which photographs could address artistic issues yet still retain a peculiarly photographic quality, establishing a realm in which the aesthetic and the utilitarian document coexisted.

The final chapter of this study addresses a primary tactic in the quest for an artistic photography: the establishment of legitimizing institutional structures such as societies, publications, and salons. While organizations of photographers and photographic publications were founded in the United States soon after the invention of photography, the structures and foci of institutions underwent significant transformations in the 1880s and 1890s. Where earlier photographic organizations were primarily the realm of professional photographers, the increasing popularity of photography encouraged societies of amateur photographers to publish their own journals. Inspired by European paradigms in London and Vienna, these amateurs endeavored to legitimize their medium through the foundation of a salon tradition. In the 1880s and 1890s, the character of these exhibitions changed drastically, as selection and award processes were hotly debated and as the participants increasingly embraced the current conventions of art photography.

An outgrowth of legitimizing institutions was the delineation of internal divisions within the practice of photography. With the multiplicity of uses of photography in an increasingly industrialized and commercialized society, art photographers strove to construct a unique space for the medium unfettered by associations with less lofty photographic applications. Before the invention of the dry plate and the subsequent growth in the number of amateurs, the photographic amateur was, by necessity, a member of a wealthy leisure class. Earlier photographic equipment was expensive, and the mastery of the photographic process required a significant investment of time. The early, upper-class amateur was particularly prevalent in England, where the difference in social status between the working-class professional and the leisure-class amateur was often pointed out.[9] In America there were fewer upper-class amateurs, and until the 1890s, class distinction was less of an issue. Over the course of the 1890s, Stieglitz and his circle reinserted the class distinction of the early art-minded amateur and shared an affinity with the antitechnology values of the Aesthetic movement. Americans in particular celebrated the supposed democratizing effect of photographs, yet the elite photographers effectively negated the democratizing effects of the accessibility of photography by making art photography a selective social sphere.[10] In doing so, Stieglitz looked to the more socially stratified model of the British photographic community. While the Photographic Society of London (later the Royal Photographic Society of Great Britain) had long been the realm of the privileged photographer, the Linked Ring was an even more exclusive assembly, one to which Stieglitz himself was the first American elected. Amateur photographers, presenting themselves as the true champions of photography as an art, elevated their work by contrasting it with what they saw as the unfeeling, uninspired work of professional photographers. Furthermore, amateurs with artistic pretensions felt the need to distinguish themselves from amateurs with less lofty goals. Indeed, in America, photography had an immense appeal to a general public fascinated by new technology and social status. The "artistic" amateurs detailed the characteristics demarcating their pictures from the snapshots of the horde. Yet the differentiation between amateurs was much more subtle, with one set of practitioners of highly aestheticized methods, Stieglitz and the Photo-Secession in particular, condemning the work of other, very similar groups in order to cohere an exclusive synthetic alliance.

I chose 1900 as the later temporal boundary for this investigation because it is the year of the Third Philadelphia Photographic Salon, an exhibition in which legitimating strategies take a firm hold. Stieglitz and his circle emerge as an elite core group of photographers who manage to manipulate not only formal characteristics of the medium but also photographic institutions. By purposefully fostering an air of selectivity in the photographic club and exhibition, these elite artist-amateurs created a unique space for photography amid the fine arts. The Third Philadelphia Salon set the stage for the Photo-Secession, the first American forum for art photography in the twentieth century.

Amateur and Professional: The Impetus Behind Legitimization

The invention of the dry plate opened the practice of photography to a hugely expanded body of practitioners, and it was the amateur who made the biggest impact on the photographic scene. Without the technology of the dry plate, the photographer had to coat the plate with liquid emulsion and expose the negative before it dried. Consequently, the preparation of the plate had to be completed in close proximity, both spatially and temporally, to the exposure of the photograph. The advent of the dry plate allowed the photographer to prepare the negative in advance, thus giving much more flexibility to the picture-making process. More important, the dry plate could be manufactured commercially, and a photographer need not be concerned with the preparation of the negative.[11] Looking back in 1894, F. C. Beach, editor of the *American Amateur Photographer* and first president of the Society of Amateur Photographers of New York, assessed the gravity of the dry plate on amateur photography: "The practice of photography as an amusement did not assume much importance until early in the eighties . . . [with] the introduction of the modern dry plate . . . Many people who never imagined they could master photography were attracted by the new process and gave it a trial."[12] In the wake of the dry plate came smaller, more portable cameras, commercial processing, and eventually the Kodak, a hand camera with roll film requiring that the photographer do no more than simply "press the button."

The opportunities made available by the dry plate were not welcomed by all photographers, for the new ease of the medium created competition, and the vast technical expertise of the commercial photographer was at less of a premium. To many photographers, the dry plate was the catalyst for a diminution of photographic standards and a source of tension within the photographic community. The ease of process could afford a lack of seriousness that many professionals and amateurs alike found difficult to respect. Factions formed within the growing ranks of photographers, with their varying levels of dedication to the medium, factions discussed in chapter 4.

The ever-growing number of photographers catalyzed the impulse to claim art status for photography. The motivation for this claim varied from one segment of the photographic field to another. At the risk of oversimplifying the various photographic camps (the boundaries between these groups are not always well defined), several categories of photographers can be identified. There were professional photographers, who believed that the trappings of art helped them retain a share of a market increasingly diluted by the price-gashing commercial hacks and recreational amateurs, who no longer required the services of the professional. Other, more principled professionals regarded art status as the right of a medium as capable as any of the standards of art: they took pride in their work and integrated their mastery of the optical and chemical nature of photography with an informed intellectual investment based on conventions of the traditional graphic arts.[13] Finally, art-minded amateurs underscored their freedom from the demands of the commercial market, challenging notions of what made good photography and how the photographic image could achieve the rank of art.

Many photographers in the early 1880s adopted the term "artist" to bolster their professional reputation. The commercial photographers cared little for the traditions of art or for the placement of photography within its ranks. Instead, the term was intended to appeal to the consumer. In a market being made increasingly competitive by "Cheap Johns," cut-rate operators to whom technical and aesthetic standards were of little account, countless established professionals could ill afford to concern themselves with lofty issues like high art status.

In contrast to the photographer who appealed to the title of "art" simply as a business ploy, other commercial photographers attempted to legitimize their medium because they truly believed in the potential of photography to produce works of art. The stand of the professional dedicated to procuring photography's place among the fine arts was most forcefully proclaimed by Edward L. Wilson. A well-traveled and successful commercial photographer and editor of several of the most widely read American photographic journals, including the *Philadelphia Photographer, Wilson's Photographic Magazine,* and *Photographic Mosaics,* Wilson was tremendously influential in the discourse of photography as art in the last two decades of the nineteenth century, yet his significance has been lost in most accounts of this period.[14] While he epitomized the technically adept, institutionally active, and conservative professional photographer, the type likely to resist much of what "art photographers" would attempt to establish, Wilson was actually a major influence, initiating strategies to legitimize photography as a means of artistic practice. He consistently published essays by well-respected academicians (most notably John Burnet), painters' thoughts on art (like those of William Hart and Xanthus Smith), and articles by English theorists Robinson and Emerson. Remarkably open minded, Wilson published a broad spectrum of theoretical and technical approaches to photography.

Unlike professional photographers who might be subjected to commercial motivations, facets of the amateur photography community defined themselves as the true champions of photographic art. Early on, photographers were quite conscious of the avenues opened by the introduction of the dry plate and were aware of how amateur practice might differ from that of the professional. Many photographers saw the future of photographic artistic endeavors in the hands of the burgeoning amateur movement made possible by technological advances in the medium. Free from what was expected of photography, the amateur had the potential to reconcile the photographic art/science paradox. Amateurs gained the means to subvert characteristics that many professionals considered inherent to the medium, for "with them the pictorial effect and the pictorial *motif* are the first thing to be considered in their photography. Photography to them is simply one more medium of expression, and they can handle it as freely as their limited technical knowledge will permit, embodying ideas which, under ordinary circumstances, they would put into oil- or water-color."[15] This notion of the photograph as a tool of expression as legitimate as any other accepted art medium was often invoked by those attempting to create photographic art.

The argument that photography could produce works of art often centered upon adherence to academic rules of the established graphic arts. Amateurs served not only to inspire a desire for a higher standard of professional work, they also began to challenge the very conception of the nature of the medium. The theorization of the 1880s was dominated by the professional and tended toward compositional convention, while the next decade saw an increasing influence of some amateurs on the definition of what constituted photographic art.

America and Europe: An Uneasy Exchange

The legitimization of photography in America was by no means an insular process. While the development of photographic practice in America was quite different from that of Britain and continental Europe, texts and photographs from overseas played a significant role in the formation of American art photography.[16] In fact, many of the most influential theorists in America were British, most notably Henry Peach Robinson, Peter Henry Emerson, and George Davison. In the last decades of the nineteenth century, American journals reprinted major essays and addresses from European publications; British photographers and writers regularly corresponded with the most important American photographic journals; and books published by major photographers, Robinson and Emerson in particular, prompted much debate among American writers. Foreign photographers were invited to submit works to American exhibitions, and Americans sent their works to the English societies for exhibition and criticism. In addition, near the end of the century, the most famous of the American art photography apologists were being offered membership in exclusive European art photography societies like the Brotherhood of the Linked Ring. London was to photographers like Stieglitz what Paris was to the American painter of the late nineteenth century: an elysium of institutional legitimacy and recognized artistic archetypes.[17]

While over the course of this study I will often examine the theories of these British photographers, I focus most intently on the way they were received in American journals and exhibitions. The American reception of European paradigms varied greatly: American photographers at once aspired to British standards and resented them. Like American artists early in the nation's history, American photographic theorists wavered from unrestrained patriotism and the celebration of a uniquely American vision to unashamed proclamations of American photographers' inferiority to the Europeans.

Many of the photographers and writers who emerged as the most prestigious and prolific champions of art photography in the last decades of the nineteenth century looked intently to British photography as a model of superior practice. In his early years in Germany, Stieglitz was said to have been alone in his exploration of the art in photography: "his best instruction was derived from the English journals, which were the real teachers in the art side of the science of photography." Stieglitz was encouraged by Peter Henry Emerson's response to his first exhibit in 1887, and his admiration of the British was reflected in his "chief desire . . . to see America standing photographically on a level with England."[18] Invoking a sense of nationalistic pride for his American audience, Stieglitz asked why "the American amateur should not turn out as beautiful pictures by photographic means as his English brethren across the long pond?"[19] In the same tone, the painter, amateur photographer, and frequent contributor to photographic journals Xanthus Smith also looked to England for examples of well-fostered artistic effort and "truer taste," hoping that, with time and effort, America would nurture as strong an art photography tradition.[20] Like Smith, Catharine Weed Barnes, another prolific member of the American photographic community in the late 1880s and early 1890s, had no qualms about measuring her country's photography by English standards. "It is no special sign of patriotism," she explained, "to shut one's eyes to merit if it be not American, or to shrink from receiving deserved criticism when the results of our work fall below the standards of more experienced camerists."[21] Often the comparison to English work led to an evaluation of American work as distinctly inferior. In response to an 1893 exhibition Stieglitz concluded, "the work shown by Englishmen is proof positive that we Americans are 'not in it' when art photography is in question."[22] In order to be recognized as art, American photography had to meet international standards of the most progressive art practice.

In contrast to the critics who called for an adherence to foreign standards and found American work inferior to European were those who identified a distinctly American style and found it superior to the work being generated overseas. Writing on photography as art, an author identified simply as "one who observes," recognized the integral role of English photography in America, but asserts that

> the ultimate decisive recognition of photography as an art will come from America. . . . Our art methods are drawn from different schools of foreign art, and in our best art-schools the instruction covers a wide field of European theory and practice. But from this eclecticism is gradually rising a native and national art. American Photography has been passing through the same phases, assimilating the artistic and the mechanical sides of foreign photography.[23]

The identification of particular American dispositions in photographic practice reflected positivist tendencies and a willingness to embrace technology.[24] While she saw an essential part of the photographer's education in the study of Europe and its art, Charlotte Adams believed "we Americans are forming a distinct school of photography as well as of art . . . ," and she shunned English "pseudo-idealism," celebrating in its stead American art "grounded root and branch in realism and love for hard, positive facts, so natural to the American temperament."[25]

The celebration of "pure photography" and a propensity toward positivist investigation made the struggle to legitimize art photography in America especially problematic.[26] An American tendency to embrace technology caused photography to be especially fascinating to the American public. Statements comparing photography's significance to the railroad were frequent. But this virtual obsession with technology made it difficult to accept photography as an art, for in many minds, technology and art were at odds. Even many of the American photographers who genuinely believed photography could be elevated to an art clung tightly to the technological capacity of the medium. In what I label in chapter 3 the "photographic aesthetic," they embraced photography's ability to present a seemingly transparent record of nature, tempering it with compositional rules associated with the traditional graphic arts.

The American romance with technology may account for the resistance to legitimizing strategies like those discussed in chapter 2, which purposefully undermined the verisimilitude of the photograph. The subversion of the photographic alienated many photographers and much of the general population. While this alienation fostered a fortified espousal of the photographic aesthetic, it also allowed the development of a separatist art photography circle, the elitism of which was a primary factor in achieving space within the fine arts for photography. Ironically, the legitimizing impulse was accelerated by the popularization of photography, but as I will elucidate in chapter 4, it is the negation of the egalitarianism of the medium that procures its place among the accepted arts.

The Legacy of Legitimization

The gap in conventional photographic histories that leaves the period studied in this book so underexamined is largely the legacy of Alfred Stieglitz, the most successful champion of photography as art. Stieglitz only half-heartedly embraced the formal characteristics of pictorialism as a means to escape photography's reputation as an objective recorder incapable of aesthetic content, but he was perhaps the most masterful manipulator of photography's institutional structures. After establishing the artistic possibility for photography, Stieglitz discarded the conventions of pictorialism, endorsing the "straight" style associated with modernist photography. With this model for artistic photography firmly entrenched, pictorialism became understood as the origin of photography as art in America, and the diversity of the theory and practice from which pictorialism evolved was overlooked.

As photographic historian Marianne Fulton Margolis points out, even as early as 1899 writers like Joseph T. Keiley claimed Stieglitz and his *Camera Notes* essentially "originated the movement for artistic photography and had overseen its success."[27] Stieglitz's account, which tended to make pictorialism hegemonic and denied the resolute resistance it received, was inherited by the most influential writers of photographic history and is still generally accepted.[28] While I acknowledge Stieglitz's key role in creating a legitimate sphere for photography as fine art, I will demonstrate that the aesthetic bases of art photography are far more complex than many histories suggest, for they neglect the two vital decades that set the scene for turn-of-the-century American photography. In fact, my investigation will show that Stieglitz's own aesthetic was far from revolutionary, but his orchestration of photographic institutions facilitated radical changes in the conceptualization of art photography.

There is, however, a recent trend in scholarship on American photography of the late nineteenth century toward a more complete analysis. The essays in Martha Sandweiss's edited collection *Photography in Nineteenth-Century America* probe the interrelationships of American culture, art, and photography much more deeply than most previous studies. Peter Bacon Hales traces the revolution of photographic production and its impact on the American commercial landscape photographer. Keith Davis, in the opening chapter of *An American Century of Photography,* begins to address many facets of late-nineteenth-century photography that are examined more fully in this study: technology as shaping factor, the rise of the camera club, photographic exhibitions, for example. Sarah Greenough's astute essay traces radical changes in photographic practice over the 1880s and 1890s and some of the motivations behind defining and limiting the art of photography. Her text is perhaps the closest in spirit to this study, most particularly the analysis of institutional strategies of legitimization in chapter 4. A two-part study by Ulrich Keller also parallels several of the concerns of this work, reexamining some traditional assumptions about art photography. Keller analyzes art photography's roots in amateur practice, its institutional manifestations, aesthetic principles, and elitist strategies.[29]

The entrenchment of canonical narratives is certainly not new to the history of photography, for the mythification of photographic history dates to the mid nineteenth century, as Mary Warner Marien aptly points out in her *Photography and Its Critics.*[30] In contrast, this study reinserts an awareness of the complexity of photographic theory and practice in America at the end of the nineteenth century. The significance of my work lies in two areas: our understanding of the practice of photography and our understanding of the practice of photographic history. My project underscores the primacy of a decisive and essential defining period in the formulation of artistic photographic practice. Yet the implications of this examination of legitimizing strategies resonate beyond the way photographs are made, pointing out the manner in which historical narratives of photography are constructed and renovated by subsequent theory and practice.

CHAPTER ONE

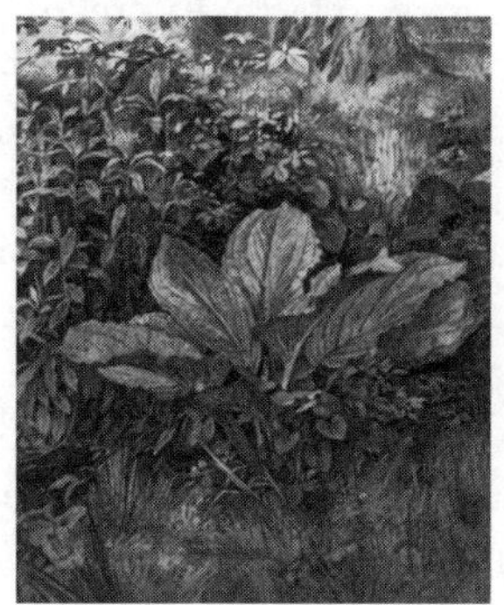

"THE GRAMMAR OF ART": AN APPEAL TO TRADITION

"The refusal to rank Photography among the fine arts, I consider, is in a measure unfounded, its aim and end being one in common with art. It speaks the same language, and addresses itself to the same sentiments."

—JOHN MORAN, "THE RELATION OF PHOTOGRAPHY TO THE FINE ARTS"

Faced with the criticism that the photographer simply did not have enough control of the camera's record to adhere to the standards of art, in the late nineteenth century scores of photographers and writers attempted to prove that the medium could appeal to artistic tradition. An early enthusiast for the artistic application of photography in America, John Moran insisted on an affinity between photography and painting, where both media could embrace nature with a shared formal language. In this chapter I focus on the appropriation and application of compositional principles by photographers like Moran and his successors. I will often cite Moran as a prototype for the discussion of the nature of the "language" and "sentiments" that writers would like to apply to photography, an impulse that became quite popular in the 1880s and early 1890s. Many photographers believed these conventions not only established a visual kinship with the established arts but also offered proof of photography's capacity to facilitate creative investment and aesthetic impact.

Moran serves to introduce many of the arguments that are applied both for and against photography's ability to achieve fine-art status. He represents a link between the post–Civil War expedition photographers and the following generations of both commercial and art-minded amateur photographers, for he pursued photography as a livelihood, an obvious underlying motivation to professional practice, and he tried to define an artistic photographic mode, an enterprise to which many amateurs would attend.[1] Moran made some of the most remarkable American arguments of the 1860s and 1870s for photography's status as a fine art, setting the stage for two decades of intense debate. Yet despite his optimism for the medium, Moran's most significant act was his ultimate denial of photography as art. Finally, he abandoned photography for painting, unable to reconcile the verisimilitude of photography with a need for creative intellectual investment.

Writing in 1865, Moran introduced prototypes of a number of the strategies employed by the next generation of photographers as they ask, "What is art, and how can photography produce it?" Moran began addressing this question by setting forth the standards of art by which photography's status could be tested, its ability to imitate, present truth, and communicate beauty. Few would have argued with Moran's assertion that photography could imitate, and he saw the only weakness in photography's presentation of truth in its lack of color, a feature that it shared with other accepted graphic art forms.[2]

Addressing the final test of photography's artistic potential, its ability to engage beauty, Moran revealed an affinity to the Kantian notion of the subjectivity of aesthetic experience, that the value of art lies in the viewer's experience of "a certain class of feeling" and that "we may claim for photography the ability to create imagery which call forth ideas and sentiments of the beautiful."[3] This notion of subjective aesthetic experience was the basis of many photographers' theorization of their medium's artistic potential, although the formal realizations of this theoretical basis varied greatly. For Moran the aesthetic experience was catalyzed by a "faithful image" of certain "combinations of nature." What exactly constituted a "faithful image" in photography and how one identified and photographically reproduced those "combinations of nature" were the subjects of heated debate for the rest of the century. For the next generation of photographers who hoped to solidify their medium's claim to fine art, models of the "combinations of nature" Moran suggested could be found in the traditional graphic arts.

Defending Their Medium

Building upon the notion that mental processes created art rather than the handiwork that realized an image or object, champions of the medium admitted that photography per se was not an art but neither was any other graphic process in and of itself. However, just as with the other graphic media, a properly educated, motivated, and talented operator could produce fine art through the photographic medium. A widely published 1886 address by the young photographic theorist Frederic Hart Wilson, son of the influential Edward L. Wilson, presented photography's place among the traditional arts as an obvious given, the general acceptance of which was only hampered by "mossy critics and artist-bigots."[4] Like many of his colleagues who considered photography as legitimate a mode of representation as any other graphic media, Wilson argued that the process of representation was irrelevant and that the end justified the means.

When art status lay in the product rather than the medium, the scientific nature of photography seemed less troubling. "My ideal of the art-science," wrote Catharine Weed Barnes, the thoughtful and prolific essayist, photographer, and editor of the *American Amateur Photographer* in the 1890s, "is a high one, . . . it appeals most strongly to all who, besides artistic taste, enjoy the study of optics, chemistry, mechanics, and that indefinable mental quality which can blend them all into a homogeneous whole."[5] With the proper motivation, the photographer became the "disseminator of a true art," but success depended on his or her role not as a scientist but as an artist and was "proportional to his ability to rely less upon his chemical and mechanical appliances and more upon himself."[6] J. Traill Taylor, editor of the *Photographic Times and American Photographer* suggested that the thoughtful and critical photographer must not be seduced by science and accept unquestioningly the photographic medium as art in and of itself, nor should he or she accept the categorical denial of its artistic capacity. The photographer was told to rise above the scientific side of the medium. Essentially, the photographer must prove that photography was not merely an uncontrollable physical process but one that included creative intervention, like any other form of fine art.[7] An assertion of individuality and authorship arose: the recognizable investment of individuality carried the artistic significance.

The Language of Art

Writers provided very specific parameters for art and the photographer's ability to achieve it, standards that, according to Taylor, conformed to the "rules and conceptions of art" that govern aesthetic response.[8] Art, these writers insisted, was measured not by the mode of representation but by the established standards that guided the creative process. Photography had the same capacity to communicate, and it was the content of the communication that carried significance, not the mode of communication. Moran believed that aesthetic impact could be attributed to learned formal devices: "When the photographer can face nature with calmness—the calmness of knowledge—this stubborn nature will seem to mould itself to the forms and shapes of his own mind." With a mastery over the photographic process and the grammar of art, the photographer was able to impart his or her thoughts on selection of subject, compositional structure, thematic harmonies or contrasts, light, and the work as a unified compositional whole.[9] Like many of his colleagues and successors, Moran looked to established paradigms in the traditional graphic arts that could be applied to photography.

A major tenet in many of the claims for photography's artistic potential was that very specifically defined, universal codes of art could be identified and applied to photography, thus producing photographic art. The aesthetic was presented as a result of definable, rational, and stable rules, distilled to a set of virtually scientific principles. Many photographers exhibited the firm belief expressed in a painter-photographer's address to the Society of Amateur Photographers of New York that "principles of composition . . . faithfully followed can aid in raising photography to recognition as an art" and that traditional artists' hesitancy to accept photography as an art stemmed not from the nature of the medium but rather from the weaknesses of the skills and knowledge of photographers themselves.[10]

The theory that the same laws of art that apply to painting apply to photography attested to lingering platonic notions of empirically definable, timeless, formal elements that begat art. As a speaker before the Cincinnati Camera Club phrased it: laws "govern and underlie all art. . . . [They] are not my individual interpretations; nor are they the conventional opinions of any one class, or set of men, artists or critics. They are simply the meanings of nature, expressed through the manifold forms of, lines and colors, found in the whole universe."[11] The appeal to a universal set of rules equated art to an empirical science, implying that art could be derived from a set of explicitly defined principles.[12] This project of artistic infusion led photographers and writers to seek out examples on which they could model their pictures. The photographer was told to draw on the established arts, for they were the most obvious manifestations of universal codes of art.

John Burnet as a Practical Foundation

To many writers, a major prerequisite to the ability to create a picture through the photographic process was an academic knowledge of art and artistic practice. As they struggled to secure a place for photography among the traditional arts, these writers turned to texts by respected theorists of the traditional graphic arts that codified the conventions of pictorial representation. The application of the codes detailed in texts on painting, a process that reflects the artist-photographer's intellect, became a strategy aimed at establishing photography as a medium of artistic expression. In the 1870s, John Moran found archetypes for artistic theory, seeing John Ruskin as "a giant among art writers." Moran also pointed to Philip Gilbert Hamerton's ideas, and, more important, referred photographers to Burnet's *Practical Essays on Art*, calling Burnet one of the best of those who had attempted to "formulate to laws and rules the fine arts."[13] Indeed, the text to which American photographers were consistently directed as a pedagogical resource is Burnet's *Essays*.

Virtually forgotten today, Burnet's *Essays* were originally published over more than a decade: "Composition" in 1822, "Light and Shade" in 1826, and "On the Education of the Eye" in 1836.[14] Rescued from slipping into academic obscurity in the last quarter of the nineteenth century, Burnet's essays, while perhaps conservative or passé in the eyes of contemporary progressive artists, enjoyed a period of revitalization by the American photographic press, making them the most frequently cited source of established art. In 1866–67, the *Philadelphia Photographer* published "Some Art Principles Applicable to Photography," a series illustrated largely from Burnet; in 1875–76, the journal reproduced Burnet's "Hints on Composition."[15] However, the expansive application to photography of the essays of John Burnet may be credited largely to Edward L. Wilson, a tireless advocate of imbuing photography with the artistic. While visiting London in 1873, Wilson found a rare compilation of the essays. He published a facsimile of the essays in the late 1880s, although he may have already significantly diminished his market, for he had published some of the essays as a series in the *Philadelphia Photographer* in 1880. However ill-conceived the marketing for the new edition of the essays, Wilson managed to foster new interest in Burnet's work and the ways in which the treatise on painting might be applied to photographic representation. Upon releasing the 1887 reproduction of Burnet's *Practical Essays on Art*, Wilson and the staff of the *Philadelphia Photographer* declared that, despite the expense and risk of such an undertaking, "the present status of photography now, however, *demands* such a work be done. . . . We have derived more art instruction from these works than from any kindred ones we have ever studied. . . . They should be in every photographic library."[16]

Wilson's enthusiastic support of Burnet as an artistic source book for photographers and his stalwart marketing of the facsimile reverberated in the texts of other writers. British photographer Andrew Pringle stated, "The book was not written for photographers; yet, leaving out the question of coloring, there is not a word in it which might not serve as meat and drink to any one of the meritorious band of photographers who are now aiming at raising photography as high as it can be raised in the realms of art."[17] Suggesting that they find inspiration in Ruskin, Burnet, and Hamerton, Enoch Root, in his widely published address to the Minneapolis Convention of the Photographers' Association of America, implored photographers to strive beyond technical perfection to the "aesthetical" in order to secure for their medium the "true position . . . as a fine art."[18] Root described Burnet's essays as "the most practical instruction book on the principles of art, . . . a concise, methodical and, exhaustive text book" useful to advanced artists yet intelligible to the beginner.[19]

The photographic venerators of Burnet clearly relished the establishment of a legitimizing paradigm of art practice in a text written for painting, and they were not concerned with the vintage of their resource. In fact, the more conservative theorists who tended to cling to Burnet's compositional conventions used him as a basis for their resistance to more progressive art practice. Henry Peach Robinson pointed out that even in 1888 "there is still a plentiful lack of appreciation of the value of art in photography" and that the renewed availability of a resource like Burnet was heartily needed. Long familiar with Burnet, Robinson wrote, "Although published many years ago, these essays are as fresh and useful as if written yesterday. Nothing new has been added to or taken from the principles of art since Burnet wrote, except, indeed, by the impressionist or naturalistic school, which," he notes with scorn, "ignores all that has gone before in art."[20] Similarly, Xanthus Smith, who also cherished a copy of Burnet's *Essays* before Wilson's republication, applauded the book for the period it reflected: "Written, as it was, at a time when art had shot up with a new and vigorous growth, it comprises a clear fountain-head of knowledge upon the subjects of which it treats, free from all the rubbish

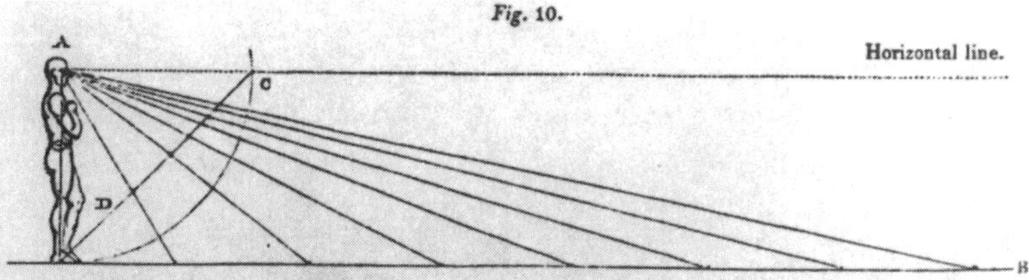

FIG. 1. John Burnet, Diagram of ratios of diminution. "The Education of the Eye," *Practical Essays on Art,* p. 8.

of 'ites' and 'isms' with which we have since become more or less befogged."[21]

Burnet's "Education of the Eye," included in Wilson's 1888 facsimile and published in series in the *Philadelphia Photographer* in 1880, began with the development of a basic understanding of measure and form, as well as geometric perspectival lines and angles. He outlined essential theories of linear perspective, a mode of representation that, in the minds of many writers, finds analogies in the geometrical optics of photography.[22] The "visual rays" in Burnet's diagram of ratios of diminution treat human perception in the manner of a ray diagram. The same linear model serves to illustrate light passing through a series of lenses, suggesting photography's fidelity to the real as it records on its sensitized plate.

The art-minded photographer was met with the challenge of mediating the camera's record, a mediation that could rely on educated selection. In order to develop a sophisticated method of selection, Burnet encouraged the student of art to "look abroad upon natural objects, and contemplate the various changes produced in their forms by their situation, so that his eye may become familiar with those alterations in form, and his mind enriched by a variety of examples."[23] This model of a self-conscious shifting observer could be co-opted by the photographer in support of the claim that choice of view was a facet of artistic investment. Burnet's text justified the photographer's search for universal codes in past artistic archetypes, for he advised his readers that the

> power of discernment is . . . to be acquired by the study of the works of those who have excelled in the different departments of art, and afterwards perfected in searching out and contemplating the

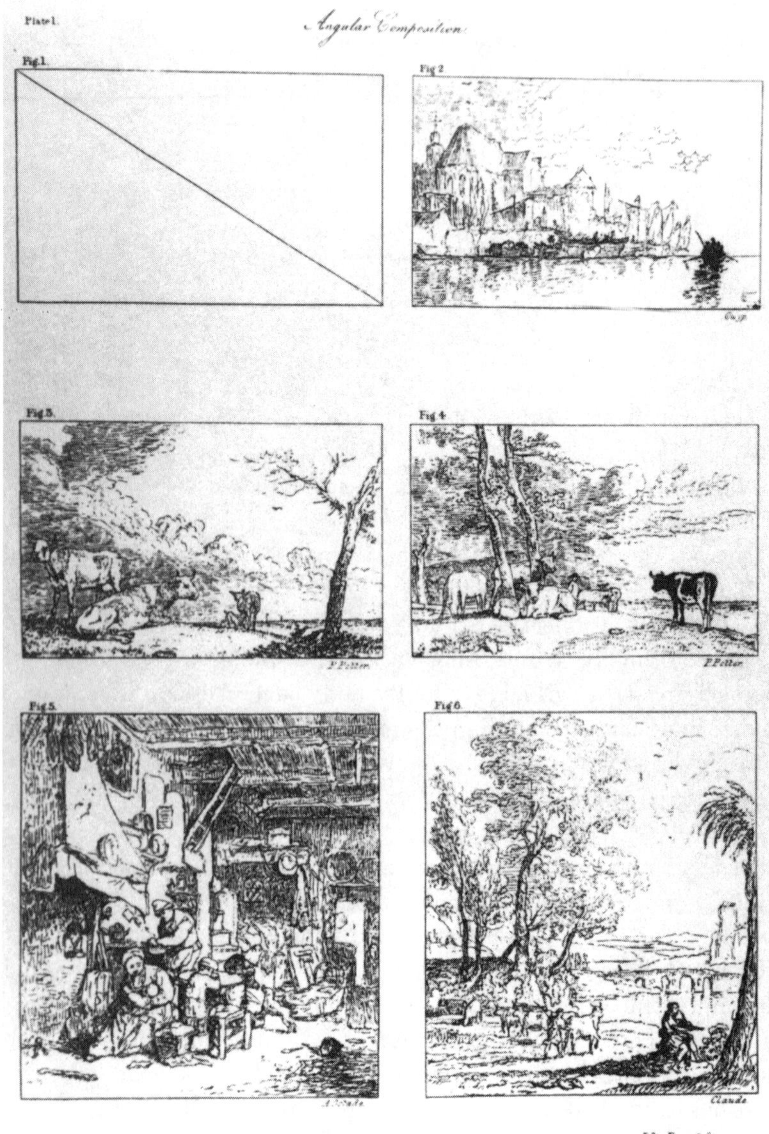

FIG. 2. John Burnet, *Angular Composition.* "Composition," *Practical Essays on Art,* plate 1.

> beautiful combinations which lie scattered in the endless varieties of nature. . . . This mode of study alone can enable one [artist] to surpass another in the power of selection.[24]

Drawing on the examples of Albert Cuyp and Claude Lorraine, Burnet discussed the creation of representational space and described basic compositional strategies such as angular and circular compositions, providing engraved examples accompanied by individual commentaries.[25]

Burnet presented a notion of a visual language that appeared in the writing of many photographers: the artist's "mind has been educated," rendering "a numerous assemblage of lines intelligible to him, which to others, uneducated, appear like a species of hieroglyphic." He described principles of design upon which painting "depends for its operation on the mind and places it in the same rank with poetry and music."[26] There were rules that made art, rules that reflected the operation of the mind. If the aesthetic could lie in the reference to tradition, then the thoughtful, educated photographer could speak the language of art and thus create photographic art.

Compositional Conventions

An objective, platonic notion of order and harmony cultivated this proclamation of particular formal rules of art.[27] Specific formal relations endowed an image with an appeal to universally defined, transcendent concepts of beauty. Yet, other than Burnet's, commentaries on and specific references to the theoretical bases of composition were not especially frequent in American photographic literature of the 1880s and 1890s: writers tended to prescribe formulae without explaining how and why they imbued aesthetic value. Most discussions of compositional principles and conventions shared the attitude of an 1884 *Philadelphia Photographer* article that stated, "Now we shall not enter into philosophy or seek to divine the cause of artistic effect, but only point out the principles upon which that effect depends, that they may be of service in the selection of beautiful pictures in nature."[28] Still, the belief in universal codes of art led many writers to prescribe explicit conventions of photographic composition that would make a photograph artistic. The scores of formulaic descriptions of compositional rules that appeared in the photographic journals of the last decades of the nineteenth century were as tedious as many of the pictures they inspired, yet they are worthy of at least a brief survey.

Photographers were told the proper light, time, and atmospheric

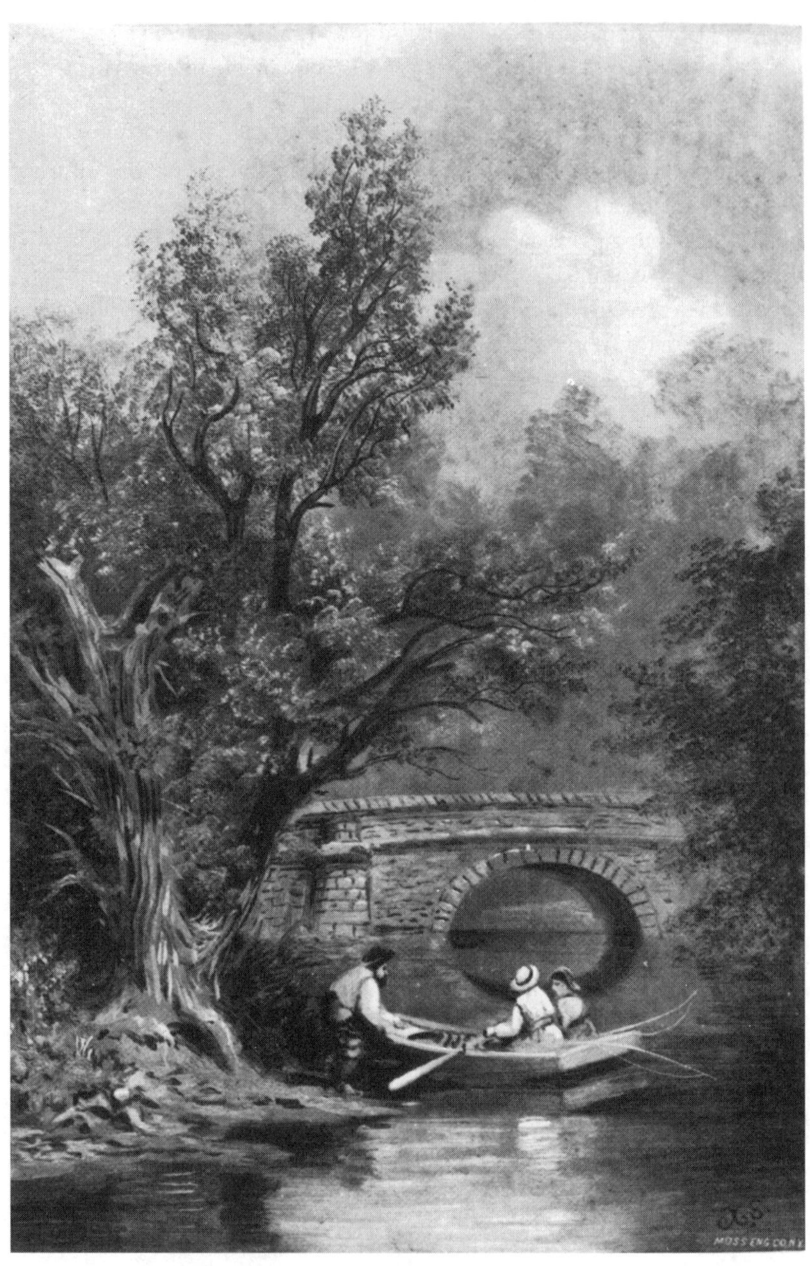

FIG. 3. Xanthus Smith, *On the Pennypack,* monochrome oil drawing. *Philadelphia Photographer,* July 17, 1886, frontispiece. Library Company of Philadelphia.

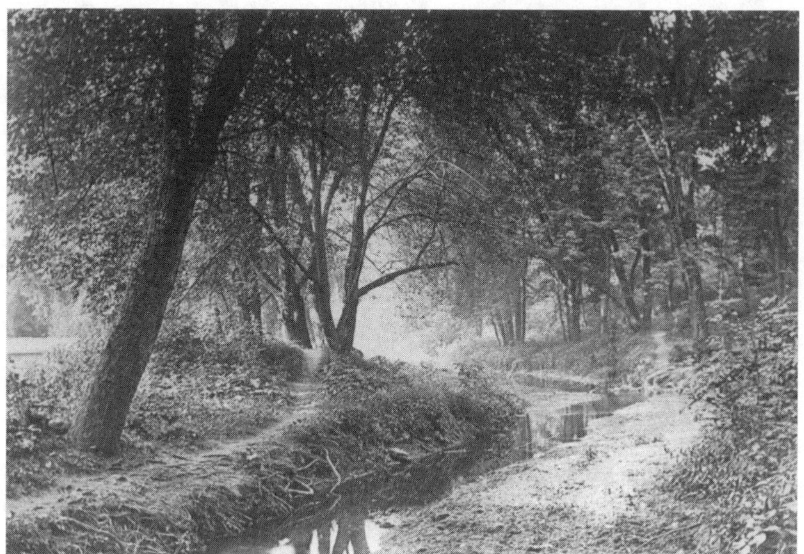

Fig. 4. George Hanmer Croughton, *East,* albumen print. *Philadelphia Photographer,* May 1, 1886, frontispiece. Library Company of Philadelphia.

conditions in which to create art.[29] The placement of the primary point of interest was also a concern for the photographer constructing artistic compositions, as was the proper ratio of landscape to sky, sun to shade, and so forth.[30] Many texts described compositional manipulations designed to enhance the illusion of space and facilitate the viewer's comprehension of the scene.[31]

The construction of an artistically accomplished landscape composition was addressed at length by the painter-photographer Xanthus Smith. In a widely published paper read before the Philadelphia Amateur Photographic Club, Smith made a point of listing a variety of means to lead the eye into a scene, and take away from the appearance of flatness. Self-consciously aware of the two-dimensionality of the picture plane, Smith explained, "Working, or rather presenting as we do, our subjects on a flat surface, every artifice should be used to overcome this perpendicularness of plane and have the effect of leading the eye into the picture."[32] He favored variety and atmospheric depth and urged photographers to avoid flattening repetitive linear elements such as the "parallel sides, lined with stiff fencing, and rows of straight-stemmed cedar trees" of a country road photographed on or near the axis of the image.[33]

Smith's paintings, reproduced in major photographic journals, reflect his advice on the construction of pictorial composition. His monochrome oil study *On the Pennypack,* from the *Philadelphia Photographer,* exhibits a careful construction of space based on common conventions of painting. Photographers were offered his example of framing trees, the gently curving receding path and creek, layered planes of foliage, and rustic foreground figures.

Like Smith, George Hanmer Croughton, painter, photographer, and president of the Camera Club of Rochester, focused on the linear construction of a composition.[34] Croughton asserted that "straight lines are to be avoided, curved lines being more graceful; lines crossing at right-angles or lines forming angles are abominations."[35] Croughton's *East,* which appeared as the frontispiece of an 1886 *Philadelphia Photographer* and was accompanied by an editorial evaluation, exemplifies his advice. The intimate wooded scene in Philadelphia's Fairmount Park, with its curving stream echoed by the footpath beside, is framed by trees that lean into the picture. These basic formal rules, enforced by the selective eye of the photographer, allowed theorists like Smith and Croughton to ally the photographic picture with the traditions of art.

Even Stieglitz, despite his self-constructed emergence as a radical presence in both general and artistic photographic circles (discussed more fully in chapter 4), was in the late 1880s and 1890s best received for his more conservative work. In such pictures, Stieglitz draws upon the Düsseldorf taste for classical organization and sentimental genre rather than upon pictorial effects of diminished focus and textured tones. In fact, this conservative approach won Stieglitz praise and earned him top billing among the *Photographic Times*'s "distinguished photographers of today":

> Artistic composition forms the chief element in every one of his pictures. There is no striving after absurd effects. He thoroughly believes in the possibilities of producing work of real art value by means of photography by means of hard work and conscientious study, and proves it by such pictures as *The Card Players, Stones of Venice, At the Brook, Wanderer's Return, The Last Load,* and many others. (See fig. 43.)[36]

Indeed, these images, cited as the best of Stieglitz's work, share a remarkable affinity to academic genre painting not only in subject matter but also in their conservative compositional structure.

Drawing on Eugène Véron's Model of Aesthetic Experience

Occasionally a writer carried the appeal for the careful study of art and an adherence to formulaic prescriptions to more complex issues: what exactly were these formulas meant to achieve, and what was the nature of aesthetic experience? Norman Macbeth, a respected commentator on the relation of art and photography, began to suggest the elusive nature of aesthetic impact, even with seemingly hard-and-fast rules of art: "Aesthetics, . . . the science which manifests the genius of art—is so much the result of personal forthputting, the emanation of an individual mind, that at times it ceases to be a science."[37]

Unlike many of his contemporary writers, Macbeth was inclined to seek out an explanation of the actual mental mechanics of the subtleties of the "aesthetic faculty." He urged the photographer to be "a thorough artist in feeling, well read in all books relating to art." In addition to the work of Burnet, he identified Eugène Véron's *Aesthetics* as containing "perhaps the most advanced notions concerning art of the present day."[38] Véron's highly influential book, published in 1878 and translated into English in 1879, offers a number of insights into contemporary notions of aesthetic qualities photographers attempted to apply to their work and theory. References to Véron were much less common than those to Burnet, and the challenge of his theories to traditional notions of artistic subjectivity made his ideas less likely to be widely accepted. Nonetheless, several influential photographic writers like Macbeth looked to Véron, and his text provided a basis for rigorous theoretical foundations for models of art photography.

As mentioned, the sources to which photographers turned for models of artistic practice need not be intended for them, and photographers rarely seemed to hesitate to look to authors who were openly antagonistic to photography. The English graphic artist seen by photographers as a source of artistic convention, Hamerton, who occasionally made photographs to record "memoranda of isolated facts," found the photograph unthinking and less likely to access nature's truths: "Photography is not a fine art, but an art science; narrow in range, emphatic in assertion, . . . always telling distinctly the one truth that it is able to perceive."[39] In his denial of photography's fine art status, Hamerton voiced the medium's vexing ties to the empirical, ties that many photographers later attempted to dissolve. Nonetheless, because his writings provided such a rich source of compositional convention, writers on photography like Moran and Wilson found in Hamerton a legitimate model of artistic endeavor.

Writers also referred to Ruskin in their celebration of photography's ability to record nature. Ruskin expressed enthusiasm for early photography; however, over the course of his career his opinion of photography changed dramatically, for he came "to regard all photography as a literal and figurative *bête noire*, yet another example of a machine undermining the creativity, spirit, and dignity of human labor."[40] In its journal, *The New Path*, an American analogy to the English Pre-Raphaelite *Germ*, the New York Association for the Advancement of Truth in Art echoed Ruskin's condemnation of the mechanical photograph.[41] In their view, photography's seemingly vast distance from the hand of the artist and the verisimilitude of the photographic record drained photography of its potential to produce art.

Véron, too, disliked photography as much as he did academic art principles, yet photographers shared many of his ideological bases in their quest for the acceptance of their medium into the established realm of the arts. Because of the seemingly scientific objectivity of the medium and its apparent transparency, Véron probably would not have seriously considered the artistic possibility of photography. At several points in his book, he used "photographic" as a derogatory term describing unmediated transcription from nature, a practice that would have made art photographers cringe. Nonetheless, in describing a psychophysical basis of aesthetics and the optimal direction for art—the manifestation of individual impressions—Véron voices ideas that champions of art photography turned to their advantage.[42]

In keeping with an empirical, positivist mind-set, Véron asserted that aesthetic pleasure is reducible to cause and effect.[43] Nonetheless, early in his introduction to *Aesthetics*, Véron set forth an idea that he took much further than Burnet: the aesthetic is controlled by formal features yet must include an appeal to human experience.[44] Through Véron, the compositional tropes tirelessly presented by formulaic descriptions of artistic infusion seemed to mimic accepted formal devices in painting; they also reflected more sophisticated aesthetic theory. Véron, editor of the journal *L'Art*, for which positivist critics often wrote, described a new, modern physiological basis for aesthetic experience that served as a foundation on which photographers would build claims of an inherent perception of such ideals as beauty and truth. Aesthetics became more than the application of simple compositional devices, finding explicit bases in subjective physio-psychological processes. The 1875 introductory statement to the first issue of *L'Art*, attributed by Richard Shiff to Véron, underscored the primacy of the individuality of the artist. In models like that set up in Véron, the individual's "temperament," or physiological makeup, shaped the impression of nature into a subjective phenomenon.[45] The sort of psychophysical basis of aesthetic response in Véron related to earlier nineteenth-century writers like Arthur Schopenhauer. Jonathan Crary explains how Schopenhauer, in *The World as Will and Representation,* interlaced scientific and aesthetic discourses. Psychophysical responses could lead to aesthetic experience, a process "grounded in the specificity of human corporeality described by contemporary empirical science."[46]

To those concerned with photography, the "art-science" medium seemed especially appropriate for an aesthetics dependent on physiological processes.[47] The photographer with a self-image as an artist-scientist might easily have been drawn to compositional conventions not merely as the formal markers of fine art but as the scientific basis for the perception of that which is artistic. The notion of aesthetic pleasure as the action of light upon a sensitive surface reflected both the photographic process and Véron's physiological characteristics of aesthetic pleasure.

Véron attempted to quantify the psychophysical processes of aesthetic pleasure, essentializing the reception of art. He posited a timeless, universal human experience of the aesthetic qualities of certain formal arrangements. Given this supposed uniformity of experience, Véron sought to "discover the rule that governs such preferences." Building on a model of basic sensory experience, he explained aesthetic experience in terms of perceptual stimuli. With the underlying notion that the aesthetic depends on the proper stimulation of nerves, he discussed how and why certain forms are pleasing, rarely attending to the role of experience in the formulation of taste except in a general, almost universal response to smile or frownlike curves.[48]

As he moved on to more sophisticated aspects of the experience of art, based more on content and less on form, Véron began to give the photographer ground from which artist status might be claimed: the possibility of authorial investment and controlled subjective response.[49] The characteristics of apprehension Véron described, which lead to the optimum art experience, became more intellectual but were still tied to basic physiological responses. Criteria for judging the value of a work included complex intellectual reactions catalyzed by nervous responses and the choice of subject that reflects "the intellectual power of the artist."[50] This point offered fodder for those photographers with artistic intention who insisted that the supposed imitation of the real in photography also reflected intellectual investment—a marriage of art and science that paralleled Véron's psychophysical model of aesthetic response.

Authorial infusion, argued Véron, came from choice of subject and arrangement and accentuation of parts. Through formal devices, the individuality of the artist was manifested in the work. Compositional conventions, like photography, were a means to an end, and the art lay in the product's ability to induce an aesthetic response in the viewer. Véron stated that the mechanical perfection of realism was impossible: "Man puts something of his own nature into everything he does . . . he always adds something which is not actually before his eyes, which comes from himself, from his personal emotions and impressions."[51] Véron returned repeatedly to the importance of the communication of the author's individual personality by the work: "We must feel the hand and individual genius of the artist."[52]

This evidence of the artist's intellect through the proper appeal to the senses could be the theoretical basis for photographers' claims to art, and the declaration that a photographer's individuality could be detected in his or her pictures was often made by writers like Henry Peach Robinson and Elbridge Kingsley. Kingsley claimed that the camera can be a tool for remarkably individualized representation: "I have often been surprised at the wide results brought home by different individuals, with the same camera, over the same ground."[53] Art value, in Kingsley's terms, lay in an expression of individuality that transcended the mechanical aspects of the photographic practice.

Photography as a Means of Expressing Individual Creativity

Art status hinged, in many minds, on a recognizable sense of individual authorship. The assertion of a human element in photography should be considered within the larger context of a late-nineteenth-century society increasingly dominated by the mechanical, the impersonal. In this context, the expression of individual identity became more urgent, especially in attempts to build a paradigm of artistic photography, for photography seemed to many to embody a mechanized estrangement from creative individuality. The imprint of the artist's creative intellect was theorized in a formal structure embedded in photographic composition, a structure based on accepted artistic models. For many writers, one of the loftiest goals of artistic expression was "the cultivation of that most precious power of individuality," which in turn "cultured in an atmosphere of an ordered imagination, sooner or later bears the fruit of originality" and "brings forth works of creation." Individual expression, one of the highest goals of art, had to be structured by an "ordered imagination" imposed by the grammar of art, thus differentiating individuality from "eccentricity."[54] Such criteria for infusing the artistic led to evaluations where the presence of the subjective maker was revered.

Edwin Cocking, a member of the Photographic Society of Great Britain and an early contributor to American legitimizing discussions, argued for an inherent subjectivity of photography, claiming that all pictorial photographs "bear the impress of its producer's individuality, whether it be good or whether it be bad," and therefore possess a subjective side. He concluded that photography can "be made the medium for the visible existence of art conceptions."[55] Cocking emphasized the importance of compositional control in his discussion of the use of line as a means of artistic investment illustrating a knowledge of "the language of art." Like Véron, he related standard rules of composition in which the interplay of lines in the scene represented could structure the pictorial effect, from balanced pyramidal groupings to dramatic angular oppositions. To Cocking, a thoughtful picture exhibited evidence of the individual's design, "a higher development of mental power" that resulted in "*something conceived and attempted to be carried out*."[56] The conception of the photograph bore the artistic value, rather than the technical creation of the image, and that conception depended on the conventions of the established graphic arts. Cocking focused on these conceptual tasks of the art photographer: the camera may be a machine and the image may be created through physical and chemical processes, but these scientific elements were the means by which the properly motivated photographer can tap into the creative inspiration that was a prerequisite to admission into the realm of art.

Selection as Aesthetic Investment

Underlying (or even resisting) an appeal to the mediating intellect was a celebration of the recording capacity of the photographic medium. To many photographers, the apparent proximity of the photographic record to nature could be one of the medium's greatest attributes. Indeed, an American propensity toward a reverence for nature surfaced throughout nineteenth-century painting, and, by thoughtfully engaging nature under the guidance of the wisdom of tradition, the photographer could imbue his or her products with the qualities that beget art. On the relation of nature and fine art, John Moran mused, "Our simple and unselfish delight in the contemplation of nature, . . . is the foundation of all the beautiful or fine arts, and . . . distinguishes them from science or the mechanical arts."[57] Moran embraced a type of naturalism where photography's seeming ability to record faithfully certain aspects of nature was its most laudable feature.

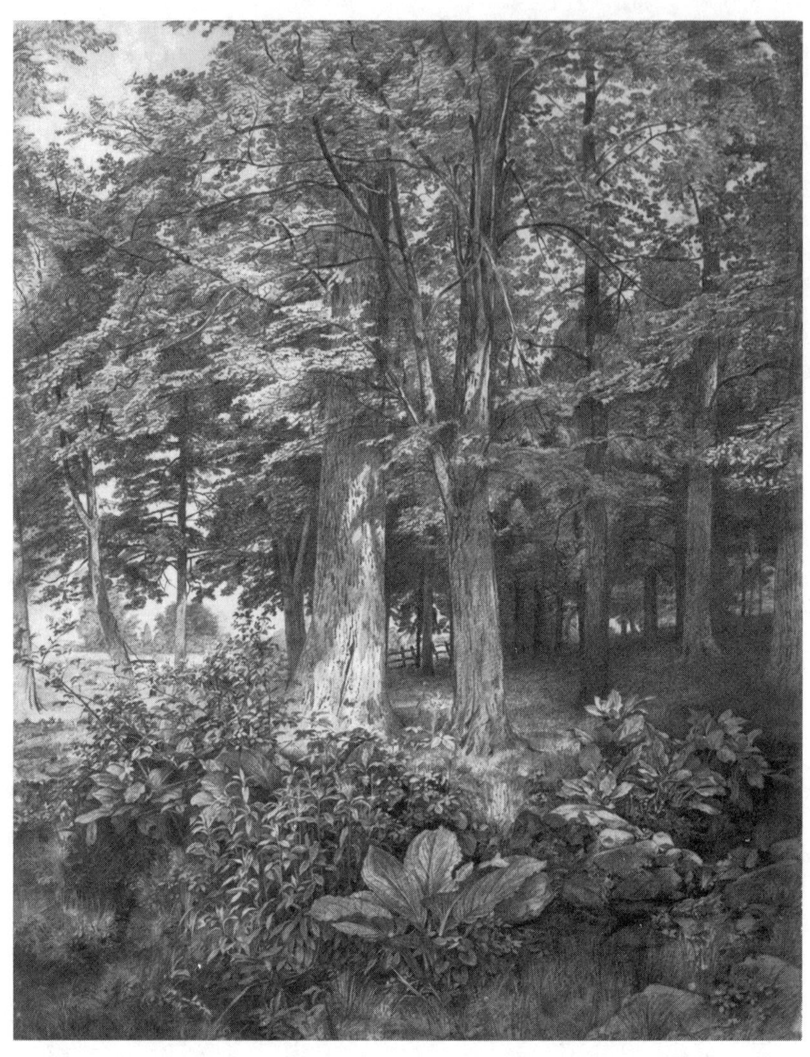

Fig. 5. William Trost Richards, *Corner of the Woods,* 1864, pencil on buff paper. Courtesy Museum of Fine Arts, Boston. Reproduced with permission.

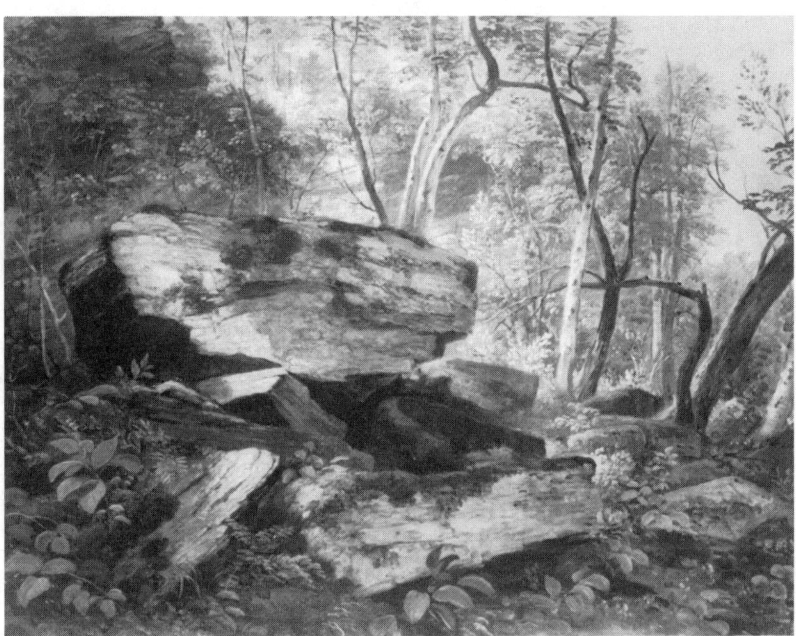

Fig. 6. Asher B. Durand, *Study from Nature: Rocks and Trees*, n.d. From the Collection of The New-York Historical Society.

This sort of praise was the legacy of John Ruskin and his American Pre-Raphaelite followers, with whom Moran was quite familiar.

Although the American Pre-Raphaelites were ambivalent toward photography, the group served as a disseminator of Ruskin's ideals and their formal manifestations to the photographic community. Modeled after their English precursor, the Pre-Raphaelite Brotherhood, the short-lived but influential Association for the Advancement of Truth in Art was founded in 1863 by a multivocational group. They based their philosophy of art, as Linda Ferber explains, on a Ruskinian concept of moralistic truth, defining standards of accuracy from the "photograph" and the "topographical report."[58] This measure of art's standards in the close observation of nature and detailed record could easily be invoked as an artistic paradigm by the American photographer, for the photographic medium seemed ideal for this kind of engagement of nature. In nature, wrote Enoch Root, "the intellect is quickened, the mind cultured, and the soul brought into nearer relationship with the Supreme Creator of all beauty and goodness."[59] The immediacy of an unmediated examination of nature is

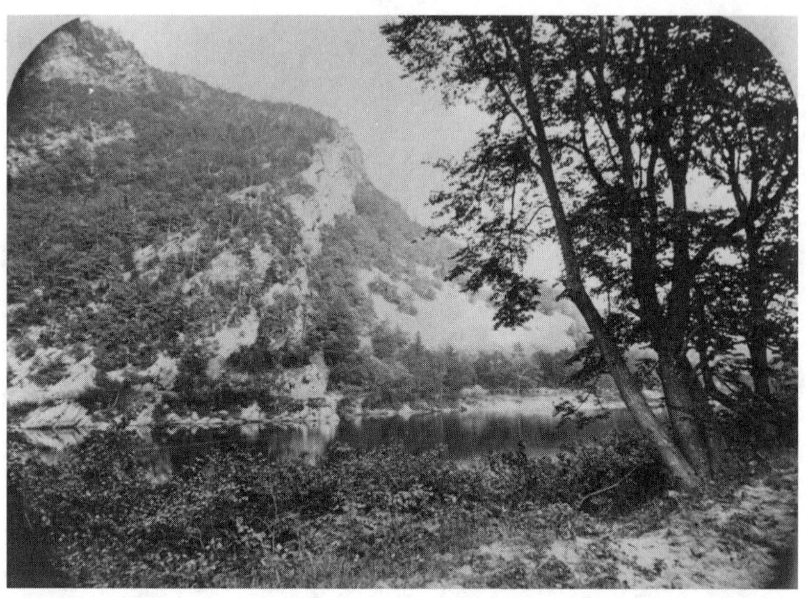

Fig. 7. John Moran, *Indian Ladder Bluff, Delaware Water Gap*, 1863, albumen print. Library Company of Philadelphia.

suggested in the informal plein air studies of the 1850s done by Asher B. Durand and William Trost Richards. The best known of the Ruskin-inspired American Pre-Raphaelites, Richards was a member of the Association for the Advancement of Truth in Art. In their captivation with nature, these works seem to find analogies in a few of John Moran's photographic landscape studies. An alternative to compositional convention lay in this direct confrontation of nature, as in Durand, and the photographic capacity for a detailed record was enough to satisfy a Pre-Raphaelite sensibility like Richards's.[60] At the height of the American Pre-Raphaelite movement in the mid-1860s, Thomas Moran reached the peak of his Ruskinian phase, and John Moran himself made informal photographic studies.[61] While the composition of Moran's photograph *Indian Ladder Bluff, Delaware Water Gap*, with its receding brook, is more traditional than Richards's seemingly impromptu encounter with an intimate forest passage, the two works share an kinship in their treatment of the intricate foreground undergrowth and delicately illuminated foliage.

Croughton's *East* (see fig. 4), which I discussed earlier as a manifestation of selective compositional convention, was also described as a bit of scenery akin to landscapes by artists such as Richards.[62] Indeed, the detailed rendering of natural forms throughout the image shares an affinity to Richards's work. Croughton's Ruskinian attention to the specifics of natural forms is tempered by the carefully structured composition, which draws the eye through the pictorial space. The advocates of the "photographic aesthetic" discussed in chapter 3 celebrated this coexistence of artistic convention and uniquely photographic qualities.

Almost two decades after the height of American Pre-Raphaelitism, the photographer John Bartlett revealed the lingering influence of Ruskinian ideals when he applauded photography's seemingly inextricable ties to nature, for "art and nature cannot be separated. Art cannot be divorced from nature and not suffer by the estrangement. It must be the imitator of nature, first and last." Photography's affinity to nature made it "realistic, and its power in art is this realism or truth to nature combined with a refinement in the selection of the subject." It seemed that photography's proximity to nature should be an asset, and Bartlett may have been coming to the medium's defense when he pointed out that "photography is derided and condemned to the province of a mere handicraft because she clings slavishly, as they say, to the actual in nature." But, he chided, "There is nothing, if viewed aright, which is common or unclean. . . . There is every variety of beauty, and he will perceive them all who looks not through the glass darkly, but face to face; and all of this capable of being translated in tone-value by the light upon the sensitive film."[63] Here the notion of artistic truth, based directly on the documentation of the real, is subject to aesthetic refinement.

As faithful a record of nature a painting or photograph may seem, the mere imitation of scene was not considered sufficient to assure its art status. An insistence only on nature's artistry suggested negation of author, so somehow individual creativity had to be inserted into the equation.[64] In fact, both Moran and Bartlett held that the record of nature had to be augmented by a process of creative thought, an inscription of author. This emphasis on the ability of the artist to imbue an image with creative thought through a carefully selected point of view was particularly popular in the late 1880s, but, like the admiration of photography's record of nature, it was articulated in the earlier writing of John Moran. Moran explained that the challenge for the artist in any medium was to successfully incite an aesthetic response, but inciting that response required a mediation of pure nature, a mediation by the artist's intellect. While there was artistic value in nature, "nature in herself speaks neither a language nor reveals a beauty;

it is the ideas and beauty of the mind that find their exercise in nature. . . . It is the mind that guilds and beautifies this world of ours."[65] The mind of the artist was the facilitating factor in the creation of art, not nature in and of itself.

Photography in uninspired hands produced uninspired work. "Looking at landscape photography from a painter's point of view," explained Moran,

> doubtless ninety per cent of the work would be pronounced worthless; they may have a value to some by association, or to science as a record of certain facts of nature, but as a language addressed to the art ideas, they are as dead as a language of which the key is lost; but when we see nature translated by men of whom Wilson and Blanchard are types, how different seems the world we live in; wherever they lead us, it is to scenes of light and beauty. No inanimate dry bones here, but all quickened to life by their own spirit and intelligence, and speaking the universal language of art.[66]

Photographers had to use the lens as a means to translate the raw information before the camera into the meaningful language of art, thus reflecting their creative intellect. The challenge for the artist in the photographic medium was to manifest thought in the photograph, to speak in the language of art. To Moran and many of his successors, the process of selection, by which observation of nature was mediated, allowed aesthetic or mental investment, a concept permeating Burnet's essays. During the summers of 1863 and 1864 Moran photographed along the Delaware and Lehigh Rivers and in the White Mountains, composing picturesque views that he issued as individual albumen prints.[67] Moran's *Indian Ladder Bluff, Delaware Water Gap* of 1863 (fig. 7) embodies what historian Bernard F. Reilly Jr. terms a "classical compositional device" of measured spatial progression.[68] Distinct features of the landscape modulate the recession of illusory space in the scene, proceeding from the foreground foliage to the expanse of river to the steep slope of the mountain behind.

With the danger of thoughtless recording in mind, Xanthus Smith established himself as one of the preeminent advocates of aesthetic investment through careful compositional construction, reasserting for a new and much larger generation of photographers Moran's emphasis on the primacy of the "power of selection" in the production of photographs worthy of consideration as art. In order to transcend the "hundreds of views . . . that are of no account whatever," the photographic artist had to endow the work with "certain intrinsic values" that were the product of a discrimination between "the beautiful and the commonplace in nature."[69] The "inexhaustible store" of nature, to Smith, was a basis on which to apply established art rules, allowing the photographer "to show his taste and knowledge in choosing those compositions that are particularly agreeable, and selecting a point of sight that will make the most harmonious arrangements."[70] Selection as a means of imbuing authorial creativity can be understood as a facet of what philosopher Jerome Stolnitz calls "aesthetic attitude," a directed awareness that allows the photographer to insert his or her presence. Stolnitz's "aesthetic attitude" is distinctly nonutilitarian, for it is "disinterested and sympathetic attention to and contemplation of any object for its sake alone.[71] The notion of "art for art's sake" certainly became a part of the art photography rhetoric of the 1890s, yet, as I will show in chapter 3, for many photographers, particularly professionals, the aesthetic and the utilitarian coexisted, one superimposed on the other.

While many writers claimed that photography found strength in its seeming affinity to realist doctrines, some were not satisfied with the simple selection of choosing a point of view. Andrew Pringle saw a major weakness in photography in its inability to idealize, "to *collect* details, aspects and expressions, and to join them into one *ensemble*."[72] These thoughts explain why Pringle would so admire Henry Peach Robinson's combination prints, a process in which the photographer combines several different negatives to piece together a scene much the way a painter can. In response to Robinson's "Letters on Landscape Photography," which had been published in installments in the *Photographic Times and American Photographer* in 1887, Pringle wrote that Robinson's work was "the closest approach to the highest artistic standard of any photographs I know."[73] To Robinson, the combination print (discussed more fully in chapter 3) was a way of more forcefully inserting convention and selection. In order for photography to be art, he insisted on photography's capacity for plasticity, thereby denying its identification as "a truthful, inevitable, stupid purveyor of prosaic fact."[74]

The Viewer's Role

While most of those arguing in favor of photography as art agreed that the picture must carry the impress of the photographer's mind, the nature of the viewer's role was not so clear. Edward L. Wilson saw a facet of artistic investment in the production of an insightful personal record of nature that communicates to the viewer of the work of art: "When the picture-maker begins to see things in Nature which the commonplace and unobserving do not notice, . . . then he astonishes his admirers by the revelation of unknown truths and translates for them a language whose charms have been forbidden to them, and then he is looked upon as possessing 'poetic feeling.'"[75] No longer was art status locked only in compositional device or even in the expression of the author's intellect—the aesthetic also depended on the viewer's response. Here, the Platonic ordered harmony was augmented with an appeal to intellectual response, a Kantian "harmony of the cognitive powers," where the work of art was not only beautiful but also "a vehicle for aesthetic ideas."[76] An aesthetic reaction, initiated by artistic convention, was required, but many writers disagreed on whether this response was inherent or learned. Some maintained that the idea transcended both the vehicle of communication (photography) and the code of its transmission (rules of art), so that the idea could be communicated even through unconscious or unmediated reception where the code remained undeciphered. Others argued that the process of deciphering the code was integral to the appreciation of the object as a work of art; in other words, one had to understand the language to understand its art value.[77]

Photographers with an affinity to theorists like Véron believed that artistic conventions strengthened and concentrated the ideas of the artist, as well as guided the spectator's response. Through standard formal devices, artists presented the work of their own intellect and also communicated to the viewer by means of psychophysical processes. These processes led to more than simple, low-level responses but also to memory, association, and morality. Because of the physiological basis of this reaction, it was instinctual. Writers put forth claims for a universal, inherent beauty and an instinctive human response to it. The conventions that were said to elicit instinctive aesthetic response were understood as scientifically based, proven over the course of centuries of use.[78] In contrast to the intuitive apprehension of the qualities of art, other writers presented aesthetic reception as grounded in knowledge of theory, not in intuition.[79]

Whether they argued that the viewer had to be educated in the language of art or not, most writers on photography agreed that reception somehow consisted of more than the sum of conventions and reached an advanced aesthetic appreciation, an idea I noted earlier in Véron's description of higher mental functions. Wilson repeatedly referred to a reception of pleasure, both by the viewer and the artist, that transcended the mere compositional rules and mechanics: proper study will "enable the one educated to give and to get more pleasure in the productions of his camera," and the photographer "will become inspired in some new and witchful way, with a delightful sense that will sway him, in spite of himself, ever after, and give him, and enable him to give, pleasure as long as he lives."[80] Thus the application of these compositional rules allowed access to a higher plane of aesthetic infusion.

A manifesto on the goals of the amateur artist-photographer published in the first issue of the *American Amateur Photographer* voiced many of the concepts underlying the theories outlined in this chapter, strategies that dominated the discourse on photography as art in the 1880s. It focused on an artist's relation to nature, which centered upon interpretation rather than record, where photography was but a means to an end: an objective higher than mere transcription of reality elevated photography beyond the scientific. Here, as with Véron, the aesthetic was intertwined with rhetoric about morality, a

> morality which springs from the purpose, single and earnest to interpret to unseeing eyes some portion, at least, of the charm and beauty with which God has filled this home of his making. . . . Such an earnest purpose as this lifts photography above the level of a mere pastime: it makes it an inspiration; an interpreter of the thoughts of God.[81]

Selection was presented as a primary means of artistic investment available to the photographer, who had to develop the vision necessary to recognize the features of a scene that would elevate it beyond a simple record. The photographer was able to communicate more than what was simply there; the camera could be more than a benign recorder of fact and could transmit something to the unthinking viewer. The art photographer somehow saw more and was thus elevated beyond the ordinary, much like artists in traditional media. The photographer's agency lay in the ability not simply to communicate beyond mere fact but to convey the moral and spiritual, in this case the wonders of God's creation.

The Insufficiency of an Appeal to Tradition

Not all photographers were willing to accept assertions of photography's art status based on compositional convention, selection, and other appeals to "the language of art" and its aesthetic consequences. In fact, some of the most convincing voices of dissent came from talented photographers themselves. As adamant a champion of photographic art as he seemed, John Moran's spirited defense of artistic infusion presented him with some insurmountable challenges. The challenges were so pervasive that he eventually eschewed photography in favor of painting. A photographer by trade, Moran articulated a dilemma that would frustrate commercial photographers for the rest of the century: could a photograph be both artistic and useful, or are utility and high art inherently incompatible? Moran hinted, even in his earlier writings, that the two were basically irreconcilable, an impasse that may account for his ultimate abandonment of the medium. Perhaps reflecting his close ties with artistic circles, Moran suggested a dichotomy between art and utilitarian photography, which many commercial photographers refused to accept yet which was nonetheless virtually codified by the turn of the century.

By late 1875 Moran's faith in the photographic medium started to waver, for he seemed to have considered the limits of photography more carefully. Occasional latent doubts began to be more fully manifested, foreshadowing his eventual renunciation of photography as an artistic practice and reflecting criticisms of the medium addressed by photographers of the following decades. Moran succumbed to the apparent transparency of the photographic record and began to place photography lower in a hierarchy, closer to artless realism than to the "poetic" of high art. Although he admired the "strong reasoning and analytic power of the realist," the poetic artist possessed a "still higher power." The "poetry" Moran believed was essential for high art required creative latitude, which photography could not afford. Ultimately, selection guided by knowledge of artistic principles was not enough, for "photography is a realistic art, and within its sphere no human hand can rival it; [yet] it is a translator, not a creator."[82] The seeming incongruency of photography's realist tendencies and his own demands for more creative investment than he could find in the photographic process led Moran to eschew photography in favor of painting, the medium that offered him a greater opportunity for imbuing his work with the poetry that begat art.[83]

Moran's desertion of photography after having found in the medium so much potential for artistic expression is evidence of the complexity of the predicament in which champions of art photography placed themselves. Photography seemed so closely linked to the empirical sciences of chemistry and geometrical optics, yet the demands on art in the second half of the nineteenth century increasingly stressed an assertion of subjectivity, individuality, and authorship.

As telling as Moran's abandonment of photography was, an even more passionate rebuttal to attempts to place photography within the realm of the fine arts was made by William James Stillman. Stillman remains a challenging character, for he created exquisite photographs that seem to be the ideal evidence for the claim that a photograph can be a

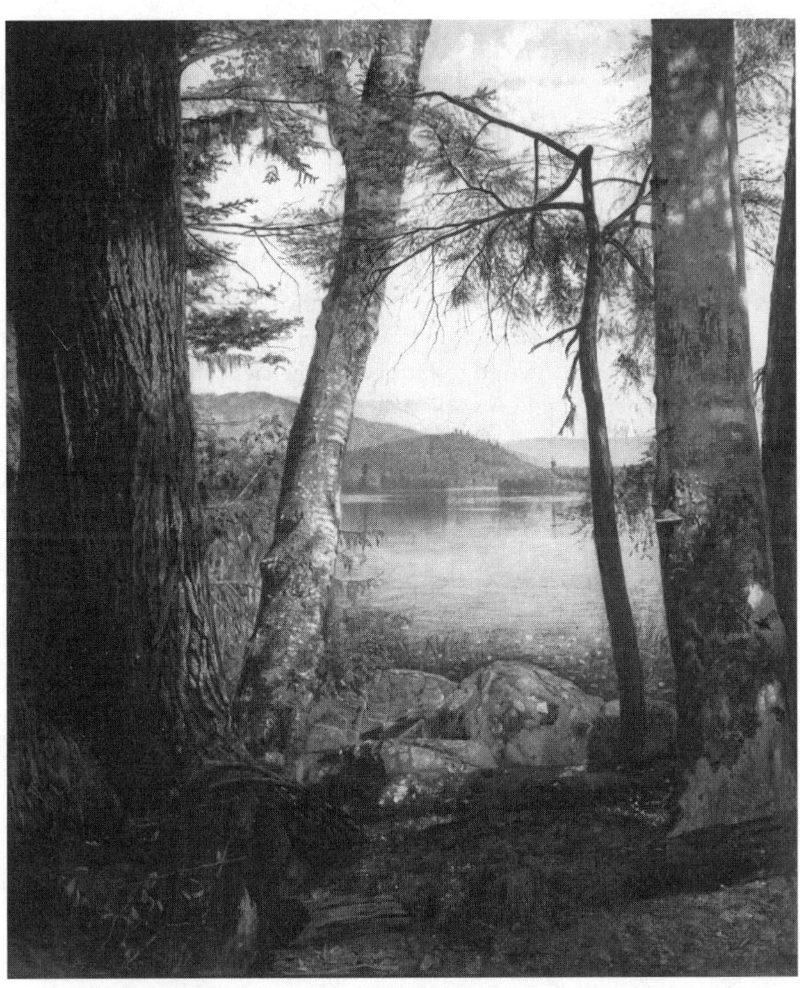

FIG. 8. William James Stillman, *Saranac Lake, Adirondack Mountains,* 1854. Courtesy Museum of Fine Arts, Boston. Reproduced with permission.

work of art. He was a masterful technician with supreme control of the medium and an eye for sophisticated, evocative, and uncontrived compositions, and his work seems some of the most likely to be acclaimed as art. Yet he did not accept photography as fine art; in fact, more than any photographer in America, he adamantly denied photography's art potential.

Stillman's work with some of the most prestigious artists on both sides of the Atlantic, along with his vast critical writings on fine art, gave him the clout to be a most convincing American champion of photography as art. Stillman studied landscape painting under Frederic Edwin Church; in 1849, he traveled to Europe and befriended John Ruskin and the Pre-Raphaelites; and he was hailed by *The New Path* as "the first American Pre-Raphaelite."[84] Stillman's 1854 painting *Saranac Lake, Adirondack Mountains* reflects an American Pre-Raphaelite engagement with the minutia of happened-upon nature, a remarkable coalescence of Ruskinian thought and the native landscape tradition.[85] Stillman's photographic studies can have the same feeling: compare, for instance, Stillman's photograph of a tree base and the surrounding forest floor with Asher B. Durand's study of a similar intimate wooded scene (fig. 6). Stillman studied in Paris until he returned to the United States in 1856 and, with John Durand, cofounded *The Crayon*, a primary source of Ruskinian principles in America.[86] Between 1851 and 1859 Stillman contributed regularly to the Academy of Design, to which he was elected an associate in 1854. In 1869, after a stint in the diplomatic service, he published a book of photographs of the Acropolis.[87]

In 1885 Stillman joined the staff of the *Photographic Times and American Photographer* as an associate editor and began contributing articles that complicated and intensified the debate over the prospects for art photography. Stillman authored the first article of the 1885 volume of the journal, which he entitled "Photography and Art." Displaying a marked skepticism about the ability of photography to achieve the status of fine art, he challenged many of the conclusions made by writers in the half decade before his appointment to associate editorship and offered spirited retorts to many of the theories used to support photography's claim to art status. Stillman accepted the standard criticisms of photography: "As a rival of art, photography is in many respects too much handicapped to do anything—it is, at its basis, a chemical-mechanical operation, and its artistic relations are only incidental." Stillman's conception of nature as it related to art differed from many of his colleagues. While other writers argued that art springs from the gifted or trained

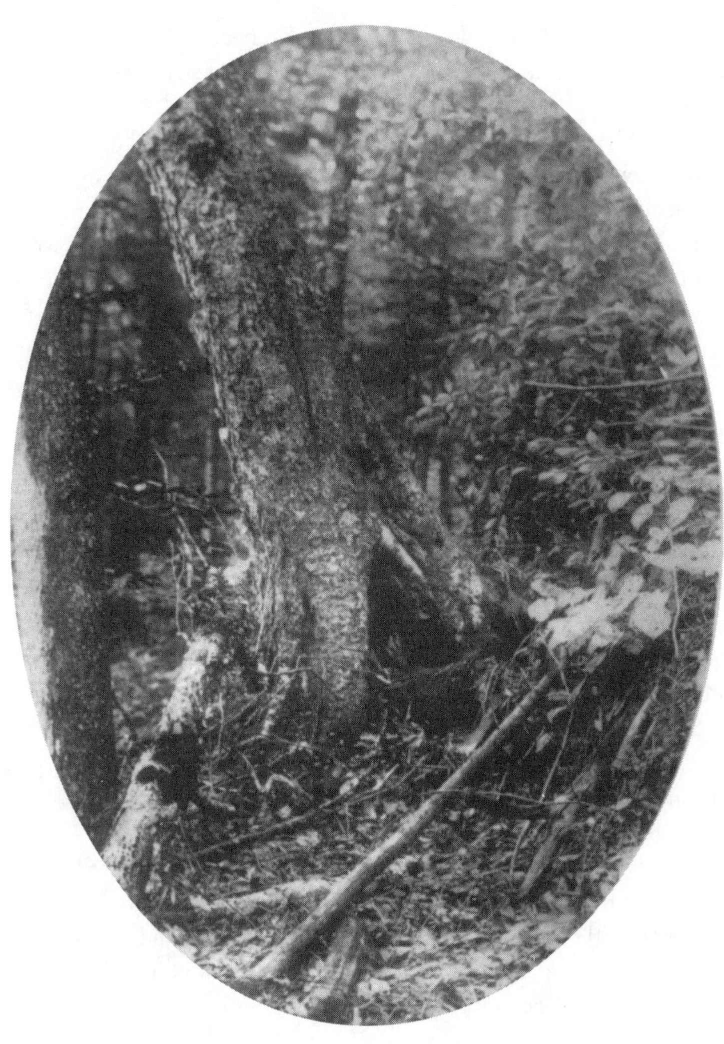

FIG. 9. William James Stillman, *Study of tree trunk, Photographic Studies by William James Stillman.*

eye that can recognize and represent natural beauty, Stillman did not accept the notion of an unmediated natural scene as art. "Now nature," he wrote,

> occasionally produces, by accident, arrangements of her material, so harmonious and happy that we consider them unusually fit subjects for the painter, they can never be confounded with the work of the artist. . . . Nature never yet arranged a subject so that in some of the minute details, at least, it shall not be discordant, and demand of art some modification to make its harmonies perfect, and this modification is beyond the power of the camera or the combination printer. They may mimic nature, but the more closely they do so the less they suggest art.[88]

"Photography," Stillman stated, "is as far superior to painting, or art in general, as a medium *for the expression of the facts of nature, or the results of science,* as art is superior to photography *as the means of expressing emotion or imaginative conceptions.*"[89] In Stillman's eyes, "the [photographer's] camera only renders the anatomy of nature, the dry unsympathetic facts, which are only his alphabet."[90]

Stillman simply would not accept the argument that creative infusion could be achieved through selection guided by compositional conventions of the traditional arts:

> there is no possibility of changing a photographic impression by any thought or effort of the photographer. We may cut down a tree that stands in the way of our view, but that is not art; and we may retouch our work and our negatives, but that is not photography, and we may choose our subject well, but that is neither one nor the other, but good taste.[91]

Stillman distinguished photography from "legitimate art," which he claimed was the "production of design," arguing that photography was "not an art of design, but an art of technical excellence."[92] In contrast to a painter who has the opportunity for creative investment at all stages of the picture-making process, "a photographer only finds a bit that suits him and puts his camera before it and the lens does the work; it is an absolutely mechanical process."[93]

Henry Peach Robinson entered into a spirited debate within the pages of the *Photographic Times and American Photographer* between Andrew

Pringle and Stillman over photography as art.[94] Taking issue with Stillman's preference for the traditional graphic arts, Robinson maintained that the artist's tools were varied and that, despite an admitted limitation in the medium's plasticity, photography did indeed have much potential for personal expression. Beyond this potential, the actual process of representation allowed room for what he called the "personal equation:" a uniqueness of style that asserted the individuality of the photographer and facilitated the expression of his or her conception.[95] Stillman, however, disagreed with this conclusion on the most fundamental level, flatly rejecting the increasingly prevalent argument that the photographic image can be a work of art because of the mental or emotional investment of the photographer. Stillman denied photography's ability to express a conception, stating bluntly, "'rendering the sentiment of a landscape' by the use of the camera and lens . . . is analogous to the turning out of poetry by machine," and he explained that "a photographic view can have neither sentiment nor expression."[96]

A gifted photographer, Stillman did not give up on the medium altogether, for he conceded that, while photography was not art, it could be artistic.[97] Stillman defined "artistic" as "resembling art"—not being art. Photography could be "improved by taste and judicious selection and treatment, such as an artist would use"; thus it could be "artistic." In discussing the ways a photograph may be made artistic, Stillman recapitulated many of the compositional conventions his colleagues published again and again. To Stillman, however, these conventions made better photographs but did not make photography a fine art.[98]

Although for Stillman photography was not an art, because by his standards photography simply did not afford the original individual investment that defined art, his motives were not the degradation of the photographic process. As I will explain in chapter 3, Stillman had an egalitarian view of graphic media: photography stood its own ground. As is evident in statements in which he discounted retouching and other forms of manipulation because they "are not photography," Stillman believed that the dignity of the medium lay not in aspirations to art status but rather in unpretentious fidelity to the characteristics that seemed inherent to the medium.

During the last half of the nineteenth century, the discourse on photography as art appealed to established formal and aesthetic traditions. These traditions offered photographers a means to attempt a reconciliation of the seemingly binary opposition of photography's deep roots in empirical science and the demands of art. Photographers appealed to respected academic texts like those of Burnet and to the work of aesthetic theorists like Véron, arguing that photography could, through the knowledgeable application of formal rules of art, express individual creativity and incite aesthetic response in the viewer. Yet, in the eyes of writers like Moran and Stillman, the paradox of photography's seemingly inextricable link to positivist science made it incongruent with art, which an appeal to selective vision and compositional convention could not overcome. In chapter 2 I will examine ways in which photographers endeavored to subvert the scientific side of photography, attempting to assert more forcefully a sense of authorship and an appeal to the psychological and intellectual processes thought to be activated by art. This process of subversion, mostly in the hands of amateurs, both challenged the standards of acceptable photographic practice and embraced new models of how the photograph could appeal to subjective experience.

Chapter Two

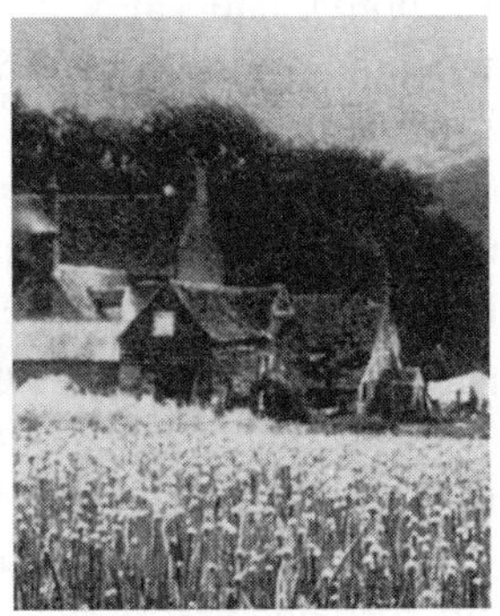

"Positive Conspicuous Defects": The Denial of the Photographic

[The photographer] is rather rigidly confined within the fixed limits of the process of photography. His lens, his plate, and his developer are but narrowly controlled by himself. Their action is preordained in their construction, and he can only inject a subjective influence over their results by subterfuge and device.

—L. P. Gratacap, "Impressionistic Photography"

Grappling with the dual nature of photography as an "art-science," photographers during the 1880s and 1890s attempted to reconcile these seeming opposites. In addition to the compositional conventions borrowed from the established graphic arts discussed in chapter 1, photographers with artistic intentions also investigated legitimizing strategies that modified the nature of the photographic image itself. Photography's verisimilitude—its apparently inherent capacity for crisp, detailed, seemingly transparent or "truthful" images—was most often the feature that led critics to deny it art status. In response to the weaknesses of the inherently "photographic," some photographers, particularly amateurs, attempted to subvert these qualities through a purposeful repression of detail, depth of field, and range of tones.

Many of these formal devices have come to be associated with a general photographic movement called "pictorialism." However, as Peter Bunnell points out, the term "pictorialism" is not a nineteenth-century designation: the title was coined shortly after World War One.[1] While "pictorial photography" is a phrase that found frequent use in the last few decades of the nineteenth century, it was incorporated in so many contexts and with reference to so many differing approaches to photography, it lost any specific meaning. In place of "pictorialism," I will employ terms that provide more of a sense of contemporary formal devices and theoretical foundations. While the formal effects can be given the general classification "soft focus," I introduce the term "antiphotographic" in order to underscore the fact that these effects were not just the result of altering the focus of the camera but rather were formal manifestations of several distinct theoretical approaches. More important, I believe "antiphotographic" makes explicit these photographers' intent to subvert qualities that most photographers considered inherent to the medium.

The multiplicity of calls for photographers to alter the photographic process reflected the zeal with which manipulation was deemed necessary. As a painter, amateur photographer, and frequent contributor to American photographic journals, Xanthus Smith divided the products of photography into three categories. First was the work of professional photographers, the goal of which was technical perfection and which occasionally contained some incidental "art in the arrangement." Second was the work of less technically advanced amateurs who neglected the artistic. The third category was comprised of the work of artistic amateurs who gained artistic sensibility through training or were "naturally possessing the art faculty."[2] This differentiation was not only significant in its creation of a hierarchy of photographic practice (a strategy addressed more fully in chapter 4); it also presented two key proposals needed for the theorization of the antiphotographic. Smith believed that a well-trained or gifted artist was able to infuse his or her work with an aesthetic content that would transcend the work of the professional and uninspired amateur, a claim that recalled the formal compositional strategies discussed in chapter 1. Even more significant, Smith's categories led to a presentation of technical perfection *at odds with* the artistic.[3]

Smith's first point, that inspired artistic investment was possible in photography, was shared by many of the writers who went on to argue for the denial of the photographic and was applied to the encouragement of compositional conventions. Yet, after asserting that art came from compliance with certain rules, Smith and other writers suggested a strategy that looked beyond compositional conventions. They maintained that photography had to be modified in order to comply with the rules of art, for art could not accommodate the photographic. New features were identified as artistic in photography, and writers turned to more generalized, intimate effects of Barbizon and impressionist landscape. Beyond compositional devices, this type of appeal sought to suppress the technical capabilities of the medium.

The increasing standardization of the photographic industry and the improvement of the optical and chemical technology of the medium toward the end of the nineteenth century constantly enhanced photography's capacity to record the specifics of optical information. To photographers hoping to divorce photography from its supposed mechanicity, the tendencies toward which photographic technology developed (for example, sharpness and detail) seemed antithetical to art.[4] The photographic artist was told to look beyond the mechanical givens of the medium, to break rules that seemed to be dictated by the technology. G. Hanmer Croughton, while embracing photographic detail, set up an opposition of the artist and the photographer, claiming that pure technical skill had become simpler and simpler to achieve because of advances in the manufacture of photographic equipment and supplies. He called for the photographer to heed the artist's aesthetic demands because technical expertise would be less and less distinctive. In order to produce "pictures," the photographer "will have to unlearn a great many things, and learn to look upon some things he has hitherto regarded as essential to good photography as edged tools that will not bear playing with."[5] Even Henry Peach Robinson, a long-time opponent of most soft-focus photography, asked if a photographer had to shun art entirely, striving after "perfect sharpness and smoothness, that terrible perfection of technique alone."[6]

The photograph's capacity for recording detail was indeed the object of ridicule of many of the champions of the antiphotographic. To critic Charlotte Adams, suppression of details could lead to an appreciation of a photograph beyond superficial technical qualities and detailed renderings of the world. Guiding the viewer through Edward L. Wilson's *A Nubian Landscape,* Adams asked the spectator to subdue the camera's recording capacity in order to see beyond the specifics of the landscape. She suggested that "to appreciate fully the truth and unity of this impression, the spectator should half-close his eyes and look steadfastly at the photograph. In this the details of the photograph will disappear, and the composition resolves itself into broad masses of light and dark. The salient features of the landscape are preserved and fall readily into their relative positions."[7]

Reflecting tensions that will be discussed more fully in chapter 4, Croughton described an exhibition viewed by an artist and a photographer, each of whom was struck by a particular photographic image. The photographer was impressed by a work showing great technical skill, "developed just right, printed and toned to perfection." The artist, on the other hand, was drawn to a very different photograph, one capturing "nature's transient moods, caught under conditions of great difficulty, where composition of line, light, shade, concentration and focus, were all there." Yet the scramble down a steep bank left the plate soiled, and the flux of nature allowed no time to secure another, so the final image was marred by the imperfection of the plate. The artist looked beyond the technical imperfections to the aesthetic qualities that made it a picture. The photographer's choice, although technically perfect, lacked the aesthetic qualities that would have made it a picture: the uniform focus of a small aperture failed to bring out the best parts of the view and challenged the recession of space by calling attention to the foreground; too much light entered and from the wrong direction; and "in short, instead of being a picture it was a photographic map" with an "utter want of artistic feeling."[8] Croughton argued that technical perfection might be neglected or even sacrificed in favor of artistic effects.

The distrust of the photographic record as an appropriate means to communicate a subjective artistic impulse paralleled a fundamental change in epistemological thought in the post-Kantian era. Analyzing Goethe and drawing on Foucault, Jonathan Crary outlines the shift from the conception of vision as an empirical mode of scientific observation to an insistence on "experiences in which the subjective contents of vision are dissociated from the objective world, in which the body itself produces phenomenon which have no external correlate."[9] The subversion of the factual in favor of the metaphysical has parallels in the literature of the period as well. Thomas Hardy, who incidentally harbored a deep-seated animosity for the recreational Kodaker, favored an internal truth not always accessible to "the outer senses alone." Henry James used photography itself as a metaphor for the "internalization of romance . . . as a way of looking, disrupting and qualifying the vision of realism."[10] Similarly, the would-be photographic artist who insisted on subjective content in photographic pictures, be it a replication of vision or a reflection of individual intellect, was not satisfied with the optical objectivity of the unmediated photographic process.

The growing stress on subjectivity and subsequent mistrust of the pho-

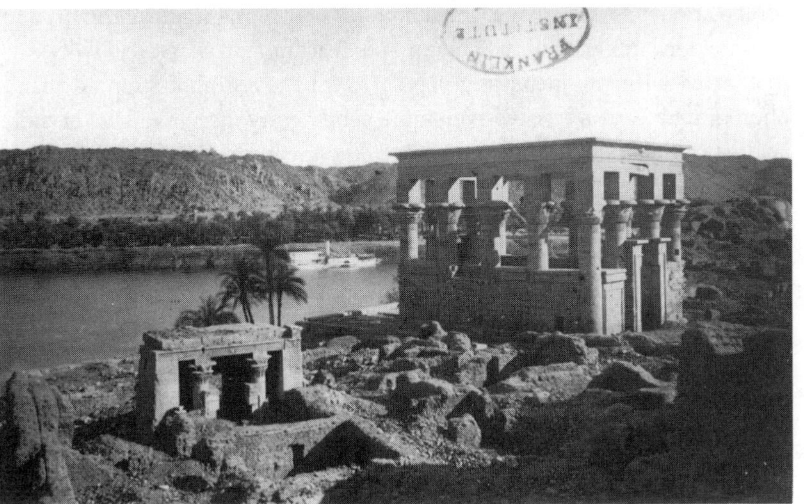

Fig. 10. Edward L. Wilson, *A Nubian Landscape,* albumen print. *Philadelphia Photographer,* March 1884, frontispiece. Library Company of Philadelphia.

tographic record as a device to access the artistic must also be placed in the context of an increasingly industrialized society. Photographic historian Keith Davis frames his discussions of the decades flanking 1900 in an economic context, underscoring the transformation of the United States from a rural agrarian nation to a largely urban and industrial one. He also notes a shift brought on by industrialization from production by skilled craftspeople to mass manufacture by increasingly automated systems.[11] Similarly, Peter Bunnell associates the antiphotographic art photography known as "pictorialism" with a reaction against "the dehumanizing effects of science and applied technology." Pictorialism, he adds, placed "its greatest emphasis on the individuality of the artist as witnessed in the work of art and idiosyncrasies of its production."[12] In contrast to an unquestioning belief in the benefits of science, which encouraged the technical improvement of photography, the negation of the inherently photographic can be attributed to a distrust of technology, and it provided a means to underscore individual creative infusion. Yet given other legitimizing strategies and the theoretical basis of the prototypes to pictorialism, the situation was even more complex. As I previously explained, photographers and writers, particularly in the 1880s, theorized the interjection of individual creativity through compositional devices that seemed both to cater to the traditions of art and to uphold the integrity of the photographic medium. In chapter 3 I will show that, faced with the increasing popularity of the antiphotographic, many photographic artists resisted even more vehemently the subversion of characteristics they believed were unique to the medium.

Invocation and Evocation

The first and most straightforward of the approaches to the subversion of the photographic I will distinguish as the "invocative antiphotographic," in which photographers deliberately made their photographs look like productions of other graphic media, most often prints. This superficial similarity to the representational quality of accepted media was a direct appeal to artistic tradition: the photograph had the look of an etching; an etching is art; so the photograph was art. As an 1894 reviewer put it, the work "resembles reproductions from paintings or etchings," suggesting that the photographers "wish to make their pictures look as little like photographs as possible."[13]

Other antiphotographic strategies were more sophisticated both in their professed relation to art and in the means by which they sought to justify this relation. Photographers began to question the equation of photographic reality and perceptual reality. The photographer John Bartlett, an admirer of photography's ability to record nature, nonetheless found fault with photography precisely because he believed it did not mimic human perception. While photography, for better and for worse, was closely linked with a purely scientific record, Bartlett doubted such a correlation between the photographic image and human perception of reality: "One can not consistently affirm that the pencil of light does faithfully translate nature upon the sensitive film; that is nature as presented to our normal vision." What Bartlett meant by photography's infidelity to "normal vision" was not simply its lack of ability to record color or its long struggle with unequal sensitivity to different areas of the spectrum. Instead, Bartlett invoked observations of human physiological reactions to strong contrasts of light and dark where the retinal receptors are "exhausted" and transmit "rays of the opposite kind" to the brain.[14] His point was that photography was actually too accurate to compensate for this "physiological peculiarity." While Bartlett dismissed photography's artistic potential, other photographers attempted to reconcile the photographic record and perceptual experience, proposing the impressionist photograph.

An impressionist photograph was meant to replicate a perceptual ex-

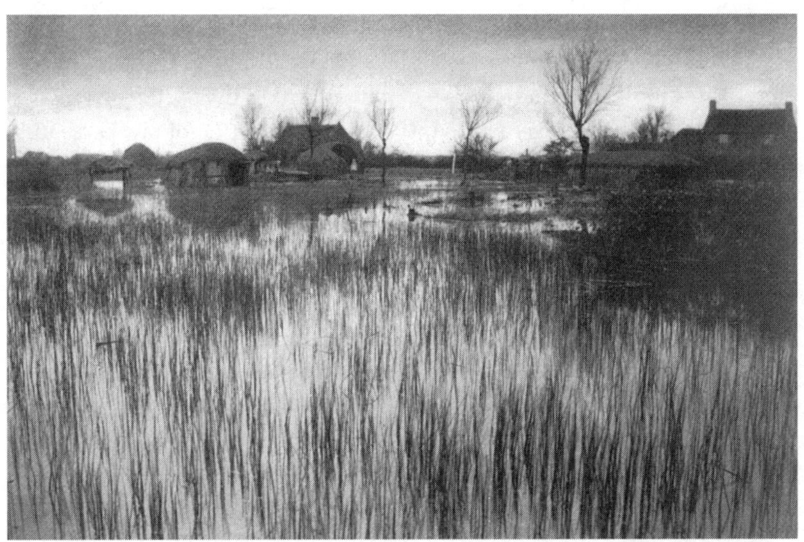

Fig. 11. Peter Henry Emerson, *A Rushy Shore,* 1886, platinum print. Private collection.

perience of a scene rather than simply cataloguing the facts of nature in an empirical photographic account of reality. Impressionist photographer A. J. Treat presented a notion of a record of pure perceptual experience as he quoted a description of impressionism: "The record of a visual sensation in all its freshness, without the complication of its simple purity by the addition of hypothetical lines or masses which the eye has not directly observed."[15] "Naturalistic photography," defined and most strongly advocated by the major British photographer Peter Henry Emerson, shared this basis in perception with its theoretical grounding in the notion of "differential focus."[16] The only narrow plane of focus in a naturalistic photograph was that of the main subject, a technique that was meant to mimic human perception.[17]

With this theorization of impressionist photography, the practice can be understood as a sort of positivism. Visual sensation was proposed as a set of scientifically quantifiable phenomena that could be replicated by photography. This sort of positivism, as it related to photography, however, was very different than that which embraced the unmediated photograph as a record of transparent truth. The photographic record and perceptual experience were at odds.

Within impressionist practice, photographers further distinguished the use of the antiphotographic by embracing a variety of views on exactly what the perceptual record was meant to be, distinguishing a positivist perception from a more subjective model of perception. In the positivist view, for instance, the impressionist photograph as a transcription of raw perceptual experience in and of itself was considered by some to be evidence of the image's artistic status. Other writers required an appeal to the viewer beyond perceptual experience, an appeal that involved higher subjective cognitive processes of memory and association. Writers found in the antiphotographic "a revolution in photographic methods," where "artists of a higher plane" eschewed "topographical accuracy" in favor of a "landscape of [their] own inner consciousness."[18] This romantic focus on the internal rather than the external engaged the metaphysical, the nature of experience itself rather than merely describing the physical attributes of the world.[19] I call this mental associative appeal through soft focus the "evocative antiphotographic," which may be distinguished from the "invocative antiphotographic" because the evocative image did not just look like art, it was meant to act like art.[20] The evocative will lead us from the positivist realm into the romantic, where photography was placed in the service of an appeal to the metaphysical.

Indeed, in American painting, one can easily point to parallels to shifts in artistic photographic practice. In painting, by the 1880s the "detailed landscape of the native school" (the Hudson River School, the American Pre-Raphaelites, the Luminists) was being eclipsed by "a more painterly and personal interpretation of nature" like that of George Inness and his Barbizon-inspired landscape.[21] In fact, in 1879 Inness saw the meticulous scrutiny of the details of nature in Pre-Raphaelitism as "a true outgrowth of the scientific tendency of the new age. It was a false philosophy. . . . It carried the love of imitation into irrational conditions."[21] In a similar vein, Carl DeMuldor, in his 1885 *Philosophy of Art in America,* criticized American Pre-Raphaelite work for its lack of "perception of larger truths, values of tone, controlling the harmonious or decorative relations." They were "*sans* soul, *sans* thought, *sans* inspiration and poetry, . . . produced through the rarest ape-like imitation."[22] Indeed, in the traditional arts as well as in photography, tolerance for the cataloging of detail, even if it were subject to organizing principles of art, was waning. Artists suspected that an appeal to such specifics reflected neither perception nor taste.

Subverting the Photographic

The photographer who wished to avoid photographic specificity seemed to be at odds with the inherent capacity of the medium, for well-performed

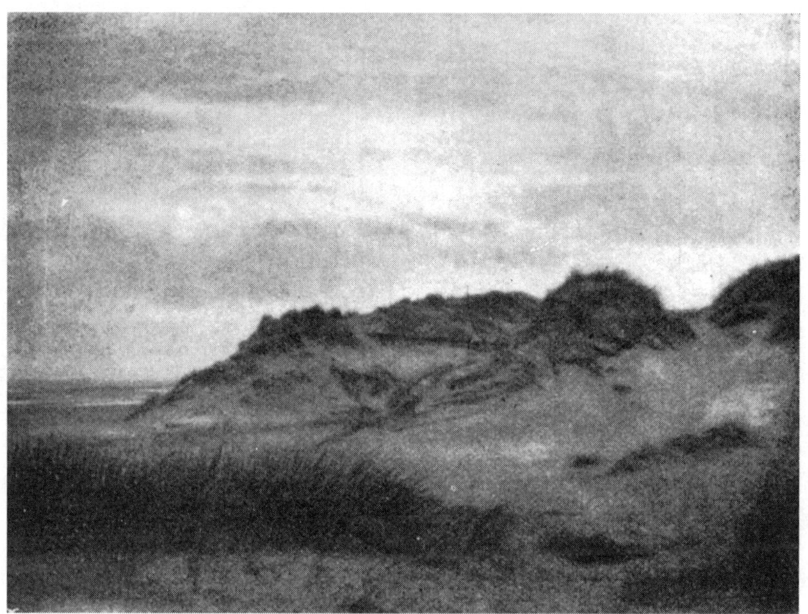

Fig. 12. F. C. Lambert, *Sand and Sunshine,* halftone. *Photographic Times,* September 1896, p. 412. Library Company of Philadelphia.

photography, as technology shaped it, lent itself to minute clarity. However, F. C. Lambert, elected to the Linked Ring in 1896, wrote of the imperfection of the process as a laudable feature, finding possible advantages in "positive conspicuous defects." By subjugating the tendency of the photograph to record precise detail, one could turn the photographic "collection" into photographic "selection."[23] Lambert's *Sand and Sunshine*—with its overall soft focus, flattening broad masses of tones, and generalizing textures—reflects this sort of subjugation.

In an 1895 address, the founder of the Linked Ring and frequent contributor to photographic literature Alfred Maskell discussed the changes he perceived in the practice of art photography since the early 1880s. He pointed out the willingness of progressive contemporary photographers to discard much of what had been valued in a photograph. In contrast to the creation of a faultless negative, he described "the art of making spoiled negatives." In his day the photographer was free to work "after the completion of the negative," unhampered by the "supposed necessities" of technical perfection. This new freedom, according to Maskell, allowed for "new capabilities and new possibilities in photography," including unique expression, compared to the older standards where "an inflexible regularity allowed no play to the individual." In fact, to Maskell, "retouching, or the alteration of the mechanical work of the lens, is the only door through which art can enter photography."[24]

In response to the use of "photographic" as a derogatory term applied to graphic representation, Washington, D.C., photographer Eugene Lee Ferguson defended the medium and attempted to define a legitimate space for what he called "the unphotographic photograph." The strength of such a photograph was its attempt to "get beyond the fixed scope of photography," to transcend the limits imposed by the common practice.[25] Such values led to positive evaluations of photographers like Stieglitz, who was not "mechanical . . . , the slave of his apparatus," but rather "knows how to handle his camera and materials to make them respond to his wishes."[26]

Photographers invented ingenious ways to undermine the features to which so much photographic technology was geared. The suppression of the minute recording capacity of the medium could take place at several different points in the photographic process. A photographer could begin this manipulation during the actual exposure of the negative. The focus could be altered during exposure, thus subordinating detail to more general effects. The aperture could be opened during exposure, changing the depth of field and spherical aberration and thus the quality of focus. The photographer could soften a picture with a large single lens and a wide aperture, with a monocle or spectacle lens, by using a small aperture with the lens racked out-of-focus, by introducing an astigmatism, or, as F. C. Lambert and George Davison did, with the use of a pinhole in place of the lens. Collodion films or diffraction gratings could be placed over the diaphragm inside the camera, softening the image before it reached the plate. Some photographers disrupted focus during exposure by causing their cameras to vibrate, drawing a violin bow across a cord with a heavy weight suspended from the center of the tripod. The image could be altered by the waves of heat from the flame of a lamp held beneath the area directly in front of the lens during exposure.[27]

Along with manipulating the camera, a photographer could soften the images in the darkroom. He or she could mask, scrape, paint or draw directly onto the negative, creating images that looked more like drawings and prints with their openly declared artistic activity. A collodion film or sheet of glass between the negative and printing paper could diffuse the photographic image as it was printed. Textured bromide and platinum papers infused with emulsion offered an alternative to more prevalent

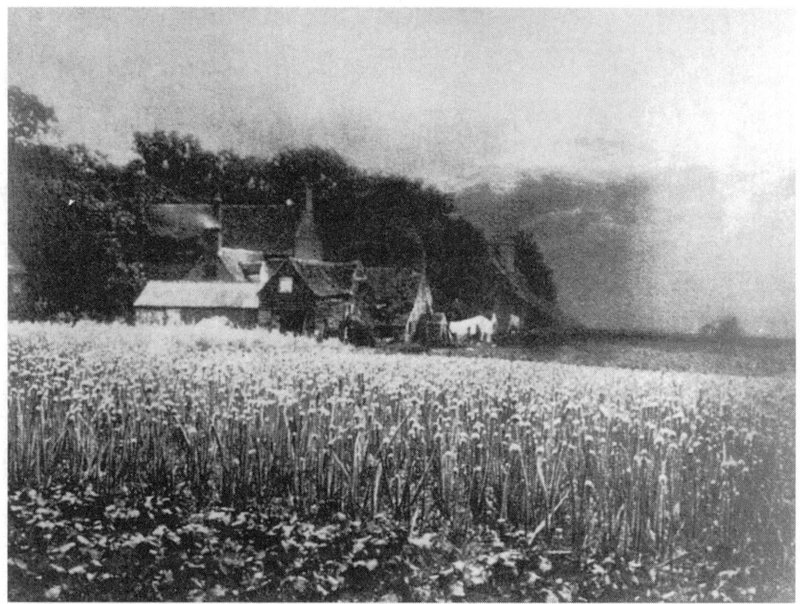

Fig. 13. George Davison, *The Onion Field (An Old Farmstead)*, 1890, photogravure. *Camera Work*, April 1907, p. 91. Library Company of Philadelphia.

glossy, smooth finished albumen papers and could be further roughened after printing. Many photographers preferred the subtle tones and surface of platinum prints to the sheen of albumen: "The fine matte surface and cool grey tones of platinum were gratefully restful to the eyes after the glare and shine of albumen."[28]

In addition to using newly available commercial printing papers, photographers coated their own paper with layers of gum-based toned emulsions, giving not only rich tones but painterly effects. Brushing these emulsions onto the paper or brushing on the developer left gestural marks akin to those of the graphic artist. French photographer Robert Demachy saw a new plasticity in pigment-based photographic processes, most notably gum bichromate.[29] To Demachy, such a process allowed the photographer to insert his or her "aesthetic culture" beyond selection and to control the scattered information of the "nondiscriminating lens."[30] The solubility of the gum bichromate emulsion gave the photographer a great deal of latitude in the printing process, for unlike gelatin-based processes, details and even whole objects could be rinsed away to the point of mere suggestion. This plasticity of the print meant that the photographic

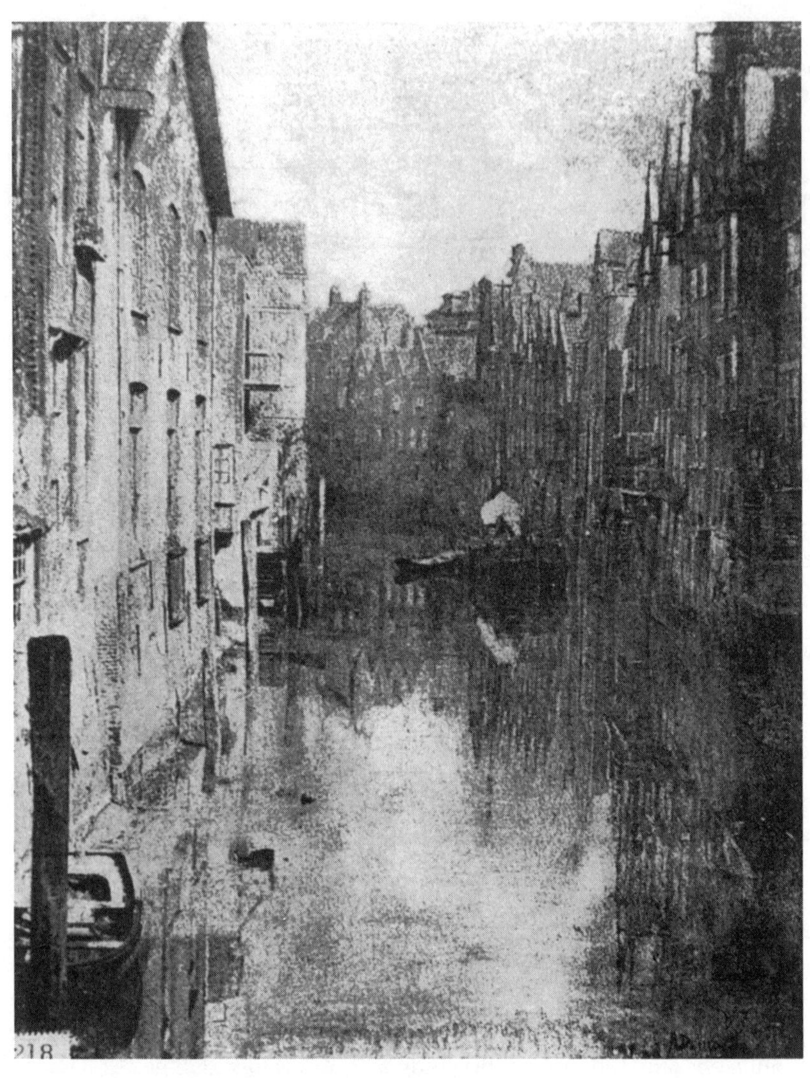

Fig. 14. Robert Demachy, *Dead Waters,* halftone. *Photographic Times,* September 1897, p. 407. Library Company of Philadelphia.

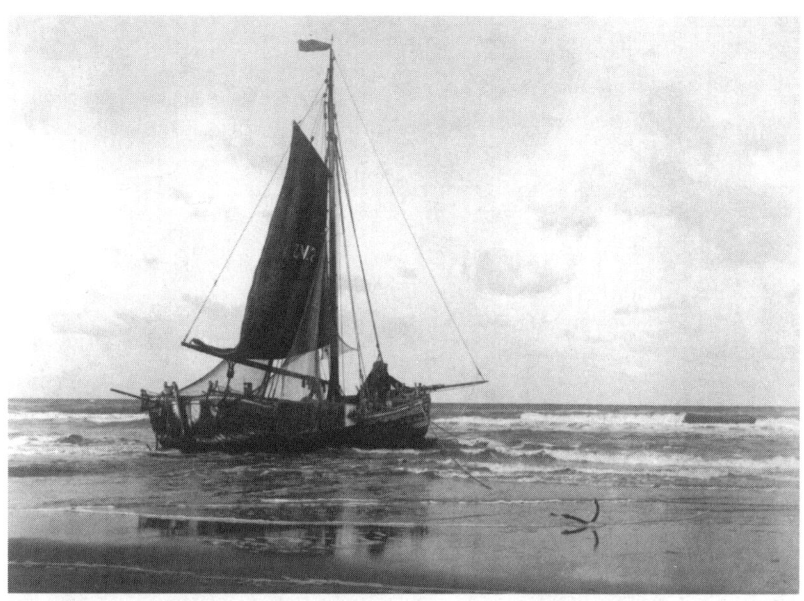

FIG. 15. Alfred Stieglitz, *At Anchor, Katwyk*, 1894, gelatin silver print. Philadelphia Museum of Art: from the Collection of Dorothy Norman.

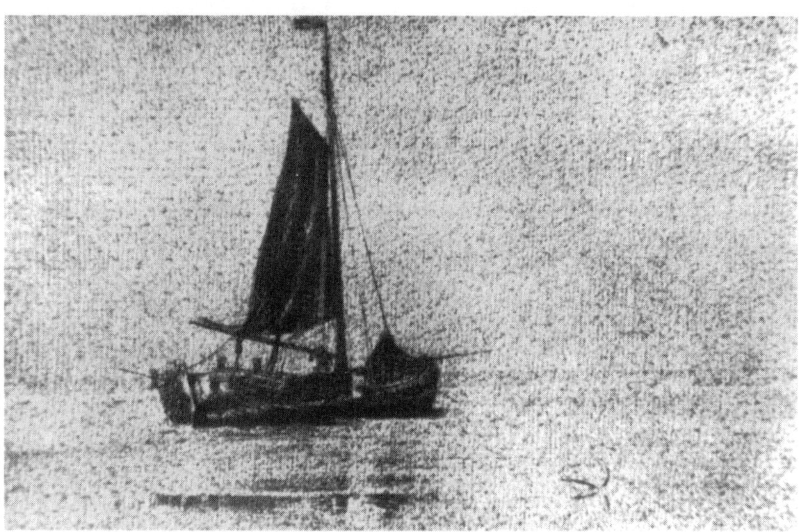

FIG. 16. Alfred Stieglitz, *At Anchor*, 1896, gum print with India ink on rough Whatman paper. *Scribner's Magazine* 1899, p. 535.

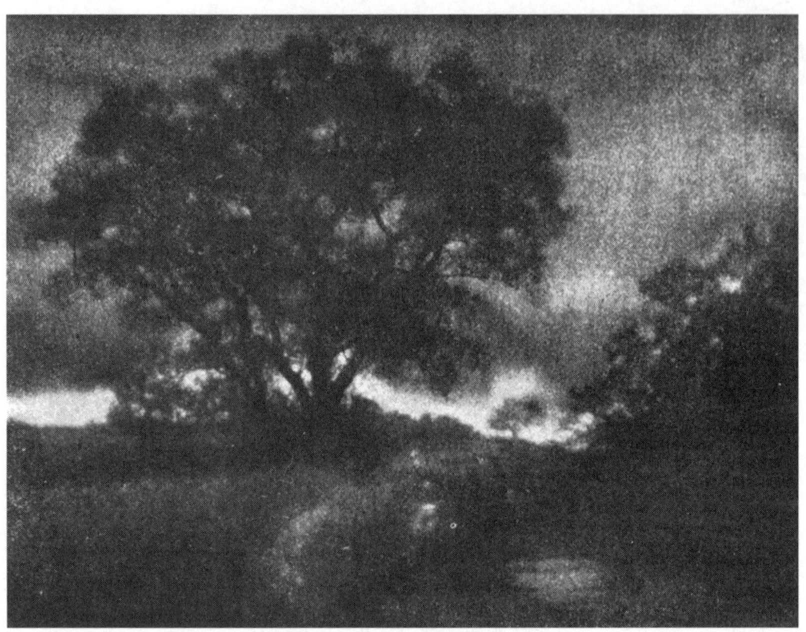

Fig. 17. Mary Devons, *The Willows,* halftone. *Photographic Times,* January 1900, p. 7. Library Company of Philadelphia.

process was even more subject to the artist's powers of control and selection. Furthermore, the gum bichromate process did not lend itself to the production of identical prints, so each photograph was more likely to be conceived of as unique. Demachy praised the process for allowing the photographer to develop select parts of the print and create unique individual prints. Demachy's *Dead Waters* was one of several prints presented in American journals as examples of how the gum bichromate print could facilitate a unique subjective rendering of a subject through its generalizing effects that create deep, textured shadows and a grainy moodiness.

Photographic historian Geraldine Wojno Kiefer juxtaposes two prints by Alfred Stieglitz from the same negative that reveal the broad latitude available within the printing process.[31] Stieglitz's first print of the small sailing vessel anchored close to a glistening wave-swept beach is printed on gelatin silver paper, which provides a wide range of tones and a plenitude of detail, down to the bubbling surf and rigging of the craft. The other print, created with a gum-based process on rough paper, reduces the boat to a shadowy mass, and the beach, sea, and sky merge into a striated, textured field that suggests a charcoal drawing or grainy aquatint. Among the Americans who followed in Demachy's footsteps was Mary Devons of Cambridge, Massachusetts, whose gum bichromate images were selected for the Philadelphia Salons and earned her applause for advances in the process.[32] Devons thoroughly mastered the artistic gum bichromate method, and the indefinite softness of images like *The Willows*, which appeared in the Second Philadelphia Salon, was reproduced in the *Photographic Times* and received high praise.[33]

The Nature of Artistic Truth

The role of art, the character of photographic truth and how it might differ from artistic truth, as well as how each related to nature itself, all became loci of the theorization of the antiphotographic. Croughton explained how photographers had to study art outside of their own field to escape the mechanicity of photography, for "to see Nature through the eyes of an artist, who has been trained to see her as she is, is very different from seeing her through the lens . . . : I would like to impress upon all young photographers the importance of studying art apart from photography, to be able to detect the untruthfulness of photography, for with untruthfulness there can be no true art."[34] Photography may have been scientifically true to some, but scientific and artistic truth were not the same, and the artful photographer had to be able to distinguish these truths and be able to transcend science for art.[35] An investigation into the particular means by which the antiphotographic can address both nature and "the ideal of the true artist" is the focus of the remainder of this chapter.

The first and simplest of the antiphotographic strategies is "invocation," defined as a straightforward appeal to the *look* of art. Here the rhetoric of truth to art was quite literal. Art photography was to look like other forms of art. Compositional strategies and the denial of photographic qualities, particularly detail and tonal range, could be used on a very superficial level simply to imbue photography with some of the formal characteristics of accepted art media, most often prints. The trappings of traditional graphic representation seemed to deny photography's apparent objectivity. Catharine Weed Barnes characterized the motivation behind such a strategy: "To say a photograph resembles a painting is understood to be, and is, a great compliment, for it generally means that the picture has nothing stilted, obtrusively photographic about it." Basing one's judgment on the standards and characteristics of painting, a photograph worthy of compliment had to have nothing "obtrusively photographic" about it.[36]

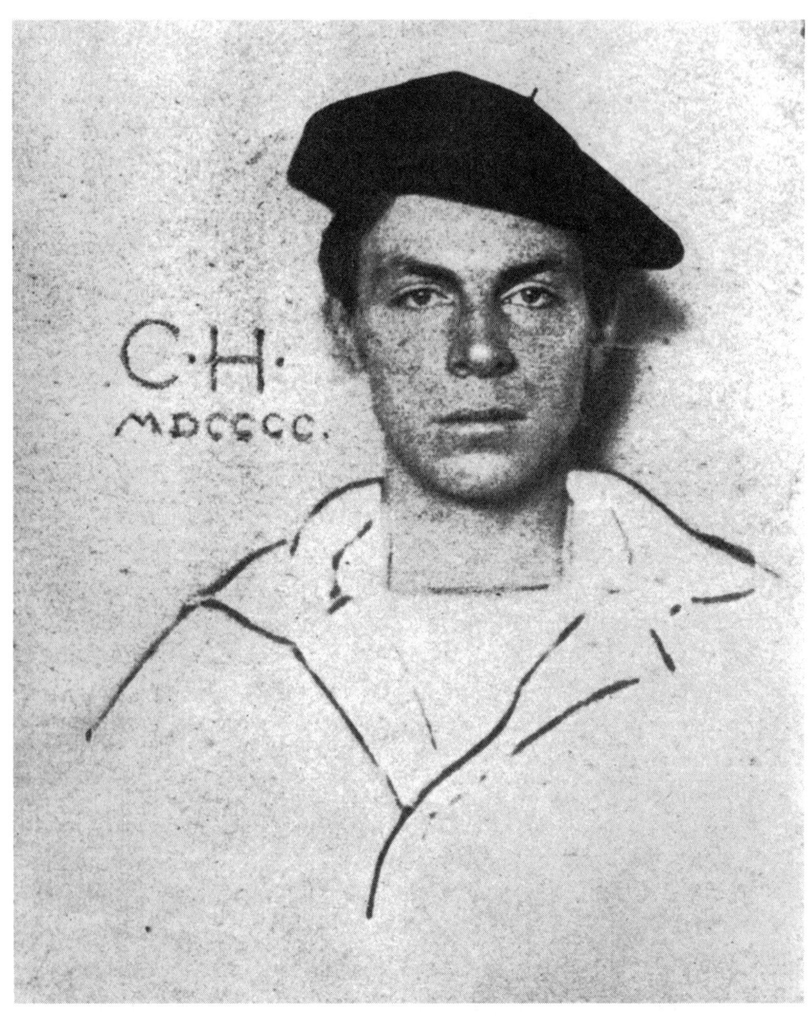

Fig. 18. Mary Devons, *A Charcoal Effect,* halftone. *Catalogue of Third Philadelphia Photographic Salon.* Philadelphia: Pennsylvania Academy of the Fine Arts and the Photographic Society of Philadelphia, 1900, p. 17. Library Company of Philadelphia.

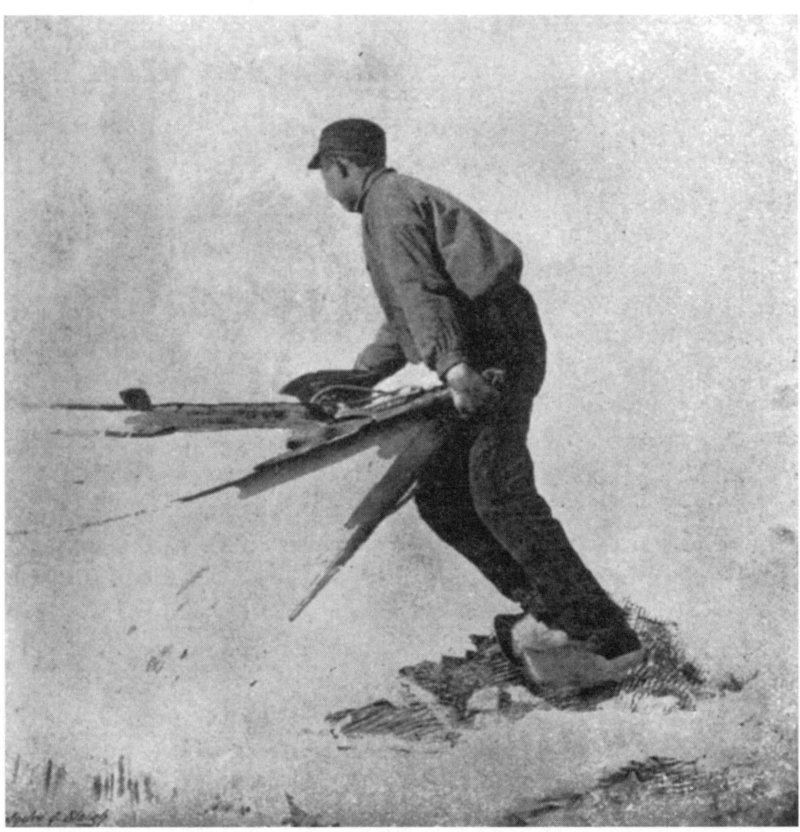

FIG. 19. J. Craig Annan, *A Photograph from Life,* halftone. *Photographic Times,* June 27, 1894, p. 64. Library Company of Philadelphia.

The fairly direct appeal to the graphic quality of accepted media surfaces in several ways. *A Charcoal Effect* by Mary Devons, exhibited at the Philadelphia Photographic Salon of 1900 (and much maligned in the popular press), juxtaposes the photographic representation of a man's head and neck with drawn shoulders.[37] The fine gradation of the photographically recorded head, with its subtle tones and romantic beret, combined with the few simple sweeping lines rendering the shoulders and chest, resembles an unfinished sketch. Similarly, J. Craig Annan produced landscapes with sections of the negative masked and manipulated to produce the same sketchlike effect.[38] For instance, in *A Photograph from Life,* an image of a boy launching a boat, all but a few fragments of background landscape and boat have been masked, and the central figure remains hovering in an undefined background. Late in the century, many photographers altered their prints by brushing on emulsion or developer, leaving gestural, painterly marks. In Edward Steichen's well-known self-portrait, the photographer (dressed as an artist: pallet, beret, and all) emerges from deep shadows and a web of brush strokes.

The most common of these invocative strategies, and perhaps the most damaging to the artistic mission, was the use of dramatic transitions of light and shade, which became known as "Rembrandt effects." These Rembrandt effects were quickly adopted as a standard in professional portraiture and became a cliché of commercial gimmickry. This sort of popularization left no room for the art photographer to be distinguished from the commercial, a perceived necessity for the establishment of artistic photographic practice and an issue elaborated upon in chapter 4.

The easy appropriation of the look of art into the commercial realm and the lack of rigorous theoretical grounding for this sort of invocative practice left photography open to many criticisms, particularly a lack of imagination and hollow mimicry. Lambert insisted that thoughtless imitation showed a superficiality in those who looked to others' work for rules rather than to genuine principles of art. So often, he lamented, the virtues of pioneering work, both artistic and technical, were diluted by a superficial mimicry that tends to magnify the faults and overshadow the merits.[39] To Ferguson, invocation was not sufficient: "To say . . . that it [a photograph] resembles an engraving or an etching is poor commendation." Instead of just looking like another form of graphic art, an artistic photograph had to bear "the impress of the artist's individuality"; it "satisfies the eye, and appeals to the imagination."[40] As Ferguson prescribed, invoking the formal qualities of accepted arts could be more substantial, for adopting the formal qualities of other art could carry more weight than simple mimicry; it could appeal to a deeper theorization of artistic truth.

Photography and Perceptual Theory: Impressionism

The application of perceptual theory as a basis for artistic validation of an image related, not surprisingly, to similar explorations in painting, but it raised uniquely complex issues in photography. In particular, appeals to "truth" were made with much abandon by artists in all media, and the term became especially precarious when used in reference to photography. Arguments spiraled around a practice that purposefully denied supposedly scientific photographic truth in favor of an artistic truth that, in turn, found

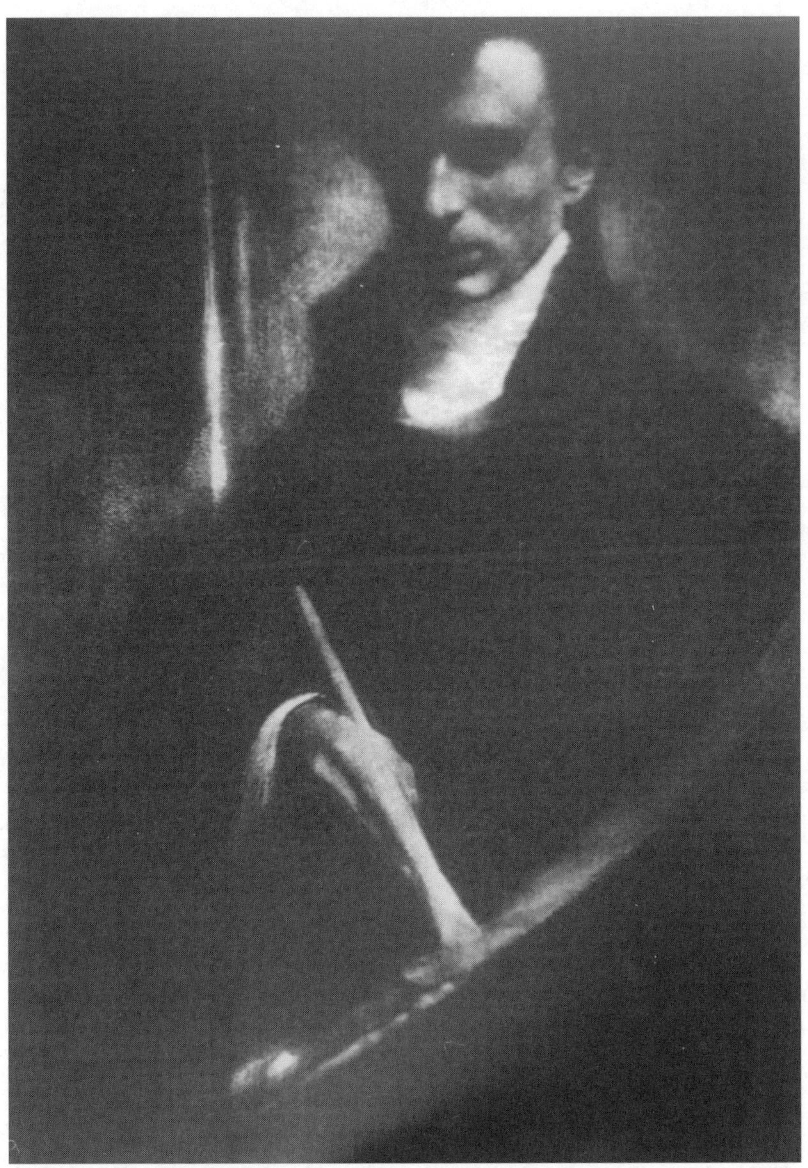

Fig. 20. Edward Steichen. *Self-Portrait with Brush and Palette, Paris,* photogravure, 1901. *Camera Work,* April 1903, p. 9.

its foundation in scientific perceptual theory. A major focus of the theorization of truth in the antiphotographic was impressionist photography. The term "impressionist" was used by late-nineteenth-century writers in a number of ways, often suggesting quite varied meanings. Occasionally the term referred to the depiction of fugitive effects in nature, as in Croughton's reference to a sloppy yet artistic picture that captured the flux of nature's transient moods. More often the term "impressionism" was more closely identified with discussions of the dependence of artistic truth on perception. Artistic value resided not in the conventions of art but rather in an appeal to direct human experience.

While these writers believed perceptual experience could be quantified scientifically, perceptual truth was quite distinct from the photographic record, no matter how mechanically veridical the medium seemed. Photography's propensity to record precise detail and spatial depth impaired its ability to reflect human experience. A. J. Treat indicated that, while some argued that the lens could not be wrong in its productions because it was mechanical, it could capture more detail than was visible to the eye. While he clung to paradigms of compositional structure and the unbending "stolid rules governing the fine arts," he revealed some influence of Emerson's naturalistic photography, describing proper depth of focus and saturation of detail in terms of perception. He pointed out that the "eye changes focus according to the distance of the object," so when "more is presented than it is natural the eye should see it," the result is "hard and lacking in feeling."[41] Treat distinguished perception and cognition, where the brain deceived the eye, arguing that knowing there are leaves on the tree was different from seeing them.[42] The pure visual record and the pure photographic record were by no means the same thing.

In essence, theorists like Treat turned the mechanical criticism of photography back on itself. Reflecting an anxiety about mechanization and a modern, post-Kantian insistence on individual subjectivity, they believed that the seemingly scientific side of photography was precisely the side that lies. In order to replicate a human impression, the photographic process had to undergo significant mediation: the mechanical had to be repressed in order to access truth. Unless the immediacy of perception was synthesized, the photograph did not reflect perceptual truth and therefore did not present artistic truth.

George Davison and Impressionist Photography

One of the primary disseminators of impressionist photographic theory in America was the prolific British photographer, writer, and founder of the English Brotherhood of the Linked Ring George Davison, whose work provided a basis for much of the photographic art theory and practice in the 1890s. He asked photographers to forego the formal conventions of composition upon which legitimating strategies like those outlined in chapter 1 were based. In his widely published essay from the *Practical Photographer*, Davison placed himself directly at odds with the many writers who found legitimization in explicit compositional rules: "It would be absurd to seek to deduce any absolute rules of arrangement or to give the particular practice of any artist or artists the prominence of laws. . . . To crystallize the methods of any man or school in the form of rules for guidance does more harm than good." Instead of adherence to firm formal rules of art, Davison argued for a direct appeal to perceptual experience and the subsequent mental processes.[43]

Despite its antecedents in painting, impressionism as a record of perceptual and conceptual experience was embraced by some photographers as a way to free photography from graphic convention. Indeed, the impressionist photographer was often accused of abandoning the universal laws of art. The preface of the catalog to the 1896 Linked Ring London Salon explained that "the object of the Photographic Salon is to give pictorial work in photography a place of its own, and to set a standard of value by which it may be estimated, without reference, of necessity, to the conventions and principles established by other graphic methods."[44] The authors attempted to differentiate impressionist photography from older standards of art, like those of John Burnet and others that were so often applied in the more nascent phases of art photography.

In formulating his model of art photography, Davison pointed out that it was the "scholarly practice of painters who have variously been called impressionist, naturalist, and the like" that freed painting from limitations of subject matter and compositional formula by looking directly to unmediated nature as a source for pictorial art.[45] He condemned the artistic conventions to which so many photographers had looked as models for aesthetic investment. Davison warned the art photographer not to be seduced by photography's capacity for recording detail and rendering images with remarkable clarity, for these features hampered the photograph's artistic potential. By promoting these aspects of the medium, the photographer degraded his or her art. Minute definition may have been possible in photography, but Davison saw no reason why it should be exploited in artistic work. Simply "because photgraphers [*sic*] have consented to smirch the fair name of their art" was no reason for the medium to continue to suffer the indignity of sharp paper and small stops. Such definition may have been unique to photography, but it was "not the distinctive characteristic of *seeing*."[46]

Here Davison's argument diverged from the invocative antiphotographic, or the superficial appeal to the look of accepted graphic arts. He did not think that photography should deny its capabilities in order to mimic art but that it should do so in order to achieve the goal of art: to communicate a perceptual impression. In effect, Davison distinguished the photographic record and the experiential record. The photograph in and of itself, with its "unnatural emphasis" on clarity and detail, did not reflect our experience of nature, and the medium had to be manipulated to do so. Thus, to Davison, the soft focus effects of the impressionist photograph were not attempts, as some would have it, to "ape the conventionalities" of sepia or wash drawings but rather a photographic mirror of an impression of a scene. Davison's theory or technique did not accommodate the painterly application of emulsion or developer. Moreover, while the formal appearance of an impressionist work by Davison may seem allied to invocative images by Annan or Devons, the intention of the work and its relation to other graphic arts were wholly distinct. The mediation or manipulation of the photographic process might have made the work less truthful to the medium, but it served to reproduce the truth of the natural impression. Once again, the antiphotographic and a quest for truth were inexorably linked, and here, the truth lay in vision.

Photography and Vision

The associations made in the 1880s and 1890s between the camera and the human eye were, as one might expect, plentiful. The camera was often considered a surrogate for vision and memory. The actual making of pictures was frequently described in terms of a replication of vision: readers, for instance, were advised that a complete picture, unless it was a panorama, should be bounded within "the limits of the radius of the human eye—that is, what is seen by moving the pupils, but not the head."[47] Similarly, photographers were often told to expose their pictures from eye level in order to replicate the way a person would encounter the scene.[48] Some writers even suggested that a photographer should use a lens with the same focal length as a human eye.[49]

The comparison of the camera and the physical anatomy of the eye reflected classical linear optics. However, as Jonathan Crary points out, the notion of the camera obscura as a model of human perception was called into question in the nineteenth century. In addition to insisting on a more subjective model of visual experience, scientists like Augustin Jean

Fresnel, with their wave theories of light, challenged linear optics itself. The camera and the technically perfect photograph seemed to uphold linear representation systems, like Renaissance perspective, but new optical theories, by challenging linear optics, disputed conventions of perspective.[50] To the proponent of subjective soft focus, the unmediated photograph might have adhered to outmoded representational systems and presented an image untrue to human experience.

Photographic educator C. Ashleigh Snow offered a detailed technical description of filters and tones that helped control the photographic process and created an image that was similar to what the eye sees.[51] In order to produce an artistic photograph that relates to vision rather than knowledge, the photographer had to intervene in the recording process, undermining crude facts in favor of a representation of what was seen, what was perceived. Snow suggested that the photographer aim for subdued detail and for broad effects based upon the first impression of a scene, yet he still based composition on a series of rules about lines, mass, balance, contrast, repetition, variety, gradation, and values.[52] In a similar vein, Lambert used the term "eye-memory" to describe the mental image, distinguishing the photographic from the perceptual record. The art image, which appealed to the "eye-memory," could not be so strong that the image was taken for reality, a sort of hallucination that did not allow the mind to distinguish image from reality. The viewer had to be aware of the image as a construction, yet one that "corresponds as nearly as possible with the main characteristics of the scene."[53] The art depended on a very subtle mediation of the real, for the reality of the photographic record was not the same as the truth of perception.

Positivism, Perception, and Naturalistic Photography

The rhetoric of truth to vision in impressionist theory was grounded in positivist science, yet it reflected a positivism distinct from the empirical cataloging of facts associated with the traditional photograph. While artistic truth depended on scientific fact, for Davison, scientific fact depended on human perception. He saw new modes of artistic thought "laying bare the natural phenomenon of the universe," leaving behind compositional conventions and artistic paradigms discussed in chapter 1, what Davison referred to as "conventionalism." In contrast to the application of universal rules of art to nature, artists of "the Naturalistic School," as Davison called them, have "set themselves to the practice of close observation of nature to gain better knowledge of the infinite mysteries of these phenomena [of light, color, and atmosphere]."[54]

The long romance with nature in the American landscape tradition, coupled with a scientific basis of observation made Davison's ideas very appealing to an American audience. "Truth to nature," exclaimed Davison, "is the first article of their faith, and the truest that science teaches concerning light and color, and the manner in which the eye sees it is made the guiding principle." Davison stated that the lens, "as used by a *trained observer*, sees very much as the eye sees" and, employed under the same condition as the eye or under conditions as nearly approximate as possible, "nothing gives a more truthful record in drawing than photography." Davison's notion of the impression was constructed in physical terms: "Our impressions are made up of light and light values in relation to one another- color, form, binocular vision effect, focus and perception." The chemical-optical nature of photography, properly used, was not inappropriate to an impression based on the physiological perception: "It is *the light* that is the first and foremost fact of any scene or picture."[55]

For Davison, the challenge to photographers lay in the proper understanding of perceptual processes and how photography might be used to mirror human perception. He cited work on differential focus and referred to the scientific explorations of tonal ranges and intensity. Davison concluded that the typical white-to-black gradation of much landscape work did not reflect human experience and that outdoor images should be much more brilliant than ordinarily rendered images. These scientific observations found their formal application to photography in Davison's choice of rough-textured paper, which helped to diffuse the image, combined with a broad luminous tonal range, which seemed to him to correspond more closely to human perception.[56]

The scientific basis of Davison's impressionist photography was clearly allied with Peter Henry Emerson's influential and controversial 1889 book *Naturalistic Photography for Students of the Art*, and the stylistic similarities of many of their photographs reveals Davison's debt to Emerson (see figs. 11 and 13).[57] Like many others, Emerson asserted that art incorporated the selection of specific facts that appealed to the emotions, yet he insisted that "the facts of nature must be truthfully rendered."[58] The nature of his truth and the truth of his nature separated Emerson from many of his colleagues. Emerson's approach to photography, although rambling and not always fully coherent, was firmly entrenched in the notion of scientifically defined perceptual truth as the basis of art. Emerson studied medicine before taking up photography, and like his American contemporary Thomas Eakins, he looked for ways to integrate science and art.[59] Emerson's naturalism was based not on the conventions of past art but on an appeal to psychophysical processes of perception. He stated plainly that "the best artists have always tried to interpret nature, and express by their art an impression of nature as nearly as possible similar to that made on the retina of the human eye," and we had better "inquire on scientific grounds what the normal human eye really does see."[60] He was disillusioned with art theory based on the whims and opinions of writers who swayed the convictions of generations. With a basis in physiology for artistic representation, "the days of the metaphysicians are over, and with them, we hope, has died all that class of pernicious illogical literature, evolved from the inner consciousness of man."[61]

With the reproduction of nature as the highest aim in art, Emerson located true naturalism in theories based on Hermann von Helmholtz's work on the quantitative relation between luminous intensities: "Art," proclaimed Emerson, "has at last found a scientific basis, and can be rationally discussed . . . I think I am right in saying that I am the first to base the claims of photography as a fine art on these grounds. . . ." Emerson founded his practice of photography on the model of human vision postulated by Helmholtz in *Physiological Optics,* prescribing that "a picture should not be quite sharply focused in any part for then it becomes false; it should be made just *as sharp as the eye sees it and no sharper,* for it must be remembered that the eye does not see things as sharply as the photographic lens."[62] Moreover, Emerson described how to emulate the eye through "differential focus," in which the photograph was most clearly focused on a single plane, but even that plane was to be slightly out of focus.[63] The practice was based on scientific theory, not on mere convention, for "all good art has its scientific basis."[64]

Emerson's theories reverberated in the works of countless photographers who embraced the antiphotographic. Taking specific aim at Emerson's chief rival, Henry Peach Robinson, who asserted that one saw detail everywhere in a landscape, A. J. Treat recommended that the camera's focus be moderated through the use of large apertures and adjustment of plate holders, subordinating local facts not typically seen because of "the peculiarities of the human eye and mind."[65] Similarly, Elbridge Kingsley expressed a notion of photography similar to Emerson's differential focus, wishing to reproduce that which the eye takes in naturally: "The eye cannot take a distinct impression of more than one thing at a time. And why should we try to make a picture on any other principle? Why should we strain after the perfection of the camera that can focus the whole horizon and twenty miles in depth . . . ? [Aim instead for] just what the mind and eye naturally takes in simply by looking."[66] Truth and recorded detail were not one and the same; in fact, detail had to be suppressed in order to achieve truth. But like Emerson's naturalistic photography, the denial of the photographic had to be in the service of this perceptual truth, not merely a mannerism. In his discussions of photography, Emerson adamantly distinguished himself from the "fuzzy school," where the means was purely for the sake of style, destroying structure rather than creating it.[67]

Subjectivity through Evocation

As one would expect with such a wide range of art practices at the time, photographers who embraced impressionistic, naturalistic, or even invocative strategies expressed varied opinions on why their supposed truth to nature via perception constituted art. Some argued that simply looking like art or being true to nature necessarily made their work an artistic production. Others needed an additional step, a process I already defined as the "evocative," where the antiphotographic was applied in an appeal to a subjective mental response to the image. The perceptual impressionist must be distinguished from the conceptual impressionist. Naturalistic photography, as defined by the replication of planes of focus meant to reproduce physiological processes of human perception, differed from the attempt to use pictorial effect to appeal to sentiment and association. The latter identified mental processes that were catalyzed by truthful representations and thus won those representations the title "art." With these cognitive processes entering the discussion, the notion of the impression became multifaceted, not only referring to visual experience but also carrying subjective meaning at the level of author and viewer. This appeal to a mental response relates to the sort of mental processes proposed by Véron that were discussed in chapter 1.

The evocative photographer faced the challenge of creating a picture that was understood as true to nature and having "art value; for it is not a mere transcription of nature we require, but a picture containing some sentiment or idea that shall give pleasure to those who see it."[68] Not only did the image have to transcend the mere photographic record in the name of truth to nature, it also had to create something that communicated on an aesthetic level.[69] Peter Bunnell describes the metaphysical aspects of photography as "an embodiment of a subjective intelligence" with a purpose "not simply to show but to *reveal* the truth beneath appearances."[70]

Lambert defined a hierarchy of mental operations that differentiated pure perception from the mental activities it inspired: "*perception* . . . of light and form," "*apprehension*, . . . the mental effort which seizes on a certain sensation . . . and hold it for the time being," and the sensation being "*registered*," the process of self-conscious reception and association.[71] Evocative art was to appeal to the higher levels of mental processes, or "advanced stages" of the faculties of the mind, catalyzing memory and creating associations within the viewer. Photographers were left wondering how photography could appeal to these higher processes. Not surprisingly, the answer was said to lie in the antiphotographic, where the suppression of factual truth in favor of perceptual truth would improve photography. Truth to perception, writers like Davison argued, was the means by which photography could catalyze higher mental processes.

Countering the theories of Stillman, who found an impossibility in photographic design; Pringle, who said photography lacks the capacity for discrimination; and Robinson, who justified combination printing by a call for the willful improvement of nature, Davison pointed out that all of these theorizations of photography presumed an "insufficiency in nature." To Davison, the aesthetic lay in an unmediated experience of nature, and an artistic image reflected that experience.[72] Unlike someone such as Philip Gilbert Hamerton (Davison's foil several times), who differentiated truth from aesthetic delight, Davison posited that "the naturalist . . . finds no opposition between the two, but derives the keenest aesthetic pleasure from the faithfulness from which his own impressions of nature are expressed for him."[73]

Truth to human perception, the evocative impressionist photographer argued, meant truth to nature, but it also included, through perception, an appeal to the intellect. This truth, while allied with scientific observation, could be subjective and emotive in the communication to a "sympathetic companion" the "feeling of exultation, when one has happened suddenly upon a subtle fact of natural light, color, air or form."[74] The antiphotographic possessed the capacity to communicate something beyond fact, abstractions such as "the subtle beauties of creation" that were responsible for aesthetic pleasure. Beyond the re-presentation of reality, the photo-artist had to inject the image with "human sentiment that stimulates the imagination to see more than the reality," creating a "distillation of nature's essences through a human soul."[75] The artistic photograph both demonstrated the imagination of the maker and excited that of the viewer: "photography is capable of appealing to, stimulating, and expressing the work of the imaginative faculties."[76]

As Jennifer Green-Lewis points out, nineteenth-century philosophical and literary debates often presented a dichotomy of logical positivism and metaphysical idealism or, as she categorizes them, realism and romance. Yet both camps were attracted to photography as a means to express their ideals.[77] The dichotomy Green-Lewis posits applies most easily to the oft-contrasted "straight" and "pictorialist" photographs, but, in fact, the antiphotographic could be called into the service of logical positivism or metaphysical idealism, and facets of both "realism and romance" appeared in the ideals of single photographers. However grounded his theories in positivist science were, even Davison began to appeal to the metaphysical. His idea of "seeing things as they are" was highly subjective, and that subjectivity could be expressed in photography.[78]

Provocation of the imagination was often the stated intent of an antiphotographic, which mimicked perceptual experience and thereby incited mental activity. Xanthus Smith named the two most important results of atmosphere in photography: aerial perspective, which enhanced pictorial space, and a sense of mystery. Because mystery begat sentiment, Smith found fault in photographs that presented too much information, thus depriving the mind of "that gratification which is derived in searching for that which is not fully apparent."[79] Simplicity, suppression of detail, and an evocative sense of mystery were often attributed to the work of Alfred Clements, an Englishman who came to America in 1867 and experimented with the platinum process in New York and Philadelphia. Though sometimes maligned by more conservative factions, Clements's work was an example of "the advanced impressionistic school," or the "new photography." He won awards at the First Joint Exhibition, and in 1894 both Robinson and Davison judged his *Struggle for Existence* to be among the best American amateur work. The image of a lone surviving windblown pine rooted into seaside dunes is dominated by sky and a broad foreground of sand juxtaposed with the more intricate textures of sand and organic debris emerging from the dune. The work seemed to reflect the mental processes an impressionist image could incite, for Davison praised the image's "unity and simplicity with strength, combined with distinct feeling and sentiment" and Clements himself observed, "the weird things where the imagination can play suit me best."[80]

For writers on photography who saw the antiphotographic as a vehicle to higher mental processes, an integral part of the process of reception of a picture lay in the evocation of intellectual responses that transcended simple identification of objects or locale.[81] With this evocation of memory also came a claim to the laudable feature of artistic individuality, a facet of the subjectivity of perception on the part of both the photographer and the viewer.[82] While the supporters of evocative theory agreed that the stimulation of mental processes was essential to art, some differed on the intellectual and emotional infusion necessary to perceive the aesthetic.

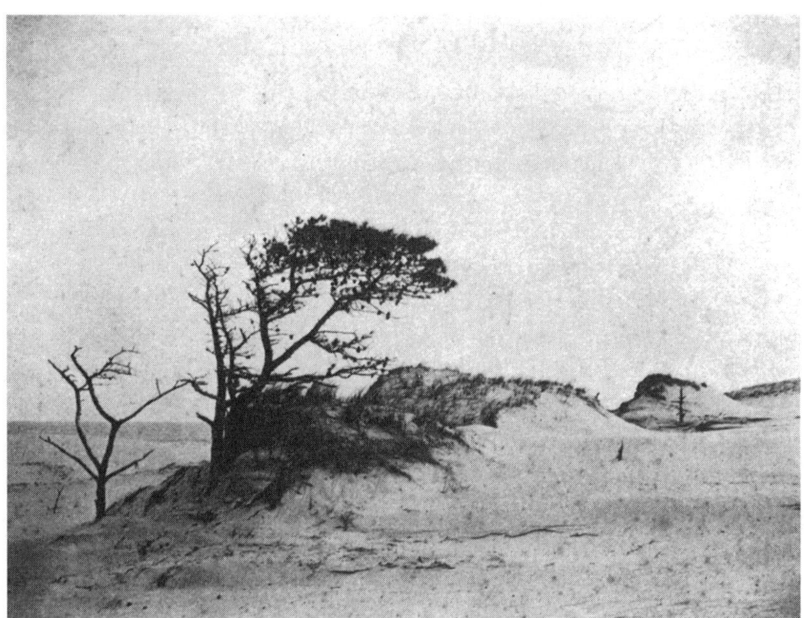

Fig. 21. Alfred Clements, *A Struggle for Existence*, halftone. *American Amateur Photographer*, February 1895, frontispiece. Library Company of Philadelphia.

The role of viewer was a key factor in British photographer and member of the Linked Ring Frank Sutcliffe's evaluation of a photograph. He considered the technical and artistic merits of the photograph as secondary to the picture's ability to "*speak*" to the viewer, arguing that works that call attention to their medium or to their author missed their mark. In a rambling, romantic recollection of associations triggered by a Davison photograph of a mill, Sutcliffe described a process of imaginative collaboration between the photographer's image and the viewer of the work. The response was individual and open-ended, and a successful photograph allowed for the viewer's participation. An overly sharp photograph providing too much information tended to close these avenues of imaginative response, as would a photograph that did not provide sufficient information to start this mental process of personal association and interpretation. The photographic medium had to be passive, so that the image was able to communicate on an individual, subjective level.[83] The celebration of the veridical photographic record succumbed to a subjective, internal vision, reflecting, in the words of Sarah Greenough, a waning of "the cult of science and positivism . . . with its promise to explain all of life's mysteries through rational scientific investigation."[84]

Unlike those writers who suggested that artistic content could be communicated to the viewer on some visceral, nonintellectual level, A. J. Treat called for an educated viewer, a sensitive observer of nature, otherwise the photographer and viewer were "not in the same plane of intellectual appreciation."[85] To Treat, mental processes incited by the replication of perceptual truth had to be mediated by knowledge or experience of both photographer and viewer. Similarly, Lambert demanded a viewer conversant in the language of visual representation: "for the appreciation of the imagination we need, above all things, a sympathetic spectator . . . ; otherwise we speak to him in an unknown tongue."[86] The reception of the work depended on a learned response, rather than on inherent perceptual abilities.

Emerson's Recantation of Naturalistic Photography

Just as I closed the previous chapter with a denial of the strategies that it addressed, so, too, will I conclude this chapter. The denial of strategies presented here is especially significant because it was not simply a denial but a recantation by one of the most influential theorists of the antiphotographic, Peter Henry Emerson. Frustrated by experiments that disproved his belief that through darkroom chemistry the photographer had full control of the range of tones, Emerson issued a proclamation, "The Death of Naturalistic Photography," disclaiming any previous assertion of photography's art potential. Emerson allowed photography the ability to sometimes give a "certain aesthetic pleasure," but he asserted that the medium always ranked as the lowest of the graphic arts. While perhaps exercising slight control over a picture, the photographer's "all-vital powers of selection are *fatally* limited" and the "individuality of the artist is cramped."

Emerson rejected the application of artistic convention. Sometimes lapsing into a bitter attack on the amateur, he asserted that because the photographic process gave but "transcripts more or less literal," the photographer could be "neither idealist, realist, naturalist, nor impressionist," the term "photographic impressionist" being "consecrate to charlatans," "photographic impostors" and "vanity intoxicated amateurs." Emerson denied the personal in photography and called claims to insert significant individuality into photography "pretentious rubbish." The camera as a machine, Emerson conceded, came between the photographer and the ideal and imposes conditions outside of the photographer's mind, thus quashing the possibility for artistic production. The photographer's intervention in selection of view, lens, focus, developer, and printing methods were, in Emerson's estimation, too few and too limited to allow sufficient artistic investment.[87] Unlike Davison, who saw photography as a vehicle with which art could be scientific, Emerson concluded that art and science were irreconcilable and that those who claimed to bridge the two were deluded and vain. The future of photography lay in the pursuit of the scientific, the literal transcript of nature, not in futile attempts at art.

Emerson's "Epitaph" names a number of essential issues in the quest for art photography and hints at issues that will be addressed in my final chapter:

EPITAPH.
IN MEMORY OF
NATURALISTIC PHOTOGRAPHY,
WHICH RAN A SHORT BUT ACTIVE LIFE,
UPSET MANY CONVENTIONS,
HELPED TO FURTHER MONOCHROME PHOTOGRAPHY TO THE
UTMOST OF ITS LIMITED ART BOUNDARIES,
STIRRED MEN TO THINK AND ACT FOR THEMSELVES,
PRODUCED MANY PRIGS AND BUBBLE REPUTATIONS,
EXPOSED THE IGNORANCE OF THE MULTITUDE,
BROUGHT OUT THE LOW MORALITY OF CERTAIN PERSONS IN
THE PHOTOGRAPHIC WORLD,
BROKE DOWN THE PREJUDICE OF THE OUTSIDE PUBLIC
AGAINST PHOTOGRAPHY'S VERY SLENDER ART CLAIMS,
ENCOURAGED MANY AMATEURS TO BABBLE AND MAKE THE
WORDS "ART," "TRUTH," AND "NATURE"
STINK IN THE
NOSTRILS OF SERIOUS ARTISTS,
ENDING BY GIVING A BRUTAL SORT OF APPREHENSION
OF ART,
AND DYING WHEN ITS
ALLOTTED TASK WAS DONE, WITH A GIBE ON ITS LIPS,
FOR THE "AMATEUR," THE "PLAGIARIST,"
THE "PRATING TRUE-TO-NATURE MAN,"
THE "IMPRESSIONIST," THE "NATURALIST," THE
"IDEALIST," AND THE HUMBUG.[88]

Emerson reiterates the refutation of a number of legitimizing strategies, including the creative conceptual act of selection, the application of traditional compositional conventions, and photography's ability to record a perceptual impression. But he also notes symptoms of, and reactions to, an elitism that I will discuss later: a differentiation between certain facets of the photographic community; a skepticism toward the application of artistic convention and rhetoric; an attitude where the amateur is looked upon with some amount of derision; and a suspicion of vacuous plagiarized theories of impressionism, naturalism, and idealism.

In retrospect, the irony of Emerson's recantation is far from subtle. He continued to make and exhibit photographs for more than a decade after his recantation, and he was one of the most vital influences on the photographers who established conventions of art photography in the 1890s, most notably Davison and Stieglitz. Davison drew inspiration from Emerson's theoretical foundation through the rest of the century. Emerson's *Naturalistic Photography* was published in full in the *Photographic Times* from 1896 through 1899.[89] And Stieglitz asked, "How many appreciate the enormous benefit that P. H. Emerson has bestowed upon photographic art? Call him by whatever name you may, criticise him from any point of view, and still the fact remains: his teachings formed the basis" of some of the most progressive and promising photographs made in America in the last decade of the nineteenth century.[90]

Chapter Three

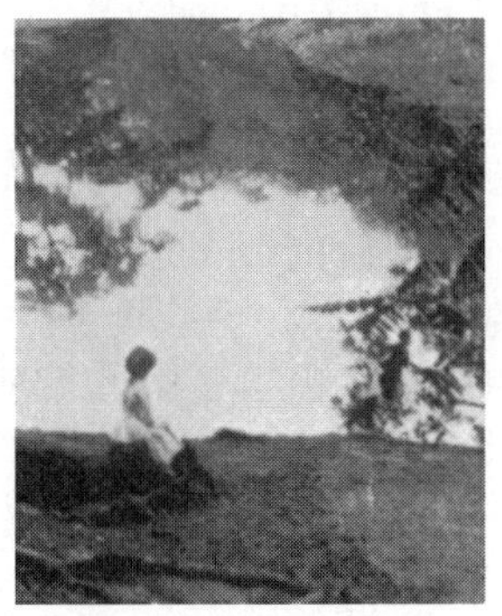

"That Legitimate Charm of Photography": Resistance to Impressionism and Naturalistic Photography and the Photographic Aesthetic

The function peculiar to photography is truth—correctness of form—the power of producing as pure a copy of nature's outlines as can be, without the human brain and hand. To this end, no artistic skill is required; photography is confined to the limits of an experimental science, and its results can only be called beautiful in the same sense that a beetle with a pin through it is beautiful—that is, scientifically so, and about as far removed from what may be called artistically beautiful as that beetle is from its former self, alive and on the wing.

—"An Artist's Thoughts on Photography"

The unnamed artist, presumably a painter, whose "thoughts on photography" were published in the *Photographic Times and American Photographer* in 1887, discussed at length the overwhelming omnipresence of the camera's scientific aspect in every photographic endeavor. The argument begins with what seems to be a strong denial of photography's potential for artistic endowment. A "faithful" photograph of a subject recorded facts, but "it will be untrue because it will not reproduce for us the picture as we saw it. Impressions made on the retina of the eye differ from those made on a sensitive plate."[1] The factual truth of the scientific was distinguished from the perceptual truth of art.

While the preceding points might easily have concluded with a dismissal of photography's artistic potential or have been used to argue for the subjugation of the photographic, the author returned to the theory that a selective eye could choose views that were able to communicate more than the simple factual truth of the scene. A great artist could devise compositions that transcended mere "*copies*," making "nature the vehicle for his own thoughts" and inspiring them "with life from himself."[2] Here, the selection argument was broadened, for the photographer was not urged simply to favor traditional artistic devices to imbue the photograph with artistic value but rather to accept and exploit the inherent verisimilitude of the photographic as a foundation for the creation of artistic truth. Photography's empirical account of reality, it was argued, could be placed in the service of artistic expression, for the mistrust of technology that drove many of the proponents of the antiphotographic to undermine the capacities of the medium did not come into play here. The writer identified "special tendencies" of the medium that should be studied and developed, pointing to the "time-honored principle of adjusting our work to the character of our tools and materials." The capacity of the photograph to record factual information was to be embraced: "There is no reason for suppressing it [detail] in a photograph. Absence of detail there is only concomitant with under exposure or bad focus, the result, in the first case, of inexperience, in the second of carelessness or affectation."[3]

Debunking Impressionism and Naturalism

To many of the vehement critics of impressionistic and naturalistic photography, the soft, or diffused, image simply failed to meet the goals of fine art as a representation of a sort of "artistic truth" free of affectation and readily apprehensible. To these writers, the photographic production of artistic truth was a process of selection that captured more than simple factual truth, and this selection could include the manipulation of photographic processes with techniques such as combination printing, which were thought to raise factual truth to the level of perceptual truth without compromising the integrity of the photographic medium.

Extensive observation of nature as a springboard for artistic success had long been promoted in American art.[4] To those whose artistic ideal was the observation of pure nature, the photographic record had unrivaled aesthetic potential, and to fetter the recording capacity of photography through diffused focus was to deny that potential. While acknowledging criticisms of photography based on its limitations in "selection, rejection, invention and in the means of technical execution," Enoch Root predicted that photography's "realistic representation of nature" would indeed be its artistic strength. He recounted advantages the photographer had over the painter in the pursuit of naturalism: once a proper vantage point and conditions of light were found, the photographer need not go through a long process of re-presentation of the scene in which memory and changing conditions altered the transcript of nature, for "the faithful sun-god speedily records it on the sensitized plate."[5]

This praise of the seeming naturalism of photography also related to John Bartlett's endorsement of photography: "It is sometimes urged that photography lacks value, from an artistic point of view, because it expresses too minutely the details of an object. But excellency of detail, if combined with breadth of conception, adds rather than detracts from the beauty of any subject. Nature does not despise detail. Why should art?"[6] Photography, Bartlett explained, "has no other resource than the representation of nature, and of necessity must be realistic in the most absolute sense of the word, it must be shown that realism, or 'the counterfeit presentment of Nature herself,' far from being a confirmation strong as proofs of holy writ against her claims to art, is the strong argument of her faith."[7] Indeed, Bartlett's *On the Wissahickon*, the frontispiece of an 1887 *American Journal of Photography*, exemplifies his notion of breadth of conception with excellency of detail. The highly structured image, with its shadowy framing foliage, atmospherically softened background, meandering bridge-spanned waterway, and pensive foreground figure, recalls traditional compositional conventions like those embraced by Xanthus Smith in his painted landscapes.[8]

While he tried to be open-minded to avoid "old fogyism," Xanthus Smith was admittedly conservative in his opinions on art and aesthetics and realized he was at odds with some prevailing standards of taste of his day. In a widely published 1886 address, he bemoaned the critical attention paid to impressionism and revealed a preference for early-nineteenth-century English landscape painting and the work of Americans like Thomas Cole (an engraving based on a Cole landscape was published in the same volume of the *Philadelphia Photographer*). Smith vigorously

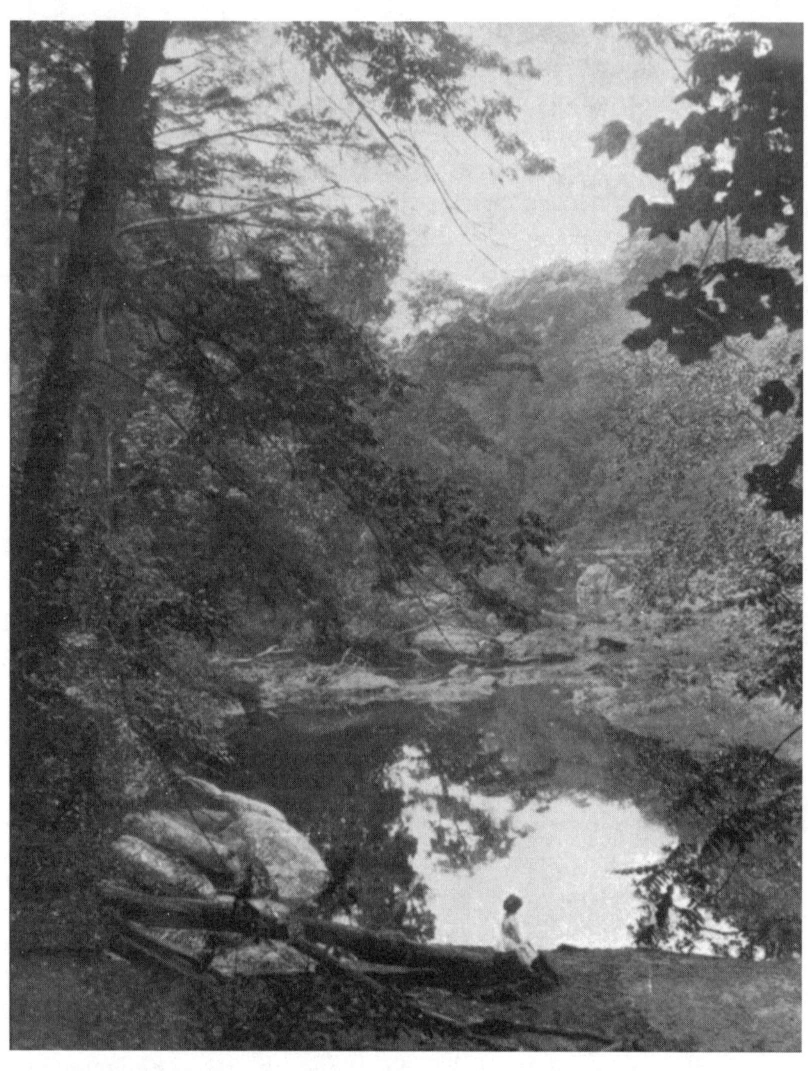

FIG. 22. John Bartlett, *On the Wissahickon,* halftone. *American Journal of Photography,* October 1887, frontispiece. Library Company of Philadelphia.

condemned French impressionism and its influence on American artists, appalled by the "conglomeration of grotesque forms" and "indiscriminate scattering from end to end of ill-shapen patches of light and dark."[9] While Smith advocated atmospheric landscape because of its sense of depth and subdued detail, he clearly had an anti-impressionistic attitude. "Why," he asked, "with all these exquisite charms in nature which a great all-ruling power has bestowed upon us, should we not be satisfied to endeavor to imitate? Why should we run mad over dirty heavy daubs of French landscapes, and call them art?"[10] To Smith, the *cultivated* veracity of photography was the medium's strength, and the photographer who diverged too far from the photographic record was misguided.

While writers like Smith argued that impressionist diffusion of focus was simply not appropriate to artistic representation, other opponents of impressionism and naturalism in photography attacked the perceptual foundations of these theories. In cogent responses to diffusion and differential focus, writers pointed out that the whole was made up of a series of impressions and that overall sharpness reflected the process of looking rather than simply a single, minute datum abstracted from the entire experience. The raw impression was less appropriate to art than a more cognitive process of looking and understanding.[11] These writers found it redundant to diffuse the focus of subordinate parts of a picture when the eye would attend to the primary object of a well-composed picture, itself defining the less important parts. Overall clear focus, they maintained, allowed the viewer to enjoy the same process of discovery in subsidiary areas of the picture, just as he or she could in nature, thus making the sharper-focused image more true to nature.

The most biting American criticism of Emerson's theories came from William James Stillman. In his extensive review of Emerson's *Naturalistic Photography*, Stillman expressed his disagreements with typical candor, commenting in the opening paragraph on "the ingenuity of the author in making so large a book out of so little matter, and, above all, so little that is applicable to the craft to which it is addressed . . . much of it is mere words which will be to an artist nonsense and to a photographer unfathomable mystery."[12] Stillman methodically undermined Emerson's use of terminology and explanations of technical apparatus and phenomena. More significant here, however, was Stillman's appraisal of Emerson's differential focus as "an absurd fallacy." This refusal to accept Emerson's theories was a manifestation of Stillman's insistence on photography as a transparent medium that was both unsuited to and done an injustice by attempts to use it to create fine art.

Condemning a Betrayal of Photographic Technique and the Laws of Art

The widening embrace of impressionistic and naturalistic photography by photographers with artistic intent inspired resolute resistance from a large photographic community who declared soft focus and atmospheric effect the refuge of the technically inept and rallied for "truth to photography." In the late 1880s and through the 1890s, the most basic reaction against the increasingly prevalent use of soft focus and general effects took aim at the ease of achieving these characteristics and proceeded to question their correlation to art practice: "Artistic photography is the higher evolution of good photography, not the lower refuge of incapacity."[13]

One of those who expressed a wariness about the formal devices of impressionism in photography was Catharine Weed Barnes. Unlike many photographers who categorically dismissed any manipulative process in photography, Barnes was willing to accept more painterly effects, but she saw a danger in the transformation of innovation into convention. With the increasing popularity of impressionist conventions, she feared overuse and a lack of technical proficiency where photographers might as well "dispose of their carefully selected lenses and save themselves much time and trouble by discarding the use of graduates, scales, and hydrometers in the developing room. The faithful workers will grow discouraged and the lazy ones jubilant."[14] Barnes repeatedly emphasized the need for technical skill, echoing criticisms that many more traditional photographers would aim at naturalistic and impressionist practice: "With altogether too many amateurs and, indeed professionals also, the tendency is often to take shelter behind the incontrovertible fact that technicality is not the one supreme good, to justify downright violation of technique, calling absolutely unjustifiable carelessness, great artistic taste, if not positive genius. You cannot find your way through the labyrinth of Art without keeping hold of the guiding thread of technique."[15]

Reviews of the American work at the Linked Ring's London Salon of 1900 suggested some of the resistance to the formal qualities of photographic experimentation and their theoretical basis. The *British Journal of Photography* criticized "the deplorable travesties of photographic work which a handful of American photographers, encouraged by the adulatory writings of neurotic 'appreciators,' are deceived into believing was 'artistic' or 'pictorial.'" A long, unaccredited quotation by Sadakichi Hartmann on F. Holland Day serves as an example of the "critical writing which is responsible for the photographic inanities." Labeled the work of "The Cult of the Spoilt Print," the American photographs were seen as

> the very negation of good photography, . . . the prostitution of a beautiful method of graphic expression to the lamentable idiosyncrasies of those whom Nature, for some inscrutable purpose, has endowed with a passion for the grotesque and the ugly, which may deserve our pity, but neither our admiration nor our imitation.[16]

Many critics of impressionist practice resolutely held to the sorts of compositional convention discussed in chapter 1. The adherence to compositional convention as a means of legitimization continued through the end of the century and increasingly became a foil to other strategies of creating art photography. Even more moderate writers resented the onslaught of self-styled impressionist photographers who were the recipients of so many exhibition "awards given to *effects* rather than to picturesque compositions." The impressionist photographers seemed to claim that "the artist is a law unto himself," when in fact, as these critics would have had it, "their work would be equally impressionistic and much more truly artistic if they would give more attention to the so-called canons of art."[17] Resisting challenges to traditional artistic principles and generally accepted photographic criteria, Xanthus Smith advised photographers that notions of clarity

> will be at variance with the views of many artists and writers on this side of the Atlantic now; but although mere whims of fashion may scoff at and cast aside as out of date many of the broad general rules which should govern art, works to be lasting, that is to go from one generation to another and retain their interest and value, must to a great extent exhibit the result of either genius or knowledge in the artist in perceiving and applying the broad, lasting principles of art.[18]

These proponents of compositional convention applied to the relatively unmanipulated photograph often aimed their criticisms at the invocative quality of many art photographs, sharing the opinion of Henry Peach Robinson, who stated succinctly, "I believe it is a mistake to try to deceive the observer with imitations of other means of art, such as etchings and water-color drawings."[19] Resenting the "strong effort of the imagination" needed to discern parts of so-called impressionist photographs, George B. Sperry assured readers that every "true photographer" would agree that photography is not the proper medium for attempts at such "pretentious" effects. While vagueness may be acceptable in wash drawings, proclaimed Sperry, "we cannot tolerate this quality or lack of quality in a photograph. Photography has still enough trade spirit to take pride in technique and has no wish to father the freak efforts that are clamoring for recognition." Sperry's photography "is primarily a reproductive art, its accuracy and fineness of detail being its distinguishing feature in comparison to other arts." "To ignore these qualities," warned Sperry, "is to take ground from under its feet. A weak imitation of another art can never ennoble photography."[20]

The controversial Third Philadelphia Photographic Salon inspired Philadelphia photographer Charles L. Mitchell to pine for an art photography that embraced more of the seemingly inherent characteristics of the medium. Like many of his colleagues, Mitchell identified much of the antiphotographic technique as an empty imitation of formal qualities of painting. The exhibition consisted of

> exaggerated copies of the peculiarities of the great masters of art, with all their peculiarities and none of their art; here are the frantic attempts to imitate some of the most divine and inspired manifestations of the painter's skill,—with the result of indecently travestying them; here are painstaking and laborious attempts to reproduce the lines of the brush or the engraver, the texture of the paper, the web of the canvas—but no attempt to produce a picture.[21]

Indeed, Mitchell earned praise for photographs like *Ellis River, White Mountains,* which exploited painterly compositional convention without sacrificing photographic qualities like range of tone and precise detail.[22]

Even Hartmann, one of the most eloquent critics supporting the early Stieglitz circle, condemned invocation as a betrayal of photography. In his discussion of the work of Frank Eugene, Hartmann pointed out that Eugene's artistic background was manifested in his incorporation of characteristics of the brush, pencil, and etching needle, often altering "entirely the aspect of the subject depicted as seen by the eyes of the camera." This purposeful reference to other media was, in Hartmann's mind, "distinctly outside the domain of photography," and despite the artistic feeling, he could not fathom "how the art of Daguerre can particularly benefit from such proceedings." He believed that photography would only reach maturity through freeing itself from the influence of painting and working within its own terms.[23]

Stillman thought that photographs should be admired for their technical quality, arguing that a good photograph was more praiseworthy than an indifferent picture. Finding primacy in exceptional craftsmanship,

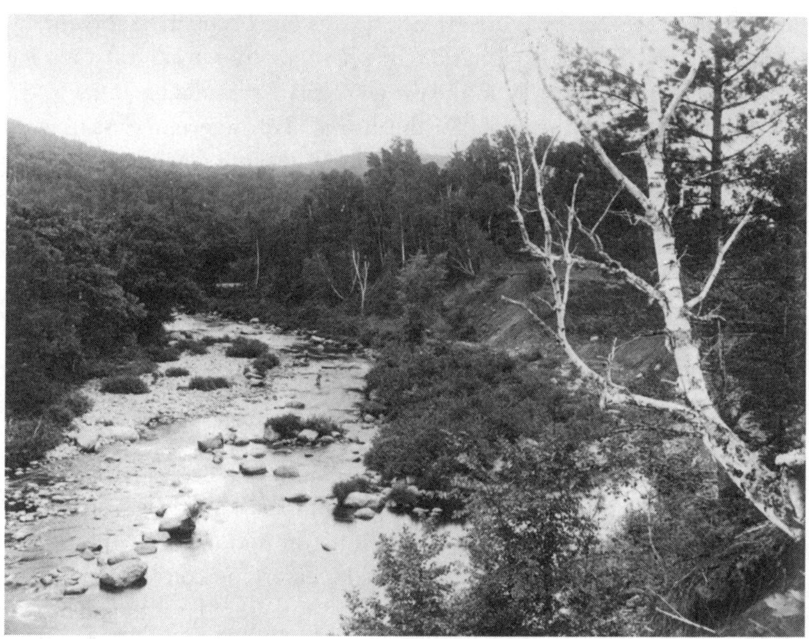

Fig. 23. Charles L. Mitchell, *Ellis River, White Mountains,* silver print, ca. 1890. National Museum of American Art; museum purchase from the Charles Isaacs Collection made possible by the Luisita L. and Franz H. Denghausen Endowment.

Stillman was appalled by photographers who seemed to deny the capacities of the medium. He viewed the painterly convention of suppressing detail as an interesting manifestation of the way the artist regarded nature, but when applied to photography, he considered it dishonest to the very nature of the medium: "any affectation of imitating the treatment an artist might give is out of place in photography."[24] Stillman called for an acknowledgment of the characteristics of the photographic medium and for photographers to resist the inclination to simply mimic painterly conventions: "it depends on photographers to stand by their colors (black and white, I suppose) to be recognized on their own merits and those of photography, and not on the fact of their doing something which resembles the work of painters."[25]

Unlike the many photographers who felt compelled to shun empirical science in favor of artistic subjectivity, Stillman embraced photography's technical side and its scientific aspects, perhaps because he made no claims for the medium's status as art. In fact, he was one of the most fervent advocates of the fullest exploitation of photography's technical capacity. Sensing a sort of hypocrisy in the denial of characteristics essential to the photographic process, he called for the dismissal of "a certain class of work which is much lauded by people who avowedly do not like photographs at all and who consider that a certain slovenliness and accidental way of using the chemicals and a want of sharpness and hap-hazard arrangement of the subject make a photograph artistic."[26] Stillman's adamant stance that photography was not a fine art led him to what I call a "photographic aesthetic," a practice that, rather than invoking the superficial qualities of other graphic media, exploited the characteristics inherent in and unique to the photographic medium.[27]

The Photographic Aesthetic

With the benefit of historical hindsight and the knowledge of the remarkable influence of the likes of Stieglitz on notions of art photography, late-nineteenth-century critics of the emerging conventions of art photography (such as soft or differential focus, textured prints, and brooding images) often seem quite conservative, if not reactionary. Yet their thoughtful resistance to many of the fundamentals of such practice emphasizes the complexity of the photographic theory at the time. The questioning of invocative practice within impressionist photography because it seemed somehow untrue to the photographic medium led to an articulation of a photographic aesthetic. Intertwined with all the discussion of truth to nature and truth to art was the question of truth to photography itself.

In his appeal for the photographic, Washington Irving Lincoln Adams, an authoritative presence in the photographic realm, asked, "Why should the photograph imitate a painting which, in itself, is an imitation?" Adams realized that this invocative strategy was aimed at high-art status, but he found these efforts misdirected and urged photographers to "make their photographs technically as good as they can. By trying to imitate paintings," he explained, "they confess an inferiority which does not really exist."[28] In his own photographs, Adams strove to engage nature in an artistic manner while holding steadfast to photography's ability to represent a breadth of light and shadow as well as fine detail. The image *The Edge of the Wood*, in which the screen of trees cuts acutely across the middle ground, shares an affinity with the earlier informal studies of the painter William Trost Richards and the photographer John Moran. Rather than imposing a strict compositional structure, Adams let the photographic

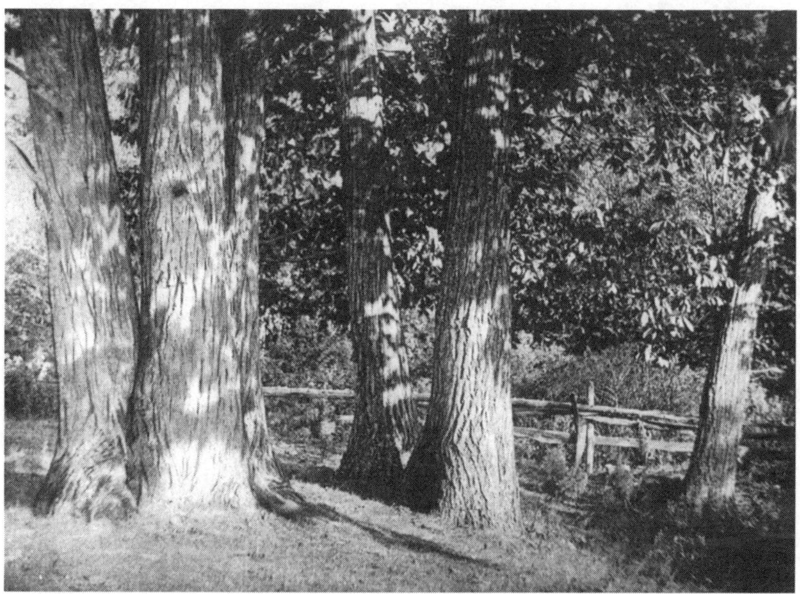

Fig. 24. W. I. Lincoln Adams, *The Edge of the Wood,* photogravure. *Photographic Times,* December 5, 1890, frontispiece. Library Company of Philadelphia.

record of sunlit forms be the emphasis of the picture, a study of nature akin to the Ruskinian spirit of the American Pre-Raphaelites.

The natural outgrowth of an appreciation for uniquely photographic characteristics was an adamant demand for a unique set of standards to evaluate photography, independent of invocative convention. Into the late 1890s many writers expressed resolute resistance to the affectations of the painterly in naturalistic and impressionistic photography, preferring to find standards for the photography within the medium itself. The professional photographer Clement Hopkins accepted earlier notions of compositional conventions applied to photography but refused to accept the legitimacy of pictorialist manipulation of the medium: "the canons of form and composition apply to all the transcriptive arts, but all other canons are proper to the art and depend on the materials and tools used. Photography, if it is to stand as an art, must . . . frame its own canons based on the experience of the tools and materials it uses."[29]

Perhaps the most impassioned and eloquent apologist for the photographic aesthetic was William James Stillman. Angered by attempts to make analogies between painting and photography through the use of terms like "sketch" and "sentiment," Stillman implored photographers to consider their medium on its own terms: "Photography gains nothing by the borrowing of the language of the painter, but the student has his ideas of art thereby confused and is prevented from cultivating it intelligently."[30] While he by no means admitted photography to the realm of the fine arts, Stillman had a great deal of respect for the medium when it remained within its own sphere. He saw honor in the photographic pursuit, and while photography might not have been an "art" it could be artistic and artful. Stillman allowed that "there is an art in photography" if "art" was used in the sense of a skillfully accomplished task, if art referred not to the thing but to the skill with which it is done.[31] Photographers who claimed to be artists, Stillman asserted, did not see it this way. Such a photographer wanted to maintain the "distinctive appellation" of artist "because of the superficial resemblance in his work to that of the painter."[32] Stillman deeply resented the affectation of photographers labeling themselves artists: "I am a photographer myself," he professed, "and [I] only feel contempt for those of the craft who feel themselves too great to be called photographers and want to borrow the plumes of the artist, evidently because they think that nothing is respectable that is not called *art*."[33] Photography, in Stillman's eyes, was to be judged by a set of criteria peculiar to the medium and should not strive to emulate other media at the expense of its own integrity: "A photograph is a good or bad photograph, as such, and is not made artistic by being bad as a photograph."[34] A truly artistic photograph was well lit, well developed, and narratively complete.

At the heart of Stillman's criticisms were a respect for American pragmatism and pride in the democratization of American culture. He found dignity in labor and satisfaction in craft and saw a photographer's wish to be considered an artist as a symptom of a synthetic elitism of the kind Stieglitz would later exploit. This yearning for higher status was, in Stillman's estimation, a great disservice to photography. In comments perhaps reflecting a socialism influenced by Ruskin, he stated: "All this nonsense is mainly the outcome of a weak affectation of a social superiority which the claimants assert over other workmen. They call themselves artists because they think that there is something, if not degrading, yet less honorable, in being an artisan, and that they will be allowed a higher social rank by claiming to be artists." Society in general decided the meaning of language, argued Stillman, and the appropriation of "artist" by photographers was like "conferring titles on oneself which nobody else recognizes." He continued to chastise those who desired the status of artist, explaining that in "aristocratic countries" a person's occupation might admit them to the "'best society,'" but "in a purely democratic country like ours, where a man is, or supposed to be, taken at his individual value, any pretension like that of the right to be called by a more distinguished appellation than that which common usage confers, is a silly vanity."[35] The quest for art status was misguided, un-American, pretentious and vain. This impassioned faith in photography's technical capacity, coupled with pride in good craftsmanship, fired many of the outraged responses to the increasingly elitist art photography sphere that I describe more fully in the next chapter.

As natural as the characteristics unique to the photographic medium may have seemed, a number of significant writers and theorists expressed an awareness that these photographic features were the product of a photographic industry that developed and marketed technology. One writer offered his take on differing schools of thought in the late 1890s, contrasting "robust" photography, "which make full use . . . of the native virility which is inherent in the particular photographic processes," and "emasculated" photography, which "may be considered as photography's lost opportunities."[36] The "native virility" of photography reflected tendencies particularly strong in America: a faith in technology and a perceived duty to nurture progress. This was the very faith that the antiphotographic questioned, and any challenge of a belief in technology inspired the faithful to become even more resolute. A contributor to the *Photographic Times* who shared the appreciation of those characteristics "inherent in the particular photographic processes employed," wrote in disgust about some of the more diffused images included in the journal. He argued that one should take advantage of the fact that "the highest skill of the optician has been exercised in the production of photographic lenses which will accurately portray . . . every line and gradation of light . . . with the utmost fidelity."[37] Another writer, reacting against the self-conscious attempt of photographers to construct a visual vocabulary for photographic art, fortified his declaration of a photographic aesthetic with an appeal to positivist science. He wrote of "the photographers who have the high art craze":

> To hear one of those misguided mortals talk, one would think that all optical science was a blunder, and that all the improvements in the construction of photographic lenses were so many steps backward. Why should the optician and the chemist conspire together to produce objectives, whose component lenses shall bring more perfectly to the same focus all the rays received by the front lens . . . if real art demands that the image shall be of artistic fuzziness, instead of a sharp and crisp delineation of all the details of the object?[38]

Supporters of a photographic aesthetic that seemed truer to the inherent capabilities of the medium, these writers displayed an underlying belief in an obligation to embrace technological progress. Like many of their colleagues, they called for a photographic aesthetic with an awareness that technical and scientific development had defined the seemingly natural characteristics of photography.

This awareness of science and industry as definers of photography's technical capabilities was just as effectively incorporated into the logic of the opponents of the photographic aesthetic. George Davison, who was most often associated with impressionist photography, understood the arguments for the purely photographic. In fact, he voiced some of the most succinct expressions of it. Calling the stand the most "dignified and honest" of the obstructions to artistic freedom, Davison claimed "that uniformly minute delineation is the natural characteristic of photography, that detail and sharp definition are the special powers of our instruments, and that these special powers should be utilized to the utmost." Still, Davison believed that such arguments had their strongest sympathies in the science of photography. Davison complained that most of the photographic journals were "under the guidance of those whose interest lies entirely in chemistry, the optics or the commerce of photography," and he saw an "absolute inability to get away from settled prejudices as to what a photograph and all photographs should be," prejudices clinging to "the traditions begotten of the optician's idea of excellence and of the mathematical point of view."[39] Furthermore, Davison pointed out, the technicians overlooked the universality of possible applications of photography, limiting photography to one narrow sphere that catered to scientific investigation. The photograph as an empirical record of reality might have been useful as one sort of scientific truth, but the medium could be applied to other sorts of truth as well. In Davison's case, photography could be utilized in another positivist project: the replication of perceptual experience, which he thought could be carried into the realm of the metaphysical.

Davison's colleague Alfred Horsley Hinton noted that the technical challenges of photography were becoming fewer and fewer as an emphasis on technical perfection shaped the development of the photographic materials made available by the photographic industry. Thus "faultless definition, immaculate surface, irreproachable gradation, and the rest of it are merely what the manufacturers intended should be possible, and we are hence carrying out *their* intentions and when successful we have only achieved what some have already done and others will do presently." Because a "clearly defined facsimile" was a common acme of photographic production, photographic means had been improved in "every way except as regards to their elasticity."[40] In fact, a self-reflective photographer like Robert Demachy could challenge the photographic aesthetic by asking simply, "What is a photograph?" Laying aside the technical standards set forth by the developers and manufacturers of photographic equipment, the call of a truth to the photographic medium could cover a range of accepted practices, from the clear documentary image to the highly diffused gum print. Some of the newer, nontraditional processes offered the "elasticity" Hinton found so essential.

Still, while some photographers like Demachy, with his richly textured, diffuse gum prints, were willing to accept as legitimate a wide variety of photographic processes, many proponents of a stricter photographic aesthetic saw plenty of artistic potential at the other extreme of the photographic spectrum: the crisp, sharply focused, more traditional photograph. Many commercial photographers and conservative amateurs resented the acrid criticism leveled at them for the creation of supposedly mechanical effects, proclaiming that photography, as they practiced it, was indeed an art. Beginning to reflect binary oppositions that would be further codified in the twentieth century, one writer even refers to the ultrasharp "64ists," who were compared to the "fuzzyists."[41] The majority of supporters of the photographic aesthetic thought that the antiphotographic lacked legible signification and failed to exploit photography's most distinctive trait: transparent representation.

Many professionals genuinely believed in the medium's capacity to foster a marriage of the artistic and the commercial. As the close of the century approached, this notion of the artistic professional became more and more paradoxical, as factions of both professionals and amateurs attempted to differentiate themselves from other photographers (discussed more fully in chapter 4). Yet mingling with the impassioned art amateurs, professionals who used art claims as a marketing strategy, and bumbling "snapshotists" were commercial photographers who essayed a consistent and calculated photographic aesthetic.

The Artistic Professional and the Photographic Aesthetic

In an 1885 article reprinted in the *Photographic Times and American Photographer* from a Buffalo, New York, newspaper, an anonymous author offered a remarkably spirited response against photographs with artistic intentions in a local exhibition: "By trying to force a handicraft out of its sphere, they made it offensive. The effects produced by such appliances were pretentious and ugly, and their pretentiousness aggravated their ugliness." Photography, however, was not completely discounted. The author praised the Niagara and Yellowstone views of the well-known commercial landscape photographer George Barker, with their "wonderful combination of minuteness of detail and depth of tone," as "the noblest use to which the camera can be put. They are, if not art, at least artistic, and highly creditable to the manipulatory skill of the operator and to the artistic eye which chose the point of view."[42] While the author was not willing to allow work like Barker's to ascend from the sphere of handicraft into the realm of art, the praise of such commercial documentary work acknowledged artistic intent and an aestheticized commercial practice that, while conforming to traditional formal devices, exploited specifically photographic attributes. Barker did, in fact, represent a bridge between photographers with artistic pretensions and those considered more documentary. His *Niagara in Summer, from Below,* dating around 1888, pictures the falls from a point of view that quite effectively communicates the grandeur of the cascade. Foreground rocks and swirling currents, rendered in rich, detailed tones, give way to more generalized features like the rising mist and plummeting surge of water. Yet beyond this selective point of view, Barker manipulated the image even further, for the picture is a combination print. Barker used a separate negative to print in the sky, a practice akin to the strategies of art photographers like Henry Peach Robinson and Alfred Horsley Hinton. Unlike his predecessors on the western expeditions of the 1860s and 1870s who often printed in skies, Barker had access to emulsions and plates that could record both landscape and sky. His decision to use the combination print to accentuate the sublimity of his subject facilitated a marriage of aesthetic sense and commercial practice.

Like Barker's work, Edward L. Wilson's *A Nubian Landscape,* which appeared as the frontispiece to the *Philadelphia Photographer* in March 1884, earned a long commentary lauding the marriage of formal and technical mastery (see fig. 10). Charlotte Adams described the image as "an admirable rendering of the external features of the landscape . . . combined with a translation upon the plate of the inner spirit of the scene." Delighting in the image for its balanced, broad masses of light and dark, Adams praised both the artistic and technical skill of the composition. She pointed out the contrasts of sunlight and shadow in the bands of sky, river, and low ruins in the middle ground. The colonnade of the temple echoes the feathery palms, which break the monotony of the long stretch of river and offset the brilliant whites of the temple and moored boat, accenting

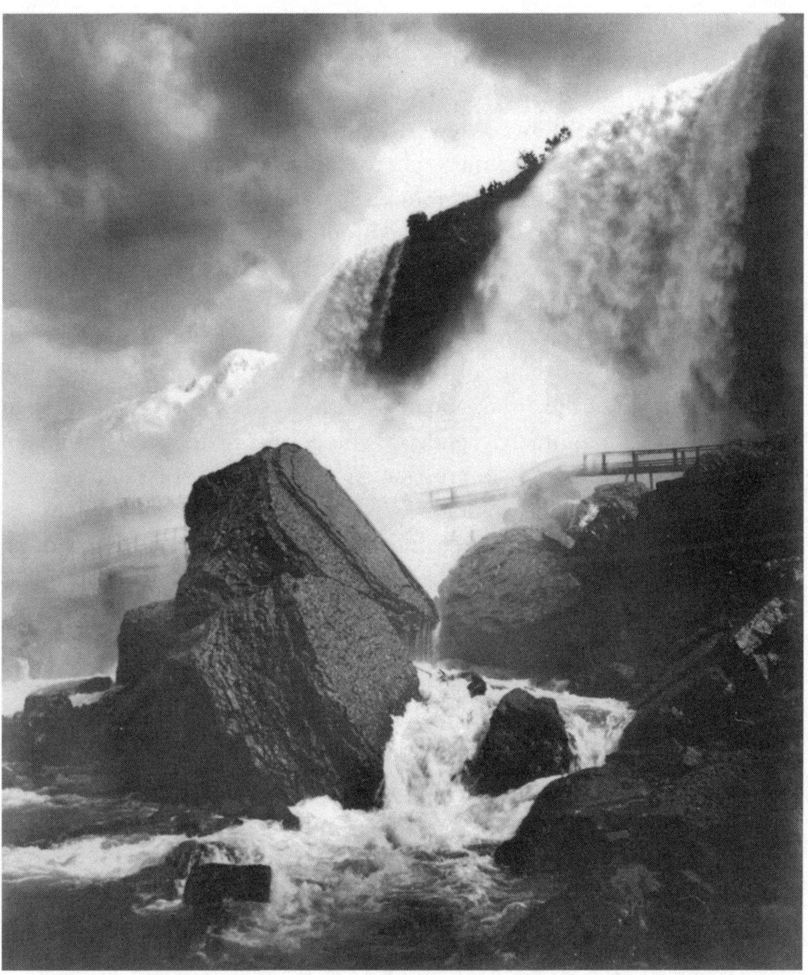

FIG. 25. George Barker, *Niagara in Summer, from Below,* combination print, ca. 1888. National Museum of American Art; museum purchase from the Charles Isaacs Collection made possible by the Luisita L. and Franz H. Denghausen Endowment.

the composition as a whole. Adams noted how the right of the foreground is kept in shadow, underscoring the prominence of the temple, and claimed for the work a rare quality of "realization" where the "sentiment and spirit" of the picture allowed viewers to imagine they were looking at the actual scene rather than a "mere photographic representation of it." To Adams, it was the masterful embrace of the photographic that enabled Wilson's work to prove that "it is the brain behind the camera that calls from its slumbers the soul of the landscape."[43] Adams theorized the co-existence of the technical and the artistic, where objective photography was not without artistic investment, for the goal of such a photograph was a compositional balance of lines and curves for pictorial effect.

While much of the discussion of work like Wilson's was generated in the mid-1880s, the commercial photographic aesthetic survived through the 1890s as an alternative to impressionistic and naturalistic photography. Philadelphia photographer William Herman Rau serves as an excellent example of a masterful old-school technician who synthesized the recording capacity of photography with traditional artistic principles. Rau, who honed his skills as an expedition photographer in the South Seas, the American West, Europe, and the Middle East (with Edward L. Wilson), is best remembered for his extensive body of images commissioned by the Pennsylvania and Lehigh Valley Railroads.[44] These pictures, designed to document the engineering feats of the lines and to entice travelers with the beauty of trackside scenery, often exhibit highly artistic conception. Recently rescued from relative obscurity, Rau combined, as Keith Davis suggests, a picturesque convention with a record "in bold scale [of] a resolutely modern subject: the impact of technology on the landscape." Rau's elevated vantage point—most often the result of photographing from atop his specially outfitted photographic rail car—along with crisp, masterfully rendered detail, led Davis to find in his work a "confidence that suggests the era's positivistic faith in both technology and Manifest Destiny."[45] In Rau's *The Susquehanna at Rockville Bridge*, the young seated figure in the foreground serves as a surrogate for both the camera and the viewer, inviting a contemplative gaze on the scenery, which is punctuated by the impressive technological presence of the railway lines, bridge, and building. The carefully included framing devices of the rock outcropping, bushes, and tree branch offset the vast recession of space that proceeds in successive planes linked by the gentle curvature of the tracks leading to the distant hills. The image presents the engineering prowess of the railway company and incorporates formal devices of picturesque landscape. Similarly, *Conestoga Bridge* documents the solid yet graceful masonry arches of the

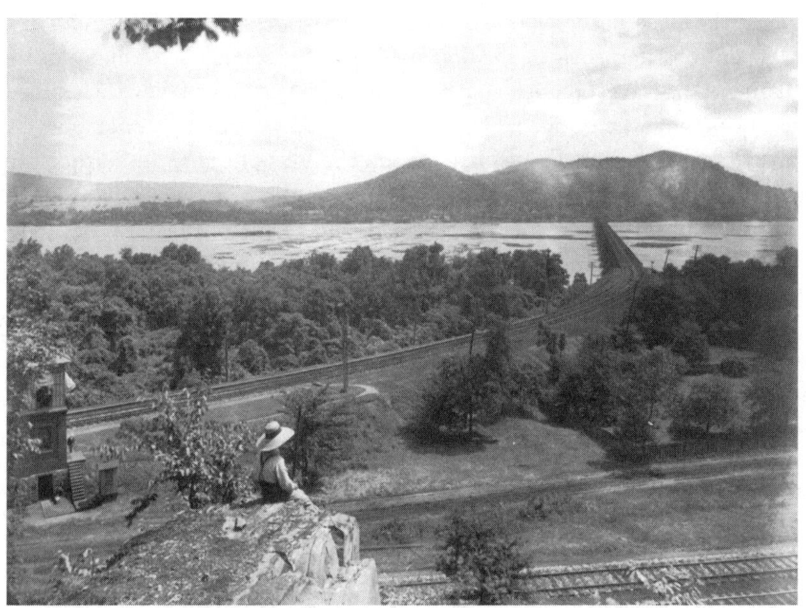

Fig. 26. William H. Rau, *The Susquehanna at Rockville Bridge,* Pennsylvania Railroad Album, American Premier Underwriters.

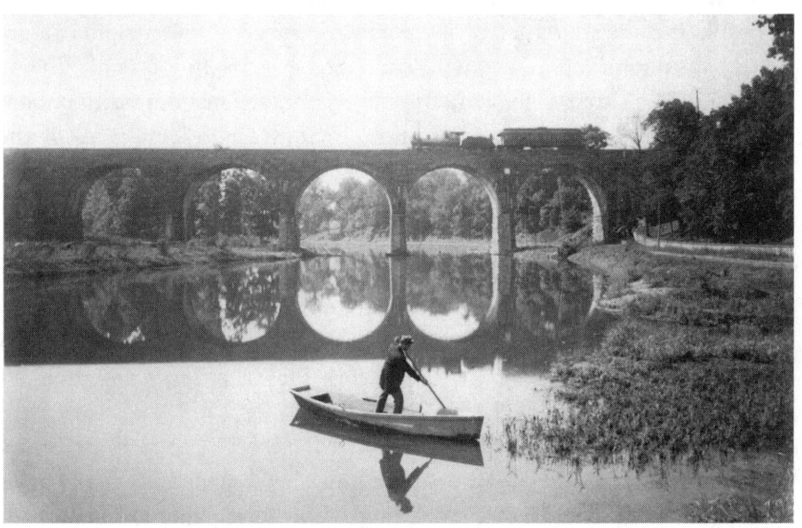

Fig. 27. William H. Rau, *Conestoga Bridge.* Pennsylvania Railroad Album, American Premier Underwriters.

span that bisects the picture perpendicular to the axis of the camera. But woven into the fabric of the document is a consciousness of many of the issues that have occupied photographers and writers I have examined. Waiting atop the bridge is Rau's own specially outfitted photographic car, which often appears in his pictures, asserting his presence, his authorship. By self-consciously noting his own intervention in the landscape, Rau stressed his awareness that the photographic process was not purely mechanical and that his images were not transparent documents but rather constructions as precisely crafted as the railways before his camera. Rau's craft included a thorough knowledge of the traditions of art and photography. The boatman laboring in the motionless water among the weeds of the bank is reminiscent of the type of subject Emerson and so many other expressly art photographers chose for romantic and nostalgic images. Rau simultaneously celebrated railway and photographic technology, articulated through the formal vocabulary of the traditional arts, appealing to both the empirical photographic record and romantic subjectivity.

Rau managed to retain a foothold for the photographic aesthetic even in the increasingly selective and elitist salons of the end of the century. Of the hundred photographers included in the Philadelphia Photographic Salon of 1898, only seven or eight were professionals (a fact that, not surprisingly, disappointed Edward L. Wilson and his editors), and Rau was among them.[46] Rau represents the school of thought that led many photographers to be supremely displeased with the 1898 Philadelphia Salon, where the photographic aesthetic lost out to the antiphotographic. To one reviewer, Rau's marriage of traditional technique and compositional device deserved the greatest admiration, in contrast to landscapes of the "pretentious" impressionistic type and figure studies displaying an "utter want of good taste." The critic ended a review of the newer trends in photography by pointing hopefully to Rau: "In conclusion, the writer does not wish to be considered pessimistic regarding the so-called new school of photography—for no one is more anxious for advancement than he—but fads or no fads, is there one of the most rabid impressionists who can fail to join him in admiring Mr. Rau's [work]? It is a *perfect photograph*."[47]

Variant Levels of Truth to the Medium

While the crisp clarity of Wilson's and Rau's landscapes and the rich, velvety indistinctness of Demachy's lie at the extremes of photographic production, definitions of images true to both art and photography spanned these bounds. As they ventured opinions on photography's capacity for artistic production, many writers attempted to define how much the

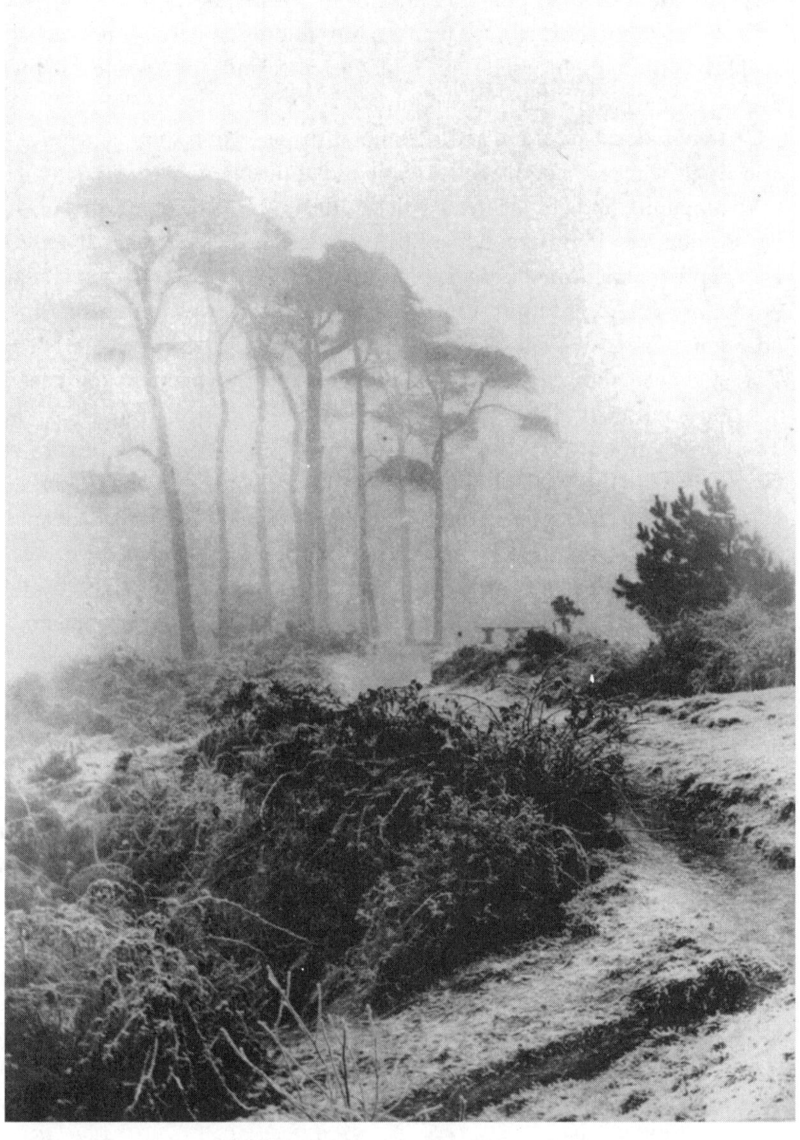

Fig. 28. John A. Hodges, *Bleak December*, photogravure, *Photographic Times*, April 1895, frontispiece. Library Company of Philadelphia.

medium could be manipulated and still retain its photographic essence. In contrast to the diffusion of focus, many photographers found ways to adapt the photographic medium to their artistic conception while still producing images that seem "photographic."

A popular purist stand centered upon the assertion that, by carefully selecting the proper conditions of light and atmosphere, one could be true to the medium and still achieve artistic effect. The landscape work of the British amateur photographer John A. Hodges, a stenographer by trade, won approval from the *Photographic Times* for its artistic effect and technical mastery. According to the *Times,* in his picturesque and sometimes nostalgic images of Wales, Devonshire, the Lake District, and the Isle of Wight, Hodges showed he was "not a supporter of the 'fuzzy school' methods but is emphatically of the opinion that breadth and atmosphere can be secured without resorting to any of the tricks and methods advocated by others." Hodges was praised for his judicious use of stops, which allowed "delicacy and softness" without being flattened by too small an aperture and its consequent overarticulation and lack of aerial perspective. *Bleak December,* included in the 1894 English Salon, was well received by the press.[48] The picture, with its contrasting masses of dark foliage and snow-covered ground, is softened by the actual atmosphere of the view, the mist-laden air diffusing the tall, tufted trees of the background. Similarly, Stieglitz's *Winter,* like his *Winter—Fifth Avenue,* was heralded as an example of an image softened by carefully chosen atmospheric conditions rather than a perversion of photographic processes. It was a "picture produced with the camera. The artist has worked with a definite purpose. It is not a chance shot or a badly exposed plate printed from and labeled 'A Misty Morning' or 'A Dull Day on the Meadows.' It is a Picture in every sense of the word."[49] The *Photographic Times* was fairly conservative, but its editors considered Stieglitz's photographs, even one as soft as *Winter,* "examples of pure photographic processes,—no retouching or hand drawing have [sic] been done on any of the negatives . . . and wherever any softening of detail or forms of the figures has been necessary, it has been obtained by the simple and legitimate expedient of additional exposure."[50]

Even Edward L. Wilson tried to come to terms with softened effects of impressionist photography, attempting to reconcile the evocative goals of impressionism with the photographic aesthetic. Wilson's reluctant acceptance of the "impressionist" mode was revealed in his magazine, where he stated that some photographers were being "hypnotized" by impressionistic photography, which "may all be very well if they do not become too drowsy. . . . It may be that there is room for effort in this direction."[51]

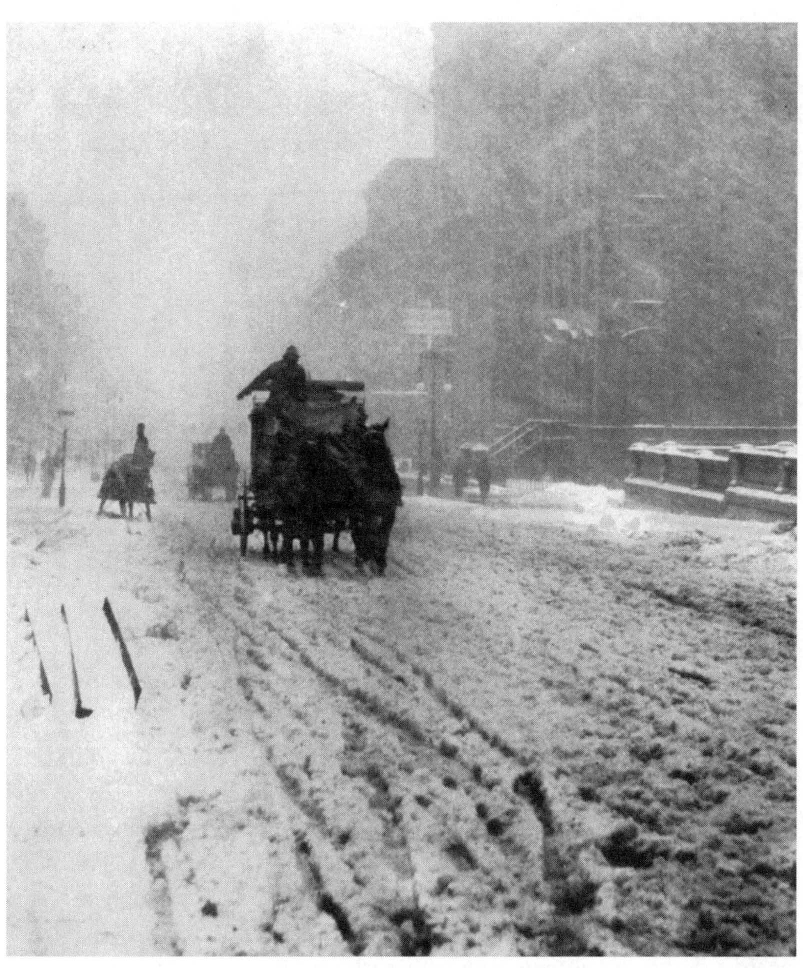

Fig. 29. Alfred Stieglitz, *Winter—Fifth Avenue*, photogravure. *Photographic Times*, April 1896, frontispiece. Library Company of Philadelphia.

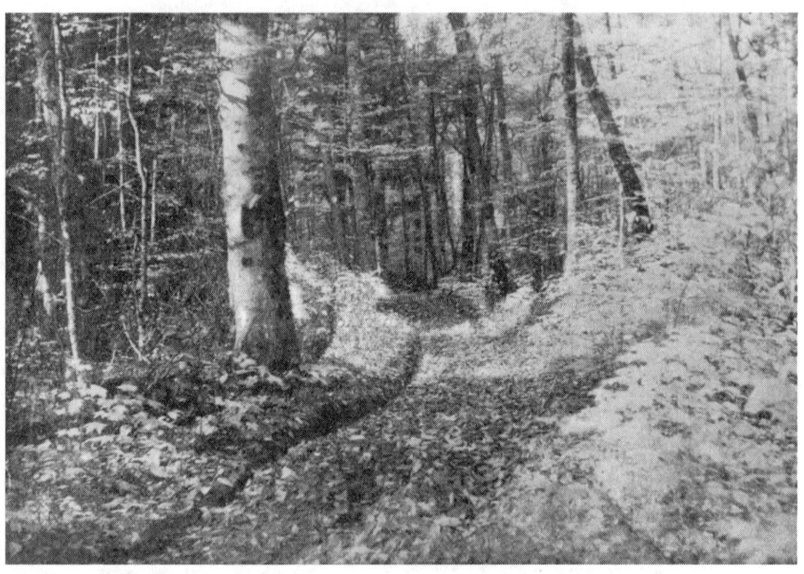

Fig. 30. Edward L. Wilson, *There Is a Pleasure in the Pathless Woods,* halftone. *Wilson's Photographic Magazine,* May 1894, p. 203. Library Company of Philadelphia.

While he clearly was not a champion of naturalistic photography or impressionism in photography, Wilson saw some good in their existence in a muted "proper place." Wilson appreciated "a mere transcript of a scene" that was at the same time pleasing, attesting to the photographer's careful thinking-out of the image.[52] To Wilson, impression was divorced from positivist perceptual theory and did not need to be antagonistic with the photographic, as it could reflect "feeling" or "the understanding of things taken by the artist—the substance of his impressions."[53]

Wilson admitted to trying his hand at this conservative "impressionist" mode, stating frankly, "Yes, I did, and I'm ashamed of it." Unwilling to eschew the recording capacity of the medium, Wilson did not base his "impression" on an appeal to perceptual experience but rather on intellectual and sentimental response to the scene. In correspondence with the emergence of art strategies of the 1890s noted by Peter Bunnell, Wilson abandoned subjects with documentary interest.[54] Photographs of unfamiliar or geographically distant subjects and places were particularly challenging to a notion of photographic plasticity, for they were apt to be accepted as truthful, objective records. In a society where the photograph was primarily consumed as portraiture or souvenir landscape and the most venerated of the previous generation of photographers were best known for their documentation of war and exploration, the art photographer in the 1880s and 1890s faced deeply ingrained expectations for a certain type of utilitarian photograph. Such expectations of both style and subject matter inspired C. A. Needham to advise photographers that "critical examination will often lead to the subjugation, for the sake of art, of that which, in an historical or commercial sense, might be considered the objective point of interest."[55]

When venturing into the realm of his understanding of impressionism, Wilson avoided the historical or documentary associations of his *Nubian Landscape* and picked views that suggested a more personal exchange with nature. Even in *Wilson's Photographic Magazine's* half-tone reproduction of the image, which Wilson titled *There is a Pleasure in The Pathless Woods*, relatively crisp detail and variety of tone abound. To Wilson, the "impression" of the northern Michigan forest scene was the "shiver which was communicated to all by the continuous flirtation going on between the woods and the breezes of the bay beyond." Wilson's impression was the communication of the response of the photographer to the scene, a sort of introversion, for he described going "out into the world again" to produce a foray into his version of impressionism.[56] Relatively detailed and conservatively composed, the image underscores that, to him, the impression was related to associations that could be communicated through the photographic mode and need not degrade the veracity of the photographic record in service of an appeal to perceptual or mental processes. To a photographer like Wilson, the photographic did not need to be completely at odds with the subjective or even the metaphysical.

Stieglitz's *Scurrying Home*, also known as *Going to Prayers*, received a great deal of attention for its play on the viewer's imagination through a comparatively "photographic" mode. A "sensation of the year," the picture received a medal at the relatively conservative Royal Photographic Society of Great Britain in 1895, was hung at the exclusive Linked Ring London Salon, and was purchased for the National Gallery at Brussels.[57] "A hundred different stories," marveled a reviewer, "can, without great flight of the imagination, be woven around these two old women hurrying to their homes or to the picturesque and old-fashioned house of worship in the distance."[58]

While some photographers insisted that their method be as technically pure as Stieglitz's, others realized that even sensitive observation, thoughtful conception, and adept technique were not sufficient to give rise to art and, moreover, that fidelity to the medium was not endangered

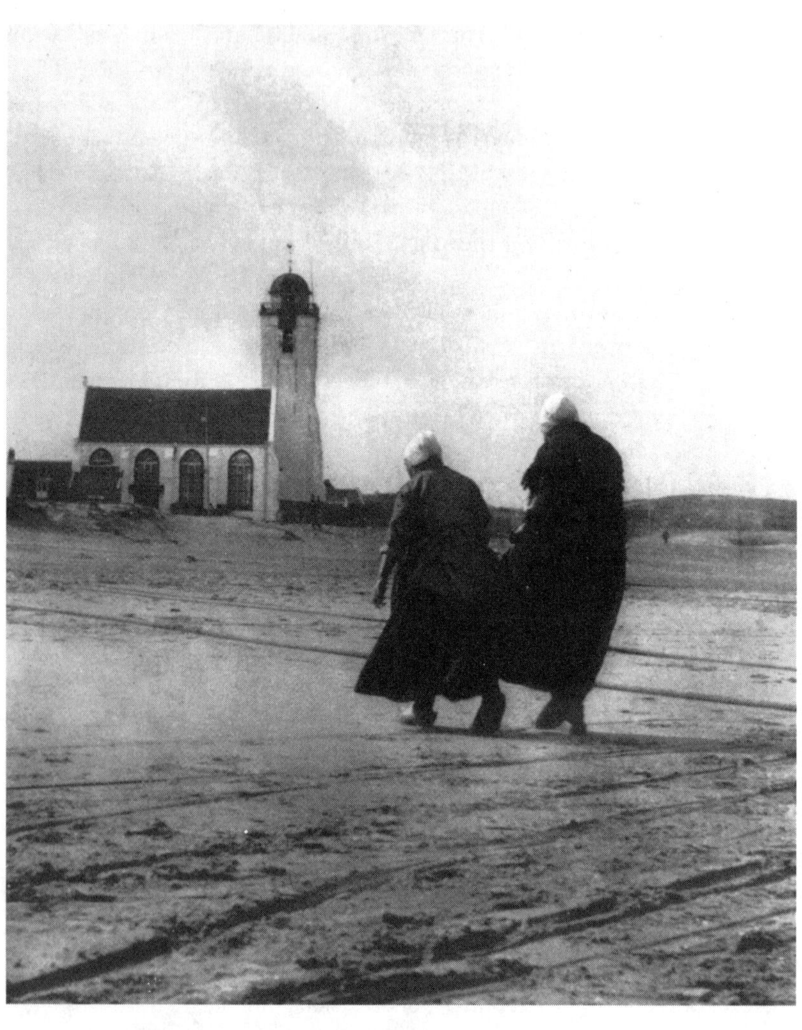

FIG. 31. Alfred Stieglitz, *Going to Prayers,* photogravure. *Photographic Times,* August 1895, frontispiece. Library Company of Philadelphia.

by the further manipulation required to produce a picture. Henry Peach Robinson took on two foes at once, debunking the naturalist-impressionist photographer while retaining a place for photography among the arts. Robinson distinguished himself as one of the most outspoken critics of Emerson and his followers and of photographers who were seduced by photography's seemingly pure recording capacity.[59]

Although Robinson argued that art photographers could distinguish themselves from the scientist and still be true to their medium through certain types of manipulation, he did not believe that the pure record of nature begat art. He declared that while one could not study nature too closely, an exact copy of it did not make art: "Nature is not art; imitation is not art; the reflection in a mirror is not art." The picture-maker could not merely copy nature but had to "assist" and "intensify" nature. He explained that one could "get nearer the essential soul of the truth of Nature by lying," and that "truth *and* Nature are not art; truth *to* Nature is an essential part of art, and that to lie like truth *is* art, and often approaches more nearly the appearance of nature than scientific fact."[60]

Robinson set himself clearly in opposition to the impressionist photographer who, he asserted, seldom said anything worth saying and "has no mission but to upset the experience and practice of centuries." In contrast to the impressionist and naturalistic promotion of the art photograph as a record of a perceptual experience (discussed in chapter 2), Robinson proposed the addition of artistic truth based on compositional conventions drawn from the traditional arts, like those discussed in chapter 1. Artistic truth, in Robinson's terms, was "a conventional representation that looks like truth when we have been educated up to accepting it as a substitute for truth." The art lay in the convention, not in the record.[61] The carefully conceived integration of several different negatives into a single print, or the combination print, was Robinson's means by which the photographer could mediate nature and insert convention (and thus artistic truth) into the photographic image. The printing-in of clouds from a separate negative originated as a strategy to accommodate early emulsions' oversensitivity to blues, and the practice continued through the century as a means of inserting dramatic skies and thus intensifying artistic effect. Robinson, whose combination prints had been highly regarded and frequently published for decades, used the strategy as a method of magnifying the photographic artist's selective powers. His *Bringing Home the May* from 1862 is an excellent example of the complexity of the process by which a photographer could assert an authoritative presence through carefully masking and printing many negatives to form a single composition. By selecting

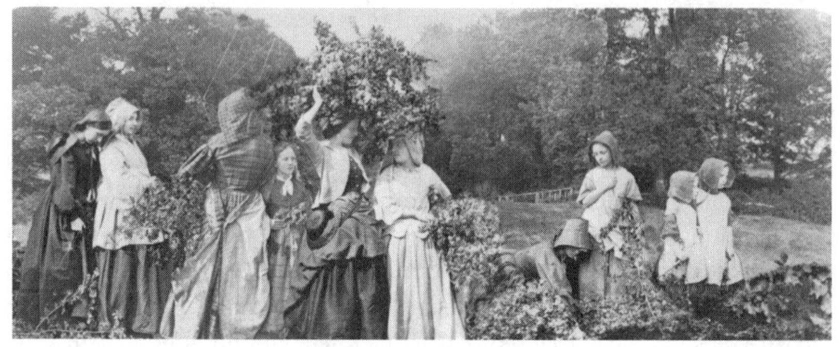

Fig. 32. Henry Peach Robinson, *Bringing Home the May*, 1862. Modern print from original negative, University of New Mexico Art Museum.

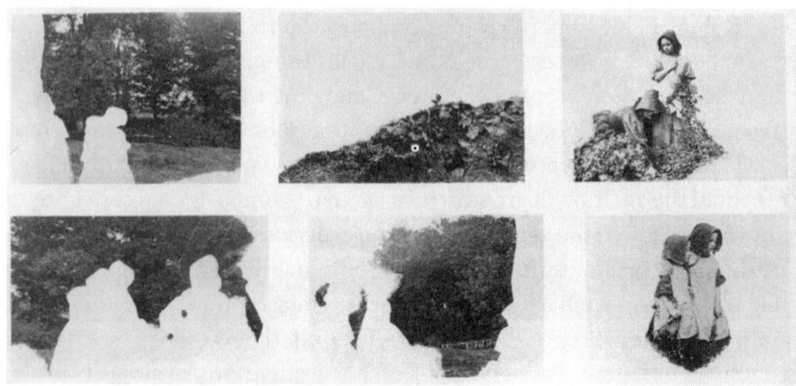

Fig. 33. Henry Peach Robinson, Studies for *Bringing Home the May*, 1862. Modern prints from original negatives, University of New Mexico Art Museum.

and combining the raw material of the photographic record, Robinson thought one could construct a work of photographic art.[62]

Building upon ideas expressed by Robinson and others, Alfred Horsley Hinton, an Englishman who was admired and defended by a remarkably broad range of photographic writers on both sides of the Atlantic, argued for manipulative practices that he believed conserve veracity of the photograph while still reaching beyond what might be considered a mere record. Hinton, a founding member of the Linked Ring, editor of the English *Amateur Photographer*, and a frequent contributor to the *Photographic Times*, advocated combination printing, masking, burning, and dodging as legitimate means by which a pictorial photographer might alter an image, "suppressing" or "emphasizing" to make a point beyond transcription.

Hinton presented an eloquent endorsement of "photographic" photography, praising the "exquisite mirror-like rendering of objects . . . [in] every fibre and detail, its fascinating exactness, or in its rich translucence of surface its finish, its fineness." Condemning invocation, he bemoaned the fact that

> irreproachable technical photography is growing far more rare amongst amateur photographers because of the false notion that the most desirable thing is . . . to make prints which at first glance have a passing resemblance to prints or pictures made by other means than photography. . . . It is the prostitution of some of the wonderful and distinguishing qualities of photography without any gain and without any apparent intention to good.[63]

However strong his praise of the "wonderful and distinguishing" features unique to photography, Hinton was not out to completely condemn the antiphotographic. Hinton himself had been accused of adhering to the vacant affectations of the "fuzzy school," and he attempted to distinguish himself from the invocative mode and unskilled amateurs. He pointed out that his softer work was evidence of his assertion that unmediated transcriptions of nature were not art. Through a selection of manipulative strategies, Hinton believed that photography could both maintain the unique integrity of the medium and produce works of art—works that reproduced the feelings and sense of atmosphere suggested by the original scene. In essence, Hinton had begun to align himself with the evocative mode in which he was "sacrificing certain valuable characteristics of photography."[64]

Hinton's ideal of photography, and his strongest link to the photographic aesthetic, was that of a *seemingly* accurate physical record. The photographer had to avoid the addition of obvious hand work, which resulted in the disappearance of photography's "value and interest" as a truthful record and with which "all confidence in its veracity is lost and it becomes proportionally valueless. "Hinton thought that photography had to retain the air of truthfulness apparent in the photographic document. "Faking" could be acceptable, but only to the point where it did not "proclaim itself by its appearing incongruous with the character of the photographic foundation." Maintaining the fiction of the document allowed the artistic photographer to access an ideal, to create images that "*appear more truthful to Nature than truth itself*."[65]

Hinton discussed the use of soft focus and suppression of detail with reference to issues that arose in naturalistic photography, explaining that then the chief concern was "what *the eye saw*, and how the eye perceived things." In Hinton's mind, however, diffusion of a picture was not a means to replicate vision; rather, it was a way to "*express the idea which its author wanted to express*." Questioning the incontrovertible value of "truthfulness," Hinton discarded the notion that a pictorial photograph had to be a record of a scene, whether it revealed the minute detail of all the intricacies of the subject or the visual impression. He described a middle ground where "truthfulness," instead of withstanding scientific analysis, could be suspended as long the viewer was not overwhelmed by artifice: "If we are photographing with a pictorial aim, that is seeking to express an idea, then the less truth without apparent violation of truth, the better."[66]

In practical terms, it is difficult to place limits on Hinton's allowable photographic manipulation because it depended on the viewer's awareness of the photographer's means. In an unusually detailed discussion of individual works, Hinton described the creation of his picture *A Deserted Shore*, in which the original photographic record underwent "suppression" and "emphasis" aimed at creating a "picture" that retained its photographic qualities. In his photographic manipulations, Hinton's tried to emphasize the "old-world romance" and "stern solemnity" of a once-bustling maritime site, the channel now choked with sand and the boat sheds in ruins, an effect that "simple negatives" would not have achieved.

He began with an image of the scene chosen for its "pleasing composition and massing of light and shade," photographing it just after sunset on a summer evening. After completing this preliminary image, *Trial Print No. 1*, he often visited the site to determine the conditions under which the character and nostalgia of the place were most effectively conveyed. Next, he spent several months scouting out cloud effects to obtain a negative that he could alter to print an appropriate sky, *Trial Print No. 2*. He printed the landscape large, 14½ by 20 inches, dodging the boathouses and water and changing the shape of the tree in the middle distance. Working with printing-out platinotype paper, which creates a visible image when printing (compared to developing-out paper, where the image is latent and therefore invisible until the print is submerged in developing chemicals), Hinton was able to examine the image in subdued light during each step of the printing process. He adjusted the cloud negative to the composition and printed it onto the landscape, again dodging the small cloud and "assisting" the rays of sunlight with carefully placed strips of paper that created bands of brightness. Removing the negatives, he then "tinted down" the entire foreground by exposing the lower sections of the unfixed print to light, darkening these portions of the image and concentrating the light in the center. He then darkened the contour between the roof and sky to correct their interrelation. Hinton's elaborate process of scouting the scene, combining negatives, burning, and dodging was inspired by his self-imposed task to transform a "simple bald negative" of a "commonplace" scene and to use it in a way that would "convey certain feelings and ideas afterwards decided upon."[67]

Opponents of combination printing abounded, and Hinton was not immune to attack. Freely wielding such derogatory terms as "faking," "fuzzyism," and "brushography" in his pro-American review of the 1898 Paris Salon, Charles Rinaldo King took particular aim at Hinton, whose pictures "seem to be object lessons of what *not* to do." King found Hinton's work spoiled by the very devices that Hinton intended to distinguish them, for Hinton's fiction of apparent truth was not upheld, revealing "at once . . . the dodgery employed."[68] A proponent of "pure photography," Norman Macbeth, who looked to Véron as a theoretical model for artistic practice, objected to the "nonphotographic." Macbeth asked the photographer to concentrate on that which was "purely and solely photographic action," denying the legitimacy of combination printing, printing-in of clouds, and retouching.[69] Combination printing, Macbeth argued, was "very unworthy of being allied to the higher associations of fine art" because the "legitimate province of photography" was in the conception, design, and completion of the photograph in singular form.[70] Likewise, Stillman saw the combination print as a vain attempt at art and an affront to photography. He called Robinson's combination prints the "most remarkable and successful examples" of the practice but pointed out that the photographer was still unable to modify nature in each part of the composition he combined, "unless he has recourse to

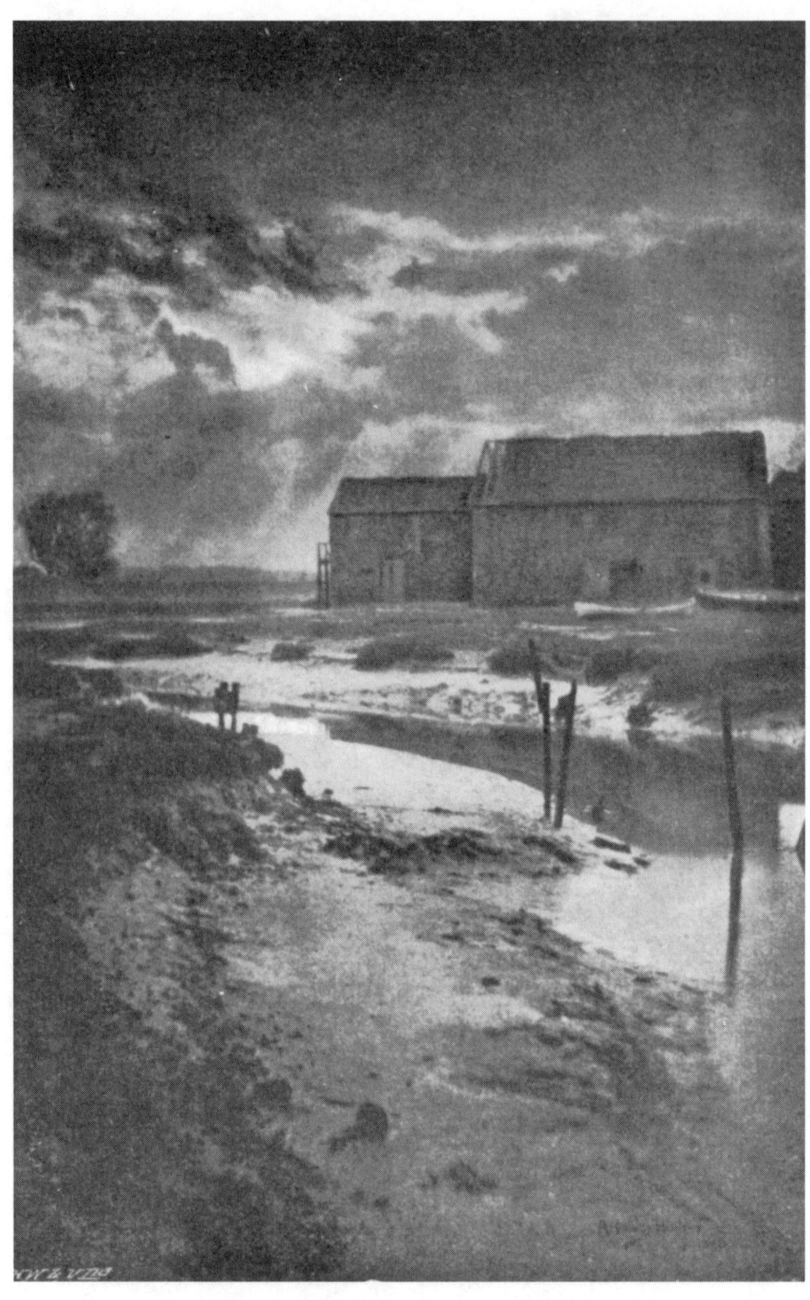

Fig. 34. Alfred Horsley Hinton, *Completed Work. A Deserted Shore*, halftone. *Photographic Times*, February 1898, p. 68. Library Company of Philadelphia.

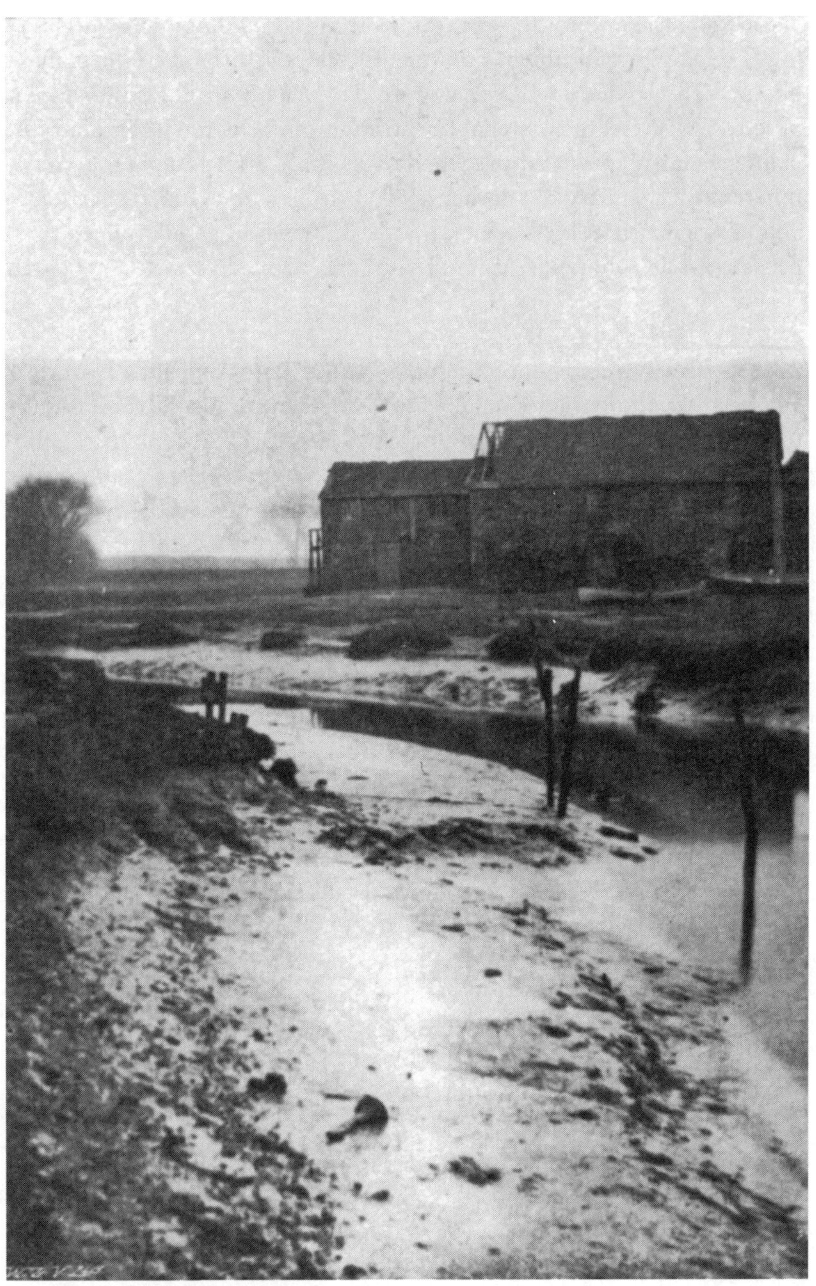

Fig. 35. Alfred Horsley Hinton, *Trial Print No. 1. A Deserted Shore*, halftone. *Photographic Times*, February 1898, p. 69. Library Company of Philadelphia.

working on the negative afterwards; which is not photography but drawing."[71] Underlying Stillman's comments was a criticism of trying to make photography something it was not, a call for fidelity to the photographic process. Why create combination prints in an attempt to emulate the painter's ability to edit nature when you simply displaced photography's inherent mechanicity to another level? Why resort to the application of another representational device, that is, drawing, in an attempt to compensate for an inherent feature of your chosen medium?

A Call for Pluralism

As adamantly as some photographers argued for a particular "truthful" approach to photography, many called for synthesis and compromise, finding strength in a spectrum of approaches to photographic art, a liberalism already apparent in Hinton's work. They sought a photography that avoided affected pictorial artfulness yet left behind the highly defined, crisply detailed photographic image, a sort of "golden mean" between "fuzzy" and "needle sharp."[72] As one writer put it, this could come only through a delicate balance, the photographer "studying Nature as she seems to him, and then depicting her as only the camera can depict her, not with the finest definition of the most highly corrected lens, but with the quality which is peculiar to the product of the camera when not aborted by the effort to get away from its limitations and into the realms of sister arts."[73] Even George Davison, one of the staunchest supporters of a science-based impressionism, relented occasionally to pleas for stylistic tolerance: "All the appeals to what science teaches about the eye and to what psychology speculates about the mind leave us in the end just where we were before, and that is, free to choose for ourselves, free to suit our method to our purpose."[74]

These moderates were not merely unwilling to take a stand; they included some of the more reflective theorists of the medium. Holding his own middle ground of focus and detail, F. C. Lambert condemned the overused device of soft focus, chiding,

> It is well to have a (hobby) horse, but is far from wise to ride him to death. . . . Among the hobby-horses now being urged to an untimely end by driving is the atmosphere, distance, diffusion, fuzzy, out-of-focus spectral steed. Its names are various, but not so numerous as its muddle-headed advocates.

Despite his spirited scorn for those who superficially adopted the formal

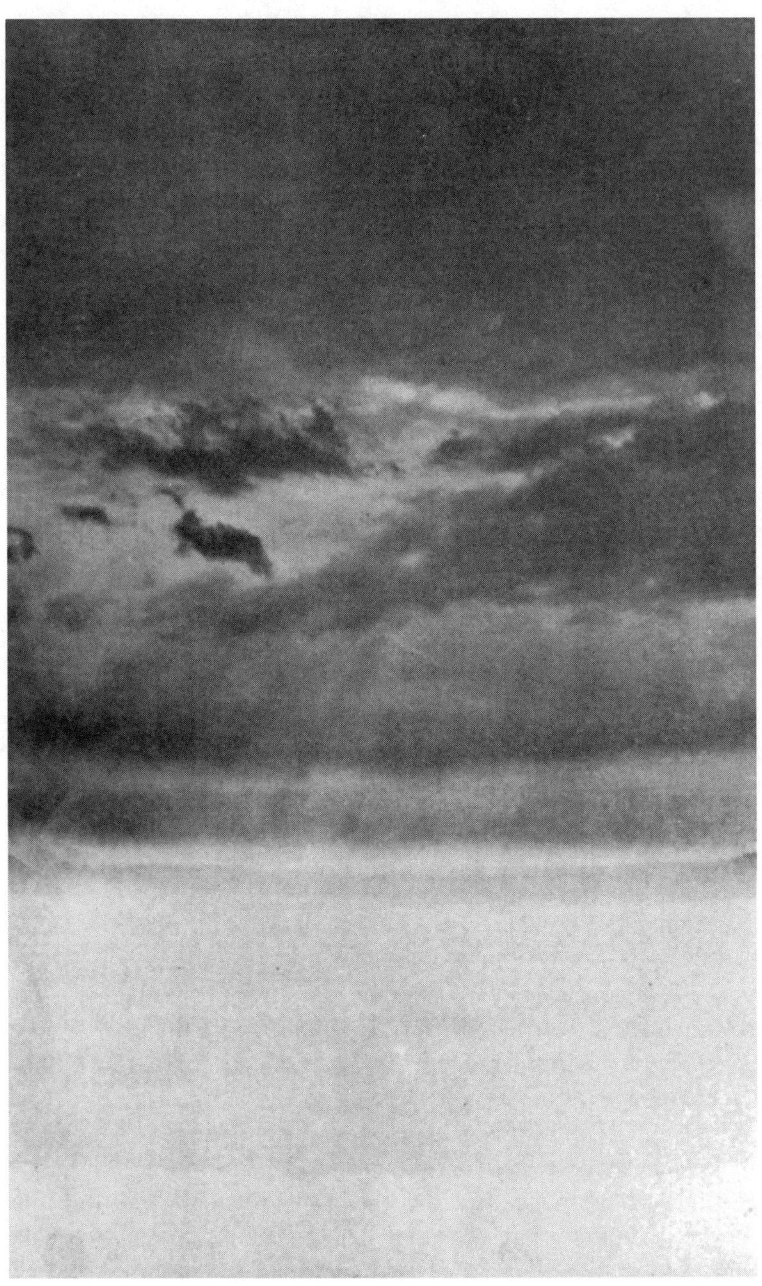

FIG. 36. Alfred Horsley Hinton, *Trial Print No. 2. A Deserted Shore,* halftone. *Photographic Times,* February 1898, p. 70. Library Company of Philadelphia.

effects of impressionists and naturalists, Lambert did not go as far as to advocate the creation of images that pushed the capacity of the photographic medium to its limits. To Lambert, captivation by "the wonderful detail-recording power" of the photograph was equally childlike and superficial, for "this power is frequently used *without discrimination.*" The capabilities of photography that were not necessarily assets included "microscopic definition, biting sharpness, topographical precision."[75] Like his colleagues who noted the photographic industry's role in the creation of photographic ideals, Lambert was aware that "the photography which manufacturers and scientists have given us, which fills our journals, and astonishes the world, is a distorted and inflated form of the photography the man of artistic instincts needs."[76] Lambert warned against "strong prejudices," calling instead for a middle ground between those who cling to fetishistic detail and those who "pin (hole) faith to other extremes" that is, the "fakers" of the "fuzzy school."[77] Like Robinson and Hinton, Lambert believed the balance lay in the correct "proportion of fact and fiction which the painter had dubbed artistic truth."[78]

By the mid-1890s, even Robinson revealed a much more pluralistic view of acceptable styles of artistic photography. While his "true painter's spirit" and "realistic tendencies" had prompted him to ridicule Emerson's theories, Robinson had "evoluted" so far as to "advocate Mr. Emerson's teachings and to substantially declare him clear-headed and far-seeing and correct in many of his assertions."[79] *Wilson's Photographic Magazine* reported that even "our aesthetic master, Mr. H. P. Robinson . . . boldly declared himself to be a hearty advocate of its [naturalism's] pursuit in photography" and claimed that "out of the preaching of many dogmas has come universal freedom. The sharpest photograph, so that it shows artistic freedom, is as welcome as any other variety of the fruit of the camera."[80] While he was quick to devalue "the rigid purism that will allow of only scientific results" and the oversimplification of the label "a one-idea'd school of the fuzzy-type order," Robinson allowed a "lawful liberty of expression."[81]

A photographer who produced engaging and unusual work and earned critical acclaim while embracing the middle ground between full-blown impressionism/naturalism and the absolutely photographic, Rudolph Eickemeyer Jr. initiated himself into the practice of photography through a unique combination of commercial and amateur approaches. Although self-taught, his first projects recorded the machines designed and manufactured by his father's hardware firm. He went on to pursue more typically amateur landscape and portrait subjects but also made extensive

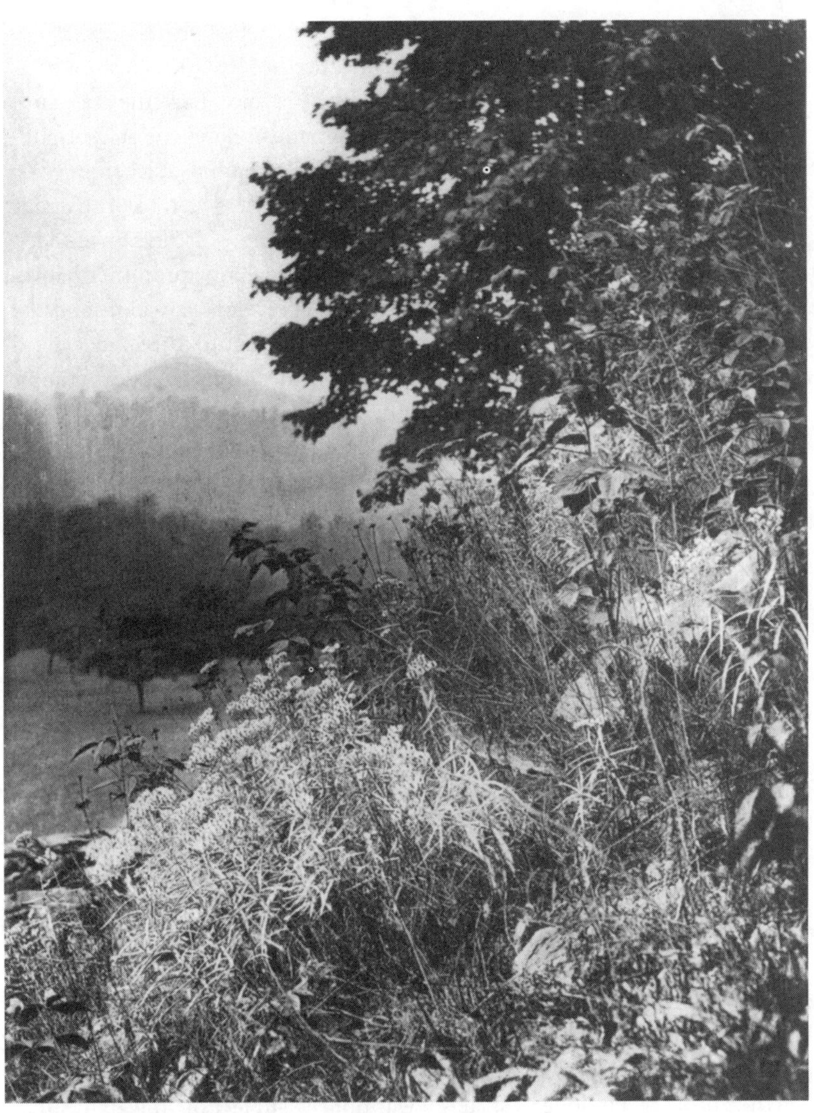

Fig. 37. Rudolph Eickemeyer Jr., *In the Valley of the Beaverkill,* photogravure. *Photographic Times,* June 27, 1890, frontispiece. Library Company of Philadelphia.

photographic travels that rivaled some of the renowned professionals, creating images at Niagara Falls and later in Europe, the Rocky Mountains, California, the Berkshires, and the Catskills.[82] In fact, Eickemeyer paralleled his "artistic" work with commercial portraiture and the sale of published books of his photographs.[83] An 1890 photograph by Eickemeyer, *In the Valley of the Beaverkill*, suggests some of the strides he took. The image of a topographically unremarkable landscape juxtaposes the atmospherically softened bands of background with an unusually prominent foreground of weeds rendered in fine detail. The choice of viewpoint and the effects present in the scene create a variety of visual textures, making it unnecessary for Eickemeyer to subvert significantly the photographic record. He combined a romantic version of Emerson's naturalistic photography with the "scientific" vision required of the empirical document.[84] In 1900, Sadakichi Hartmann praised Eickemeyer's ability to work in the "old methods" of the "purists" yet preserve "more of the truly pictorial element," creating "variety and freshness in the many facets of his work."[85]

One of the unique features of the criticism of Eickemeyer's work was its fixation on originality, a necessity high among the priorities of a progressive critic like Hartmann, who steadfastly admired Eickemeyer's work and collaborated with him on projects: "The artist who has anything worth saying must say it in an original manner—that is unlike anyone else; for if in the course of his expression he should allow himself to employ the methods that are not original with him, but merely adopted and adapted, it will mean that what he had to say was really not worth the trouble saying."[86] While individual style was praised in the work of many photographers, critics found transcending significance in Eickemeyer's vision.[87] This praise of a disavowal of convention was evidence of the expanding space for the practice of photographic art. No longer was photography required to adhere to the rules of the established arts to be considered art. In fact, photographs defined as particularly artful sometimes even explicitly challenged those rules and were praised for it. Furthermore, Eickemeyer's strategy was not the subject of "mechanically" photographic criticism: in the eyes of the critics, he had found a route to photographic art that was unique yet not too mechanical nor too pretentious. "In all his pictures there is thought, feeling and an originality which is never out of harmony or eccentric."[88]

An excellent example of this nontraditional photograph is the highly acclaimed "soft and delicate" bromide print *Sweet Home*, for which Eickemeyer received numerous awards, including medals at the 1893 joint exhibition in New York, the 1894 Newcastle-on-Tyne International

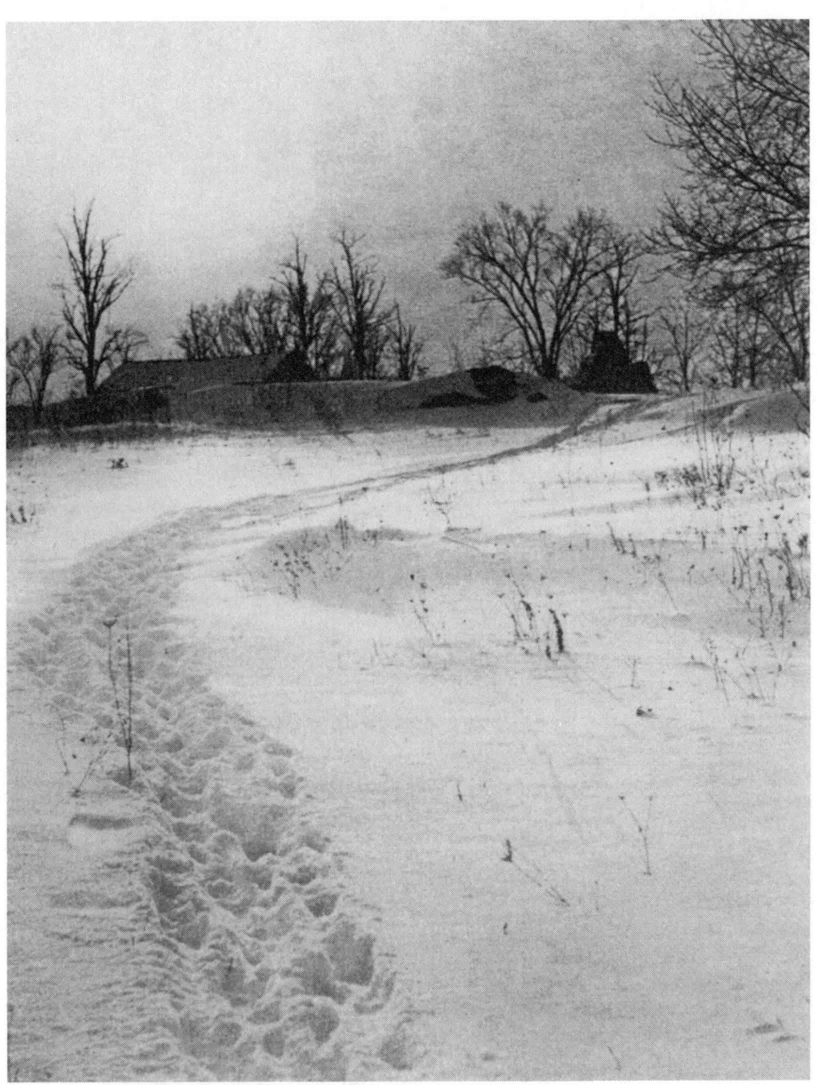

Fig. 38. Rudolph Eickemeyer Jr., *Sweet Home,* halftone. *American Amateur Photographer,* July 1894, frontispiece. Library Company of Philadelphia.

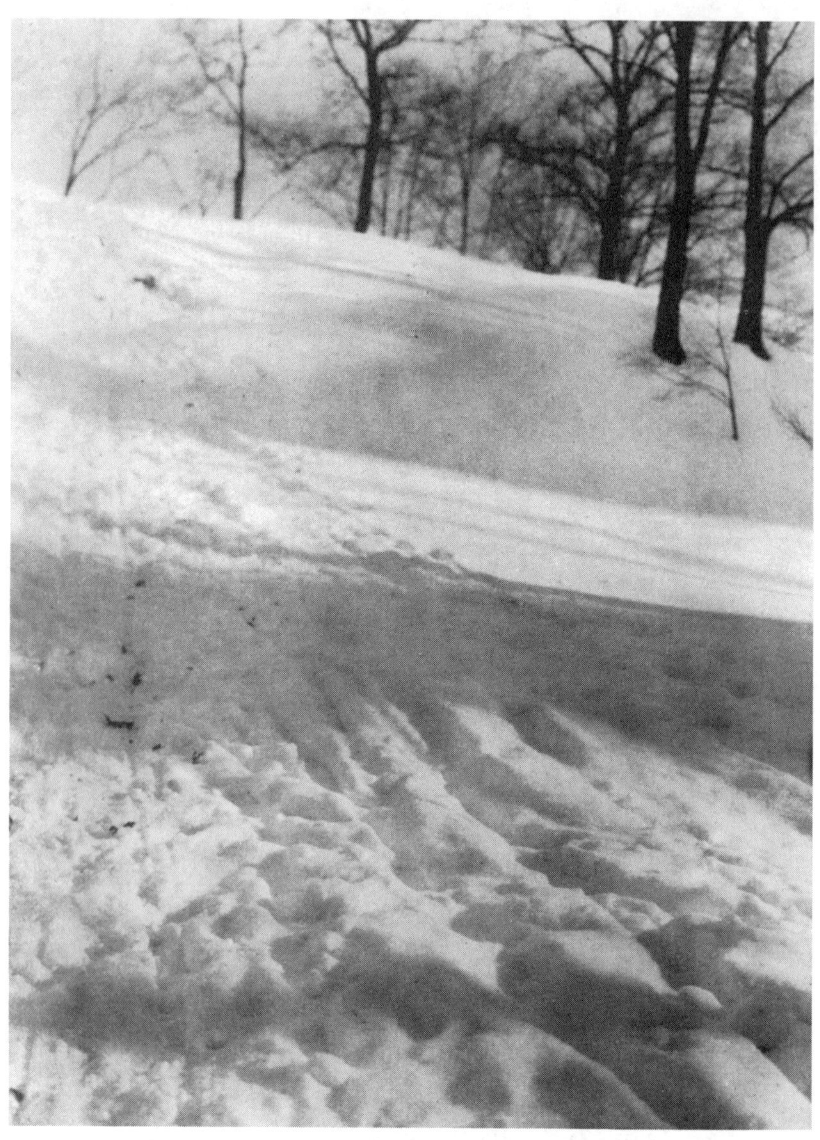

Fig. 39. Alfred Stieglitz, *Snow-Foreground Study*, photogravure. *Photographic Times*, February 1900, frontispiece. Library Company of Philadelphia.

Photographic Exhibition, and the exhibition of the Royal Photographic Society of Great Britain.[89] The image is indeed highly structured and incorporates standard compositional devices, such as a winding footpath leading the viewer's eye through the pictorial space and the masses of foliage that anchor the sides and lower left corner of the image. Yet the downward point of view, which creates a remarkable expanse of foreground, breaks pictorial conventions. The mass of subtly modulated white, punctuated only by an occasional weed and the sweeping arc of the trodden snow, dominates almost two-thirds of the picture. Hartmann particularly commended Eickemeyer's snow scenes in which "everything sleeps beneath the glimmering mantle of snow, and only the light penetrates deeper than ever into the woods with their interlacing branches and many-textured barks."[90] Stieglitz admired and in fact emulated these effects. The most remarkable facet of Eickemeyer's work, according to Hartmann, was the foreground study, and Hartmann considered Eickemeyer's *Fleur-de-Lis* to be one of the best photographs produced in America, second only to Stieglitz's *Winter—Fifth Avenue* (fig. 29): "A few branches of foliage through whose tracery the sunlight filters, a handful of nodding grass whispering to the wind, a group of nettles, spreading burdocks or tangled bracken on the roadside, or a field of flowers in which we like to pause and rest, these are the subjects which he [Eickemeyer] has perfectly at his command. In these he is unexcelled."[91]

While photographs like Eickemeyer's seemed to present new possibilities for artistic expression in a middle ground between the photographic and the antiphotographic, they still challenged traditional criteria upon which art value was based. An advocate of stylistic moderation, Xanthus Smith was troubled by Eickemeyer's departure from traditional compositional conventions, stating that high horizons like those of Eickemeyer's cause "meaningless repetition of vacuity." He denounced "the meagre apologies which are now offered us in pictures, in many instances brainless and soulless, possessing not one speck of nature or art, though lauded by the fashionable *dilettanti*."[92] This move away from conventional compositional rules was reflected in the comments of reviewer Otto Walter Beck. In a statement surprisingly published in *Wilson's*, where Burnet was so revered, Beck declared that "Burnet's analysis of composition is no longer applicable in our time, in which the decorative element forms the universal movement."[93] Indeed, Eickemeyer was not alone in his preference for decorative effect over traditional formal devices. Stieglitz's oft-published and exhibited friezelike bucolic landscape *Decorative Panel* is one of many that present a literal reference to the "decorative element."

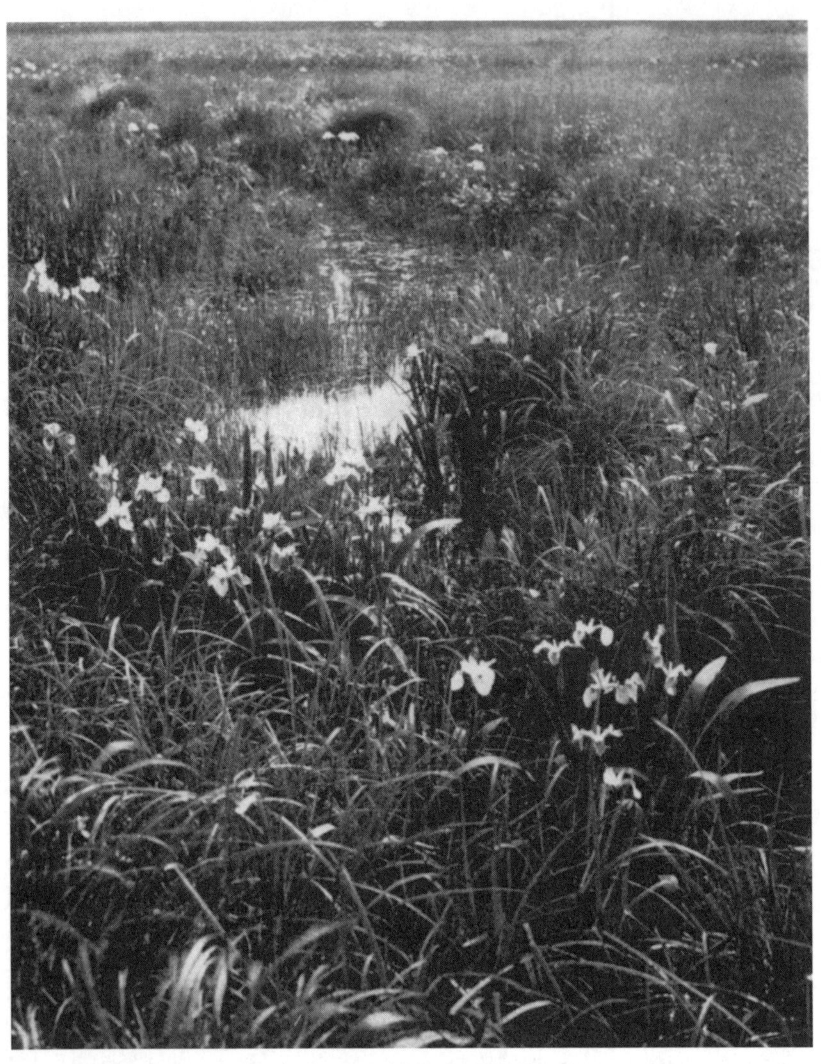

Fig. 40. Rudolph Eickemeyer Jr., *Fleur-de-Lis,* halftone. *Photographic Times,* April 1900, p. 163. Library Company of Philadelphia.

This reference to the decorative quality of photographic work is quite significant to my investigation, for it signals the entrenchment of many of the trends I have been monitoring over the course of this study. This move among some photographic circles to eschew more academic archetypes like Burnet in favor of more generalized, subjective encounters with nature paralleled trends in American painting and reflected concerns encountered in the work of artists like Thomas Dewing and George Inness.[94] The insistence on decoration allied photography with the Aesthetic movement, a realm especially appropriate for the intellectual amateur. The celebration of the dignity of the photographic craft in Stillman's criticism was ironically applied to a photographic art practice he resisted so passionately. Tendencies that consistently arise in the theorization of art photography—to resist technology, to insist on subjectivity, to demand authorship—all found allegiances in the Arts and Crafts movement and Aestheticism, with their emphasis on well-crafted, unique objects infused with a romantic sentimentalism. J. Craig Annan wrote, "We must endeavor to surround ourselves in the rooms in which we chiefly live with the most beautiful objects which we can procure, and, we must exclude everything from our immediate surroundings which is antagonistic to beauty."[95]

The elitism of art photography I discuss in the following chapter can be formulated, in part at least, as a reaction to the materialist attitudes of an increasingly commodified culture.[96] Photographers with high-art aspirations, the "fashionable dilettanti" to whom Smith referred, could retreat into the world of aestheticism, escaping association with the materialism manifested in the gadget-wielding, recreational amateur (who was likely to own a brand new bicycle and tennis racket as well). As I have demonstrated, the theoretical and stylistic prescriptions for art photography were remarkably diverse. While formal devices and their conceptual bases have thus far been the focus of my investigation, I will show in the final chapter that the institutions of photography were reshaped over the course of the 1890s to accommodate a retreat from the common, a differentiation from the masses. It was through this institutional manipulation rather than through photographic manipulation that a codified art space for photography in America was finally established.

Chapter Four

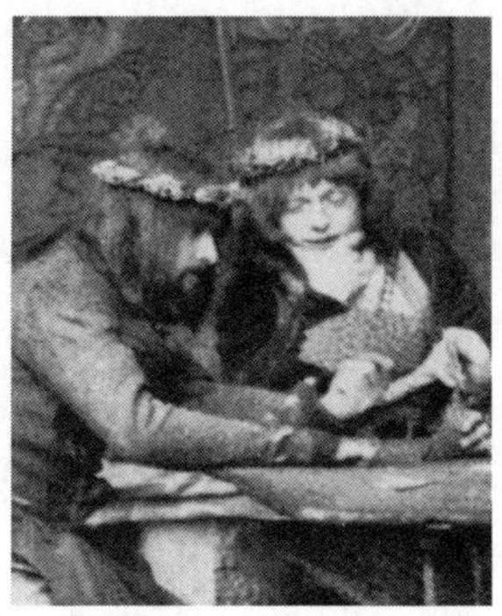

"A Certain Air of Exclusiveness": The Institutional Legitimization of Art Photography

Popular taste runs in the channels of the ordinary and favors mediocrity.

—Alfred Stieglitz, "The Seventh Annual Joint Exhibition"

In addition to the articulation of theories about the way photographs were made and conceived, the struggle to legitimize photography as art also included strategies that targeted the institutions of photography. In fact, more than any single stylistic mode, these institutional strategies ultimately allowed the establishment of a legitimized art practice in America. With one eye on European prototypes, American writers proposed photographic academies, some focused on technological development and professional education, others modeled on the academies of the accepted fine arts. While the academy did not become a major factor in the acceptance of photography as art, the photographic society proved to be a forum for intense debate over the nature of art photography. Over the last two decades of the nineteenth century, the way photographers chose to define their associations shifted radically, reflecting the growing amateur presence in the field. The photographic community became increasingly stratified, with photographers clamoring to distinguish themselves from one another by extolling the merits of their particular skills and intentions. This process of differentiation ultimately led to the establishment of a self-proclaimed elite alliance of photographers centered around Alfred Stieglitz. Through the manipulation of a final photographic institution, the exhibition, Stieglitz and his colleagues were able to create a legitimized, elite space for art photography.

The Photographic Academy

Many writers advocated the establishment of photographic academies as a means of gaining respect for photography. They called for schools modeled on European institutions, but most of the overseas prototypes and their American equivalents were more technical and scientific institutes than art schools. Although a number of photography schools and departments within larger institutions were founded, the visions of promoters of a full-fledged photographic academy that would stand on the same ground as fine arts academies remained unrealized.

To most who implored the photographic community to establish an academy, the importance of such an institution lay in the development and dissemination of technical knowledge.[1] In 1885, Charles Ehrmann, an associate editor of the *Photographic Times and American Photographer,* made a "plea for a photographic college," citing the success of the photographic departments of the Royal Polytechnicum in Berlin and similar institutes in Vienna and Salzburg. In the mid-1880s, his vision of an educational institution was based on the teaching of technical skills because "very few photographers are required to do anything artistic. Our main efforts are mechanical or scientific."[2] Even late in the 1890s, writers were still proposing a school of photography based on European models, such as the Imperial School of Photography in Vienna, a technical institute dedicated to the science of photography rather than to artistic issues. In 1886, Ehrmann became a driving force behind one of the better-established photographic schools in the United States. The school at Chautauqua, New York, which operated primarily in the summer, attracted a range of photographers but reflected Ehrmann's photographic priorities—he was primarily a commercial photographer who emphasized technique. Similar photographic programs with curricula geared toward preparing students for the pursuit of photography as a trade existed in the last decades of the nineteenth century at larger educational institutions, among them, Columbia University.

As professionally focused as many of these programs were, some facets of proposed institutions went beyond the commercial sphere and reflected the increasing differentiation within the photographic community. Extolling the educational merits of the art club, Charlotte Adams suggested that photographers model their institutions on organizational strategies of the other arts, "teaching the principles of art in accordance with the systems of the best contemporary European art institutions."[3] In the closing years of the nineteenth century, Otto Walter Beck continued to propose a photographic art school, an institution still absent from the United States. He perceived a need for an institutionalized photographic establishment, not a trade school, but a clearly defined *art* academy, asking, "Why cannot this art, with its large organizations, create an academy, finely fitted out with masterminds and masterpieces to foster comparisons with the sister arts?" Beck also underscored the need for the art photographer to be distanced from the commercial sphere: "The aspirant to the art of photography should have a period of years in which to pursue the purely artistic and therefore ideal, as apart from the mercenary considerations and temptations."[4] Despite the establishment and even occasional flourishing of photographic trade schools like Ehrmann's at Chautauqua, Beck's dream of a fine art photography academy remained unfulfilled, and the creation of a space for the acceptance and nurturing of art photography was left to other institutional strategies.

The Photographic Society: An Increasing Rift between Professional and Amateur

The photographic society was the object of momentous restructuring in the last two decades of the nineteenth century. Changes in the organizations with which photographers defined their intraoccupational associations provide telling evidence of growing factions within the photographic community, factions that played key roles in the articulation and implementation of strategies to legitimize photography as art. While photographic societies were established in the United States soon after the medium's invention, until the 1880s they were primarily the realm of the professional. These organizations catered to the needs of the commercial photographer, stressing improved techniques, new materials, and business practices. With the growing ranks of amateurs in the 1880s, a new type of photographic club emerged, one aimed more exclusively at the interests of amateurs. The Society of Amateur Photographers of New

York, founded in 1884, was designed to meet needs outside the reaches of the two primarily commercial societies in the city at the time, the Association of Operative Photographers and the Photographic Section of the American Institute. The new society was geared specifically to amateurs, "unhampered by trade interests, . . . governed by men who did not sell goods or practice photography as a trade." Professionals were allowed to join but had no voting rights.[5]

The desire of amateur photographers to differentiate themselves from their professional counterparts was linked to a struggle to define an identity for photographic art. As the amateur became a more substantial presence in the photographic community, tension mounted between those who depended on photography for a livelihood and those less motivated by economics. Many professional photographers considered the amateur a threat to business and a degradation of their trade. In 1884 the itinerant landscape photographer Robert Tramoh wrote to the *Philadelphia Photographer*, expressing unbridled contempt for the growing number of amateur photographers. Unlike the amateur of the past, whose experiments made significant contributions to the technology of photography, the dilettantes of his day were, to Tramoh, a degradation of his profession and a threat to his livelihood. They were unable to develop and print their own work, relying on a cheap technician to do it for them. "When these prints are finished, he (the amateur) takes them to his friends who tell him that they are excellent (the professional would have thrown them in the waste), and really excel those of the men who make a living by making pictures. Our amateur gets conceited, and thinks he knows it all."[6] Like Tramoh, the photographer B. F. McManus bitterly chastised the growing ranks of amateurs, complaining in 1890 of their omnipresent snapping at any conceivable subject of interest and their declarations of vast knowledge: the object of his greatest ridicule was the "press-the-button-we-do-the-rest-amateur."[7]

Paralleling the caviling wrought upon them by professionals, art-minded amateurs found essential faults in commercial practice. Amateur after amateur argued that artistic exploration and development were at odds with the demands of the commercial market. To many commercial photographers, the title of "artist" was not desired for the sake of the medium's standing among the fine arts but rather for the prestige it might suggest to potential clients. In the wake of plummeting prices caused by cut-rate entrepreneurs, or "Cheap Johns," professional photographers were often more concerned with the legitimization of their prices than with their craft. Edward L. Wilson complained to the Photographers'

Association of America that the ignorant patron "holds that, because he sees cheap prints hawked about the streets, that good ones cannot cost any more, and the artist photographer must *argue his cause* every time he asks a living wage."[8]

The pressures of public taste provoked consideration by both amateurs and professionals. To some writers, an underlying mission of photography was to educate the public and to cultivate the market, to develop, in the words of Charlotte Adams, "an educated and enlightened art public."[9] But as one writer described it, elevating popular taste was a Herculean task "of trying to educate the public so they can understand and appreciate a higher and better quality of picture . . . until that time arrives, the cheap-Johns will rule the day and carry off the spoils."[10]

In contrast to the 1880s' writers who suggested that it was the photographer's duty to popularize art photography, other critics, particularly those at the close of the century, saw popular opinion as inconsequential; and some even relished the absence of public commendation of their work as an affirmation of their elite ideals. These "progressive" factions isolated art photography rather than making it accessible on a wide level. Reconsidering his lamentations that the monthly exhibitions of the New York Camera Club were not better attended by the public, Sadakichi Hartmann commented that "there may be some wisdom in this exclusiveness while at present their efforts are strictly on the dignified line of art for art's sake, a quality which deserves unlimited praise in these mercenary days."[11] Such opinions led to the conclusion that condemnation of work by the general public might be considered affirmation of the creator's elite status.

Free from the pressures of business, the amateur, it was argued, had the opportunity to cultivate and apply the artistic, unconcerned with popular taste or commercial success, experimenting and exploring beyond the mere application of art principles and beyond what a commercial market might tolerate.[12] Technical virtuosity took a backseat to the ability to imbue a photograph with art value through a conceptual investment; the amateur was at liberty to pursue the subjective reality demanded by art, while the professional was apt to create an empirical record of reality.

Differentiation among Amateurs

The oft-made distinction between the inspired and the hackneyed, the mundane and the transcendent—one based on attributed artistic sensibility—was not limited to comparisons between the amateur and the professional. Indeed, among the amateurs themselves differentiation became a key tactic in the tumultuous search to define fine art photography, and the shifting focus of the amateur photographic society reflected this splitting of the amateur ranks. While amateur photographers who aimed at the artistic attempted to distinguish their work from what they considered unfeeling commercial and professional photography, they were also faced with the need to distance themselves from the expanding population of casual amateurs and their uninspired snapshots, recreational photographers who pursued photography as a form of amusement on the level of bicycling or yachting. The art status sought by artist amateurs required a photographic practice elevated above popular amateur pursuits.

The dilemma posed by the ever-growing ranks of recreational photographers, who on the one hand provided many enthusiastic advances in possibilities for photographic expression and on the other threatened the goal of an elite photographic art by the sheer number of casual practitioners, was evident in articles by the advocate of professional photographic education W. H. Burbank. In the *American Amateur Photographer* in 1890, Burbank applauded the popularization of photography. He compared photography to other sports and recreations, where pockets of enthusiasts organized into clubs and interest spread to gain nationwide recognition and respect, such as the League of American Wheelmen, the American Canoe Association, and the National Lawn-Tennis Association, organizations that raised their sports from "a merely local or fleeting 'fad' into a national and dignified means of recreation."[13] In the same issue of the *American Amateur Photographer*, an advertisement appeared for the *Photographic Herald and Sportsman*, a New York publication "devoted to photography, bicycling, tennis, croquet, base ball, hunting, fishing, boating and all out door sports."[14]

In contrast to his commendation of sportslike clubs promoting photography, Burbank's comments in the following issue of the *American Amateur Photographer* switched gears. Burbank indicted the recreational photographer for participating in the destruction of photography as a dignified pursuit because "it is very widely regarded as a harmless amusement or a very indifferent means of earning a livelihood. It has been degraded by its professed friends."[15] Here he argued that those who pursued photography as a "harmless amusement" were corrupting the status of photography as a serious endeavor. Many writers, like B. F. McManus, complained of insanely clicking, "press-the-button" photographers who ignored thoughtful composition, bemoaning the snapshot in which "photography descends into the line with other mechanical toys that serve to amuse" yet reflected no creative thought or technical adeptness.[16] John Bull Jr., an

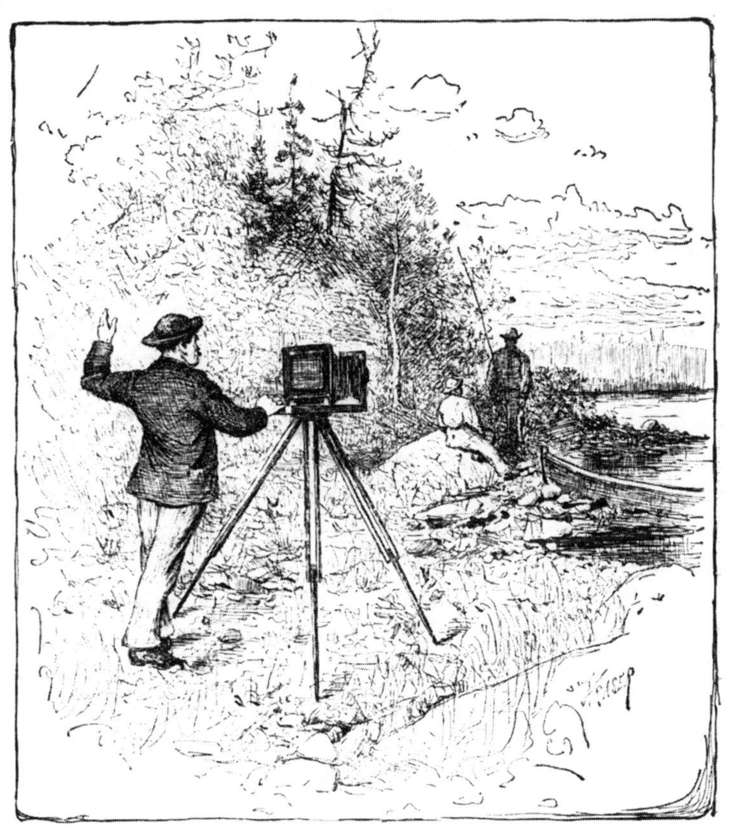

FIG. 41. Advertisement for *Outing*. *Anthony's Photographic Bulletin,* June 11, 1887, p.v. Library Company of Philadelphia.

Englishman living in America, blamed the seemingly low standard of the field of American amateur photography in the mid-1890s on the introduction and extensive advertisement, during the field's infancy, of the "press-the-button" camera by a "soulless corporation."[17]

Bull's "soulless corporation" was, of course, that of George Eastman, who in 1888 introduced his Kodak hand camera, a device that simplified the photographic process far beyond the small dry plate cameras that had become increasingly common in amateur hands over the course of the decade. Little more than a year after their introduction, more than thirteen thousand Kodak cameras had been produced, astonishing the photographic community by the manner in which the camera "persuaded thousands to the pursuit of photography, . . . [and] added largely to the ranks and considerably changed the methods of amateur photographers." The camera came preloaded with roll film, so the operator could take a hundred or more photographs, send the entire camera back to the factory, and have the negatives developed and printed and returned with a freshly loaded camera. Eastman's innovations in cameras, plates, and printing papers led many to believe that "the conservative photographer . . . sees all his good old notions subverted, one after another."[18]

In the first issue of the *American Amateur Photographer*, which appeared just a year after the introduction of the Kodak, the mission statement of the journal forcefully, and almost mournfully, distinguished between the serious amateur and the popular photographer emerging in the wake of inventions like the Kodak:

> We very much fear that in some respects photography is being belittled by its friends. . . . It has become a popular belief that all the difficulties have been removed, and that anyone can take pictures. Photography has been degraded to the level of a mere sport, and many take it up as they do lawn tennis, merely for an amusement, without a thought of the grand and elevating possibilities it opens up to them. The making of pictures is fast becoming merely an episode in a day's pleasure, not the earnest and untiring search for the beautiful. We submit that our art has a higher side than is apparent to him who uses only a detective or a small box, which, whatever their value, are far from representing all that is best and highest in photography. Indeed, were this all, amateur photography would soon die of its own too-muchness.[19]

This "too-muchness" worked its way into the photographic club as

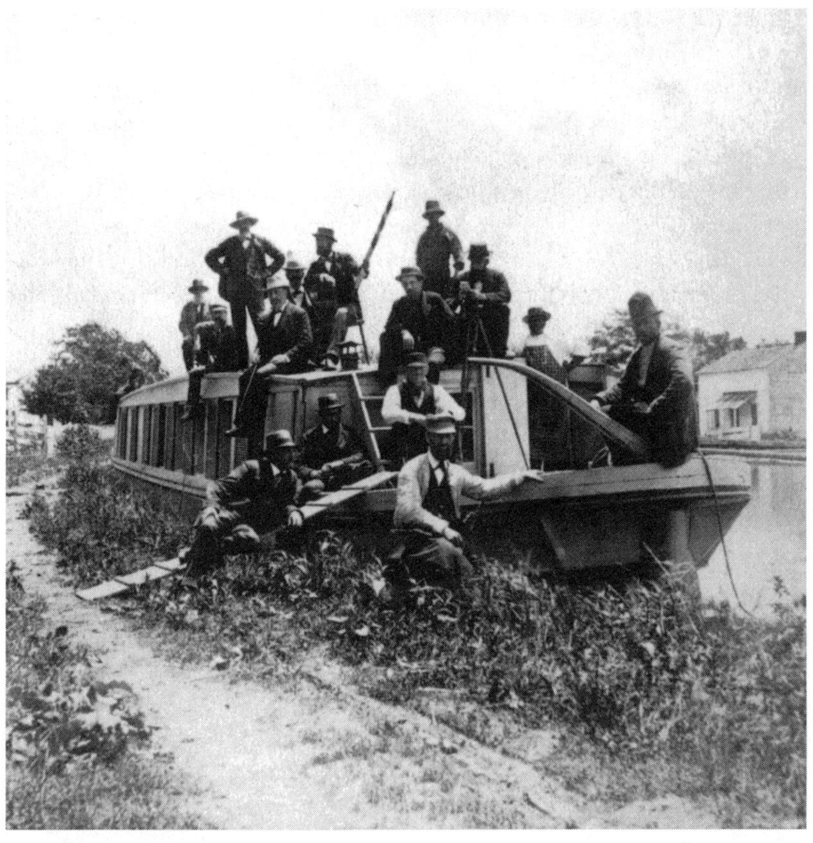

Fig. 42. John C. Browne *Excursion of the Philadelphia Photographic Society*, n.d., Library Company of Philadelphia.

well. Many art-minded amateurs were not satisfied with the institutions set up to serve their interests, finding the amateur photographic club to be the realm of either the chemist or the excursion snapshotist. In the 1880s and 1890s, the accelerated establishment of casual clubs and societies, like those Burbank described as pursuing photography as recreation, helped to foster a general acceptance of photography as a means of representation separate from commercial portraiture and documentation; however, this increased enthusiasm without serious theoretical focus also threatened the feasibility of the establishment of a legitimized photographic art.

Even though the Society of Amateur Photographers of New York was founded to address the needs of nonprofessional photographers, the society's main function was to provide a forum for the exchange of technical knowledge and "scientific matters," with demonstrations of new processes and equipment. As late as December 1895, a typical meeting of the society included the following agenda: after reviewing the minutes, correspondence describing a newly patented dark room camera was read; a model of a new English finder was shown; and a paper on developers was given. The evening concluded with a discussion of how the meetings could be made more interesting.[20] Thus even one of the most lauded "progressive" amateur societies typically focused on the technical. Often the amateur society or club's photographic endeavors tended toward the leisurely documentation of an outing. Members of the Society of Amateur Photographers of New York, for instance, made group field trips to scenic spots, like an 1884 excursion to West Point, and to dramatic events such as the lighting of the torch of the Statue of Liberty, naval parades, and the demolition of Flood Rock at Hell's Gate.[21] Amateur outings in Philadelphia also displayed this leisurely character, as is evident in John C. Browne's *Excursion of the Philadelphia Photographic Society*, in which members pose on a canal boat they hired for a day trip.

Alfred Stieglitz and the Amateur Elite

The frustration inspired by the dilettante photographic tourists and chemists dominating many of the amateur associations intensified some of the more impassioned art-amateurs' differentiating impulses. These elitist tendencies ultimately led to the construction of highly selective alliances in the amateur community, the most elite group gravitating around Alfred Stieglitz. This sense of elitism was a carefully constructed legitimizing strategy that played an increasingly vital roll in the definition of photographic art and photographic artist. These synthetic alliances were not so much a matter of style as a matter of affiliation.[22]

In his review of its contribution to the joint exhibition of 1893, Stieglitz does little to hide his contempt for the Society of Amateur Photographers of New York and his impatience with casual amateurs who "gave an impression as if photographs had been treated as sport and pastime and not as an art and science." "This is to be deplored," he continued, "for without a doubt the society contains many very talented men, who have been misled and misguided by a non-progressive majority. . . . Taken as a whole, the work shown was photographically very good, artistically very poor."[23] Separatism for the sake of legitimization reached a climax in the hands of Stieglitz, who established himself amid the general

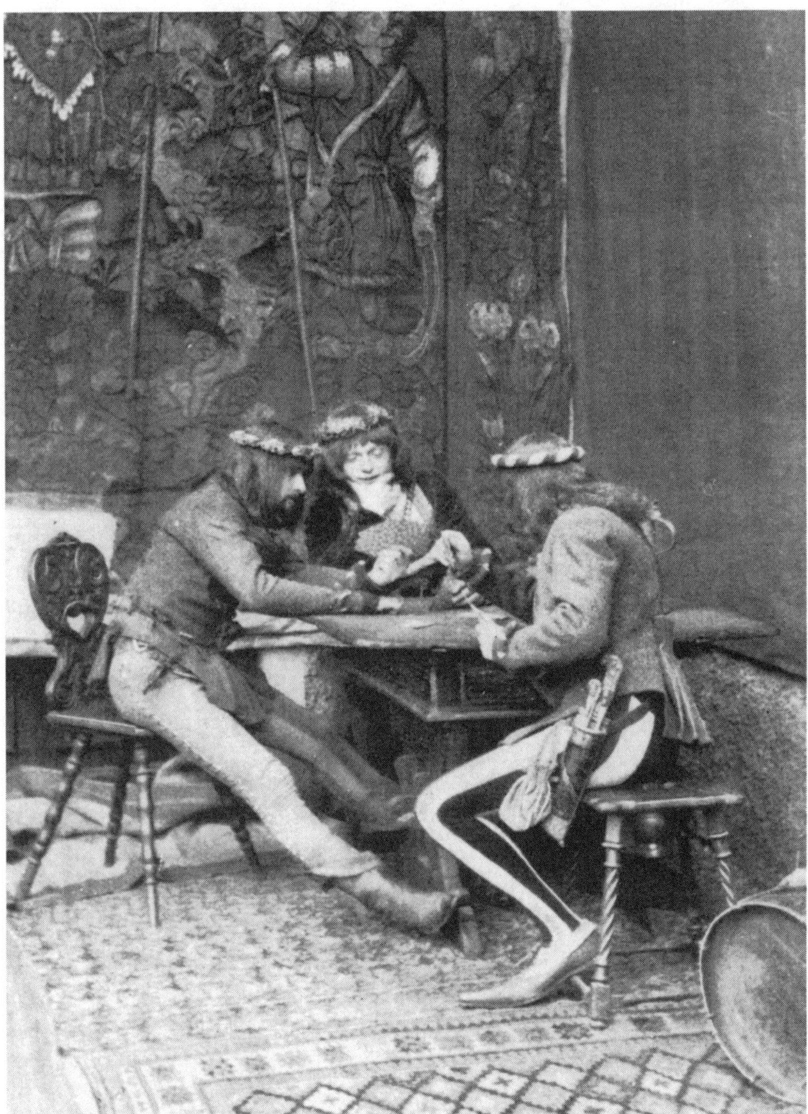

Fig. 43. Alfred Stieglitz, *Card Players*, halftone. *Photographic Times*, December 1, 1893, p. 692. Library Company of Philadelphia.

population of amateurs and continually narrowed his circle of perceived colleagues, masterfully manipulating legitimizing strategies. Ultimately, he used the Philadelphia photographic salons and the subsequent Photo-Secession to buttress the formal conventions of art photography with an institutional identity.

While his deftness with photographic chemistry reflected his studies with H. W. Vogel in Berlin in the 1880s, Stieglitz's early work is not particularly remarkable.[24] He was less an outstanding photographer than a progressive and demanding thinker. Relatively conservative in style Stieglitz's photographs were often offered as examples of good work by writers criticizing the "ultra artistic."[25] For instance, his *Card Players* is typical of many conservative attempts to impose imaginative narratives on a scene and thus produce unmanipulated illustrative photographs. His reputation earned him respect, and when he submitted his work anonymously it was not always well received: in works sent to the 1894 *American Amateur Photographer* photographic competition, Stieglitz used the pseudonym "Progressive," yet the prints elicited a cool reception from Davison, who commented, "wanting in vigor and go," "not very convincing," "the mark has been missed," and "tame and pointless."[26]

The character of his actual work aside, even early in the 1890s Stieglitz understood the power of institutions in shaping photographic practice. After he accepted the editorship of the *American Amateur Photographer*, Stieglitz became an impassioned voice for the integrity of amateur art photography and its institutions, gaining enough respect, even in England, to be elected to the exclusive Brotherhood of the Linked Ring in 1894. Despite receiving scores of medals, he placed little value on the awards and was amused at the importance many American amateurs "attach to medals gained at some little exhibition or other and awarded by incompetent judges." By January 1896 Stieglitz left the *American Amateur Photographer*, for as one writer put it, he "was too fearless and candid in his criticisms to suit the readers of such a magazine" and "was compelled to resign."[27]

In April 1896 the *Photographic Times* devoted an unusually long and well-illustrated article to Stieglitz and claimed that he stood "unchallenged as the leader in Pictorial Photography in America." Presented as the epitome of amateur artistic endeavor, he was ascribed with no motive other than the betterment of his art. Stieglitz's position as a leading champion for photographic art was constantly reiterated through a differentiation between artistic amateur work and ordinary amateur or commercial photographs. His pictures were "at once recognized as being different from the ordinary views made by the average amateur."[28] Stieglitz was the subject of one of the first major treatments of art photography in a major American journal by Sadakichi Hartmann, who emerged as one of the most insightful observers of elitist photographic practice. Stieglitz was portrayed as the leader of a select and gifted group of practitioners. In fact, Hartmann opened the essay on Stieglitz with a quote from "Hoffmann's Tales" that extolled differentiation from the masses:

> Leave the routine to the timid, clear with one bound the common track, and when thou shalt have created a path where none can follow thee . . . loosened from the fetters of ordinary rule, thy place will be fixed and thou wilt see, coming toward thee with an even step, both glory and fortune.

Although he also criticized Stieglitz's work, Hartmann praised Steiglitz's power of selection and depth of emotion, standard measures in the rhetoric of art value, as well as his "perseverance largely dependent on temperament and constitution."[29]

It is not just Stieglitz's photography that made him successful but also his drive to establish photography as art through a variety of means. Hartmann related how early on Stieglitz played a key role in the art photography realm, and members of the New York Camera Club often referred and deferred to him. Some of Hartmann's observations seemed to foreshadow Stieglitz's break with the Camera Club in favor of more selective associations. He pointed out that while the quality of *Camera Notes* was quite admirable, it consisted mostly of technical and scientific texts, a focus that changed when Stieglitz established *Camera Work,* which concentrated on photography and fine art. Hartmann also recounted attending a group criticism where Stieglitz's "slaughter of artistic pretensions" earned Hartmann's praise but left many club members in revolt "against such what seems to them ungracious treatment."[30] By 1898, when he was appointed to the jury of the First Philadelphia Photographic Salon, Stieglitz's reputation bordered on the mythical: he was labeled "the art amateur of the American continent."[31]

Hartmann recalled the phlegmatic state of the New York amateur photographic institutions in the early 1890s. But in 1896 the Society of Amateur Photographers of New York and the New York Camera Club merged, and the New York Camera Club changed dramatically. He identified such key features as the publication of *Camera Notes,* monthly public exhibitions, a new facility, and a dedication to the advancement of the "science and art of photography." The exhibitions at the New York Camera Club, explained Hartmann, differed from ordinary art exhibitions where "good and bad are hung indiscriminately together:" instead, the club presented exhibitions of a single artist's work, where the whole ensemble and its presentation "tell at once the individuality of the man."[32] The stress on individual artistic expression in his assessment of the new exhibition policies at the club is telling, for Hartmann's critical attention most often focused on those who distinguished themselves in their work and demeanor.

Elite art-photographers like those of the Stieglitz circle purposefully distanced themselves from popular culture, a realm where the ordinary photograph pervaded on a more intense level with each passing day. In contrast to the avant-garde painter who might, as art historian Thomas Crow points out, embrace low cultural forms in order to "displace and estrange the deadening givens of accepted practice," art photographers eschewed general culture specifically to define an accepted practice.[33] They construed public resistance to their art as a sign that they had managed to produce images that transcended the accepted realms of ordinary photography.

Hartmann described the increasing aesthetic elitism in New York at the end of the 1890s, an undemocratic attitude that would later put him at odds with the Photo-Secession. "There exists in New York," explained Hartmann, "a clan of Bohemians who pretend they do not care a rap for money, and who only accept it for their more or less artistic services because they have to live after all." While he suggested that such an attitude was often an affectation, he identified photographers like Stieglitz and F. Holland Day who were genuine in their high standards. He perceived ways in which these exclusive photographers, both genuine and sanctimonious, attempted to differentiate themselves from the "professionals," describing how they "claim to be superior craftsman of their trade, they fancy limited editions of their prints and exhibits in photographic salons, and understand how to surround themselves with a certain air of exclusiveness."[34]

Hartmann, while quite savvy about the benefits of developing an increasingly contracting circle, did not always approve of these art photographers' means and motives or the affectations of their advocates. He attacked the audience of seemingly advanced art: "they consider themselves the true connoisseurs, and anybody who does not share their views is not trained sufficiently to do so. For they hold that art ever remain a mystery reserved for the elect, an appendage of the fit and few—that is to say themselves."[35] Hartmann's impatience with the pseudoelite defined an even more elite group, those who did not simply affect art but truly understood. Coupled with his relentless early support of Stieglitz and his interaction with *Camera Notes* and later *Camera Work*, Hartmann was, at times, an eloquent voice of the select.

A photographer writing in *Wilson's Photographic Magazine* in 1900 made some insightful observations about the state of photography, the new significance of the amateur, and resentment within the photographic community. F. Bennett recalled the great fear that the popularization of making photographs inspired in much of the professional community: the threat to business, the plummeting prices, and the compromised craftsmanship. While admitting that these perils were genuine, Bennett pointed out a newer development in the role of the amateur. Unlike the cheap cameras, commercial processing, and lowered standards that seemed to undermine the foundation of the professionals' livelihood, the amateur, Bennett thoughtfully explained, "is invading photography from *the top* . . . with his half nebulous 'art' theories and his jargon of pictorial value."[36] Bennett understood that, to a certain extent, the successful exclusivity of art photography at the turn of the century was facilitated by bypassing and surpassing generally accepted standards and institutions of photography.

Resentment Inspired by the Elite

The selectivity of the Stieglitz group induced cries of resistance by those outside the exclusive circle who were less sympathetic than Hartmann and Bennett, those who categorically denounced the self-proclaimed elite. Edward L. Wilson, who even flirted with his own conservative brand of impressionist ideas and consistently offered commentary on the importance of imagination as a facet of the artistic, nonetheless derided the ever-tightening group of separatists. This type of Bohemian photographer, he proposed,

> will meet you at his studio door in eccentric dress, with an uncombed approach to Padrewiski hair; with bags under his eyes and an inconsolable-looking nose; brutal manners and "impressionist" inclinations. . . . This sort of person imagines that the public will stand anything from him, and does very strange things. It cannot be said that he is an agreeable person, neither can it be affirmed that he has any good prospect at permanent success, or that he will do anything very great in art.[37]

By 1900 the widening rift between the small group of self-defined art photographers and the rest of the photographic domain was large enough to agitate the restrained conservatism of a journal like *Wilson's* into a reactionary rant. The lead article of the journal's July issue, presumably written by Wilson himself, lashed out at elitist tendencies, "particularly with a noisy section of the English press and a few ambitious youngsters on this side of the Atlantic, to decry all American photography, save that produced by a certain 'school,' as something almost beneath contempt." Resenting "ponderous utterances, which abound with verdant freshness and advice of a very lofty kind" that condemned all but the most select group of photographers, Wilson took aim at the "self-anointed" critics whom he called the "godlings." With uncharacteristic specificity, Wilson attacked many writers, photographers, and institutions of which he had been rather tolerant, ridiculing the "superior 'tone' and mystic subtleties" of Hartmann's essays, the "long drawn condescension" of Hinton's theories, the outrageous pictures of Joseph Keiley's, and the "sugar-coated pills of pure Art" in a "certain club organ" [*Camera Notes*].[38] The elitist differentiation had worked, Wilson sensed, and he resented it.

While he unquestioningly admired Stieglitz, the professional portrait photographer Arthur Hewitt, like Wilson, enumerated several flaws in the pictorial movement that lived "a narrow bigoted sort of existence, . . . felt only by a favored few." He found fault in "a *narrowness* of thought and decision" in the jurying of salons as well as the construction of exclusivity by reducing the number of works accepted to salons. He also saw too much influence in too few photographers who made "a very pronounced effort to discourage any other salon, save ones in which they personally figure," encouraging the work of "a very small circle."[39] As Hewitt's resistance to the exclusivity of the art photography cliques suggested, the salon became the major forum for the implementation of legitimizing strategies. Indeed, nowhere was the revamping of the institutional structures of photography in the last two decades of the nineteenth century more apparent than in the organization of the photographic exhibition. Tensions between commercial photographers and amateurs, and among amateurs themselves, culminated in fiery debates over the mission of the exhibition, its rules and procedure, its participants and audience. Ultimately, the photographic salon became the most significant forum for the legitimization of art photography in America.

Restructuring the Photographic Exhibition

Through the mid-1880s, the photographic exhibition was often associated with a trade convention, and while it may have included photographers with earnest artistic goals, they shared space with manufacturers of photographic equipment and supplies, chemists, opticians, and everyday professional portraitists and view photographers. A myriad of awards and medals enticed exhibitors with the prospect of advertising fodder. Over the course of the late 1880s and through the 1890s, the differentiating impulse that permeated critical texts on the relation of professional and amateur, snapshotist and artist, select and uninspired, fostered a restructuring of the exhibition system. Art-minded photographers attempted to divorce art photography from the commercial and the recreational. Virtually every aspect of the traditional exhibition was challenged: the categories of work included; the awards offered; the presentation of the work; the systems of invitation and of juried selection. By the end of the 1890s, the progressive photographic art exhibition was no longer a trade show but the highly exclusive realm of the artistic elite.

To convince his or her clientele, the commercial photographer claiming the title of artist depended on official acknowledgment of his or her skill. The scores of awards and medals offered at the typical photographic convention or exposition gave the professional the opportunity to win praise that could be exploited for financial gain. The commercial photographer featured his or her honors in advertising and logos, becoming the sort of "artist" from which the art-minded amateur would have wanted to distinguish himself or herself. The label for an expensive Cincinnati studio photographer bears the title "Landy's Gallery of Photographic Art" and assures customers that "Pictures taken at this Establishment are unsurpassed for Elegance of Style and Artistic Finish." To bolster the studio's claims, the label lists medals from world-renowned exhibitions.[40] Similarly, Frederick Gutekunst, an aptly named, well-respected, and highly successful Philadelphia commercial photographer, presented a remarkable manifestation of belief in the commercial advantage of claims to art. His "trophy car," constructed for the celebration of the centennial of the United States Constitution, was embellished with banners, flowers, and burnished gold and drawn by four equally decorated horses. In addition to life-size examples of his best work, the sides of the vehicle were adorned with enlarged reproductions of photographic medals and awards from around the world. The summit of the construction was occupied by allegorical figures of the fine arts in classical garb. Two seated women represent Sculpture and Painting, flanking the standing figure of Photography, who leans upon a camera and holds aloft a wreath of laurel.

Art, to the serious amateurs and their professional allies, required more

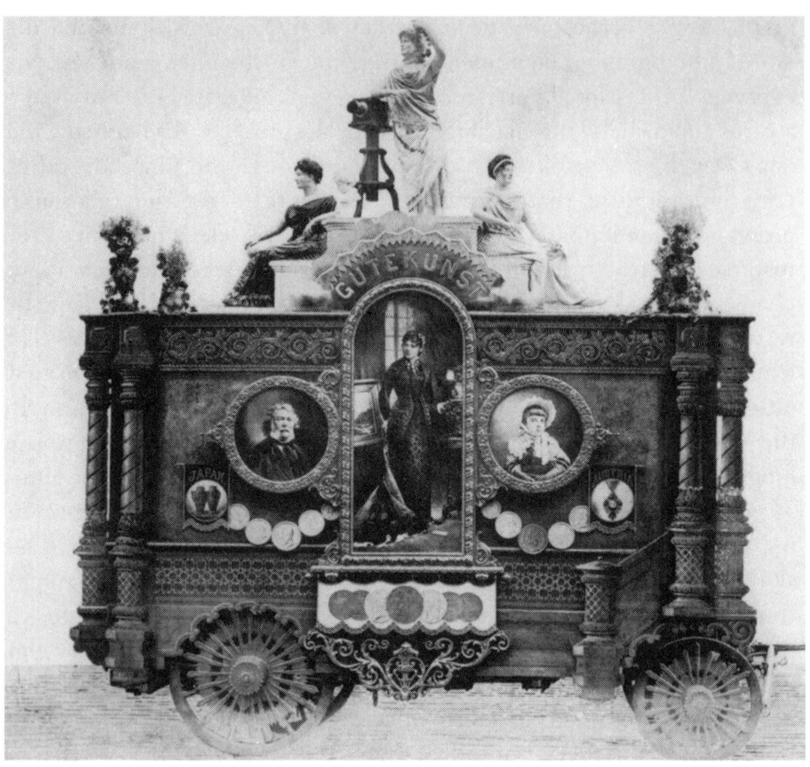

Fig. 44. Trophy-Car of F. Gutekunst, photogravure. *Philadelphia Photographer,* December 17, 1887, frontispiece. Library Company of Philadelphia.

rigorous investment and could not be a ploy for commercial advancement. The use of medals as mere advertising inspired them to call for a revamping of the exhibition and award system. In 1887, one proponent of thoughtful artistic investment in professional photography described photographic exhibitions as a place for photographers to exchange ideas, meet stock dealers, buy supplies, and "by dexterous management or by lucky chance get some token of superiority to take home and advertise upon for mere commercial advantage."[41] Henry Peach Robinson found a "state of flat mediocrity" in the field of photography, a state encouraged by awards given in such quantities (and usually for commercial reasons) that those "tokens of superiority" lacked meaning and failed to distinguish and encourage quality artistic work.[42]

The mediocrity that Robinson identified was in part due to the parameters for the artistic constructed at the traditional photographic exposition. In reference to exhibitions in 1889, Edward L. Wilson claimed great strides in his quest for the application of art principles to create pictorial effect, yet a description of an exhibition of the Photographers' Association of America reflected the state of exhibition practice. The officers of the association sought to encourage art photography by offering prizes for the illustration of a specially selected set of poems. This was the space provided for art photography; art was considered illustrative; and the great hope was that people would pay well for such pictures. Only seven contestants entered work.[43] Again in 1890, Wilson complained of a lack of "enthusiasm shown in the direction of art at our exhibitions this year."[44] Still, Wilson kept up the effort, trying "character studies or pictures illustrating some familiar phrase, [which] would constitute a much more practical and profitable field for effort, than the illustration of lengthy poems."[45] He established contests like the one in *Wilson's Photographic Magazine* illustrating the phrase "An Enticing Offer," which elicited such saccharine figure studies as youngsters with watermelons and coy yet saucy maidens.

Many photographers resented the binding of "art" contests to a given narrative, a requirement that restricted subject matter to cloying genre scenes. Otto Walter Beck called the story-telling picture "the pitfall of art of our century."[46] "When we go through an exhibition of American photographs," observed Stieglitz, "we are struck by the conventionality of the subjects chosen; we see the same types of country roads, of wood interiors, the everlasting waterfall, village scenes; we see the same groups at doorsteps and on piazzas; the same unfortunate attempts at illustrating popular poetry; the same etc., etc., *ad infinitum*." While Stieglitz himself was guilty of producing many a prosaic image at this point in his career (witness much of his European work of the 1890s), he did aptly describe much of the work his clique would rally against later in the decade. He prescribed a remedy for the hackneyed state of American photography: original, simple, atmospheric images, suggestions that are manifested in photographs of spring and winter scenes in which Stieglitz embraced atmospheric states to create tonal effects (see fig. 29).[47] More and more, the art photographer demanded that the exhibition parameter of narrative should acquiesce to an appreciation of form. "Granted that we are, in our technique, fully equal to the English," wrote Stieglitz, "what we lack is that taste and sense for composition and for tone, which is essential to producing a photograph of artistic value—in other words, a *picture*."[48]

The Photographic Exhibition and the Legitimization of Art Photography

Encouragement of the production of "pictures" was apparent in the development of a series of exhibitions sponsored by three of the most significant amateur and professional photographic societies. Beginning in 1887, the Photographic Society of Philadelphia, the Boston Camera Club, and the Society of Amateur Photographers of New York combined to sponsor joint exhibitions. These included many facets of photography, from portraits and genre to scientific and technical, but year by year, the committee in charge focused more intently on the artistic side of photography.

The adulation of British photographer and future member of the Linked Ring Frank Sutcliffe was testimony to the "art side" at the First Joint Exhibition in March 1887. By the Fourth Joint Exhibition in 1891, judges included Thomas Moran and Edward Bierstadt, and among the medal winners were Stieglitz and Catharine Weed Barnes. In 1892 Barnes herself identified the exhibition as a site for the dissemination of strategies of legitimization and formation of artistic identity, individual and national:

> All intelligent observers of the tendency of these annual exhibitions note the advance that is being made in showing the possibilities of the camera, when in the hands of a person imbued with artistic instincts, as a means of producing pictures equal to those made by the brush. Americans are rapidly catching the spirit and genius of the artistic foreign workers.[49]

By 1893 the joint exhibition expressly manifested many of the ideals that would be distilled over the course of the decade: attention to the artistic application of photography, increased selectivity of inclusion, disavowal of an extensive awards system, and a carefully defined jury. In a report on the Sixth Joint Photographic Exhibition in Philadelphia, the Exhibition Committee of the Photographic Society of Philadelphia stated,

> the main interest centres more and more each year in the artistic side of photography. . . . At future exhibitions a rigid system of selection [should] be instituted, only pictures of decided artistic merit being admitted and hung. The admission of a picture in itself would be an honor, independent of any further awards it may be expedient to offer. While an exhibition so conducted would include a much smaller number of pictures the average quality would be of a higher grade and the interest and value of the exhibition would be increased

> accordingly. An exhibition of this character, the work being selected by a careful and competent jury, would tend to greatly elevate the standing of art in the community, and would attract attention as an exhibition of pictures and not as a show of mere "photographs."[50]

Despite his contempt for the submissions from members of his own Society of Amateur Photographers of New York, Stieglitz considered the Sixth Joint Exhibition to be the finest exhibition of photographs ever held in the United States and perhaps only exceeded in quality internationally by one in 1891 sponsored by the Viennese Club der Amateur-Photographen.[51]

In light of his admiration of the English and his ties to the Continent, Stieglitz's comparative consideration of foreign exhibitions comes as no surprise, for he, and many of his colleagues, were extremely aware of art strategies overseas and stove to incorporate their successes into American exhibition practice. They took heed when Davison suggested that New York was due for an exhibition with the strict criteria of selection instituted in recent European salons in Paris, Vienna, and London.[52] Progressive American art photographers particularly admired exhibitions like the Linked Ring's yearly exhibitions at the Dudley Gallery, called the London Photographic Salon, which have "only photographic pictures on exhibition instead of a great show of photographs," underscoring "the possibilities of photography toward the creating of artistic pictures."[53] Founding member of the Linked Ring George Davison noted the conscious divergence from the type of exhibition that combines many facets of photographic practice. Davison declared the Dudley Gallery Salon of 1893 a satisfying decree for art photography enthusiasts, for "the backbone of this exhibition is no medals and rigid selection. . . . Every style applicable to artistic representation" was included but no scientific exhibits, and only about 280 out of 800 entries were accepted. "The exhibition," Davison pointed out, "ought to prove the death of the old style of show where the mechanical, scientific and industrial exhibits are all jumbled up together with very little distinction."[54]

By 1895 the London International Photographic Art Exhibition at the Dudley Gallery had developed a reputation for more progressive art content than the simultaneous exhibition sponsored by the Royal Photographic Society of Great Britain, which still included categories of scientific work. In 1896 the exhibition of the Royal Photographic Society of Great Britain (also known as the "Royal" or "Pall Mall") was again like the more traditional trade-show exhibition, paying heed to a variety of phases of photography, compared to the more art-minded salon. Despite the curtailment of much of the display of photographic apparatus, medal winners at the Royal included not only Stieglitz's "Decorative Panel" but also examples of newly discovered X rays. In addition, daily demonstrations of X rays and another new invention, the Kinematescope, suggest the wider range of photographic practice embraced by the Royal.[55]

Just as ever more abundant factions and tighter alliances cleaved the photographic society into special interest groups, so the American photographic exhibition became more specialized, spurred on by foreign examples and particularly by George Davison. Citing the separation of scientific and artistic photography in England, Paris, Vienna, Brussels, and St. Petersburg, Davison called for the art photographer to "cast off mechanical trammels" in favor of "individual and natural impressions."[56] The self-conscious distinction of art and the utilitarian would, in Davison's mind, help to free art photography from the fetter of the literal transcript. Divorcing the "artistic" salon from the "scientific" was essential to Davison in his quest to secure photography its rightful place among the fine arts.

The actual presentation of photographs became a means by which photographers asserted the status of their work as art. Throughout the 1890s art photographers refined the way in which their pictures were presented, both on an individual level and on the level of the exhibition as a whole. Presentation shifted toward the framing of individual prints rather than mounting them on cardboard, the standard of commercial practice. In addition, many art photographers opted for subtly toned mats, or no mats at all, and dark, subdued frames in place of gilt or carved oak. In exhibitions, the dense, gridlike, display of photographs typical of the commercial trade show gave way in the art photography exhibition to a more eclectic, looser distribution of pictures. An excellent contrast of "artistic" and commercial display lies in the comparison of the 1897 exhibitions of the Photographers' Association of Pennsylvania and the Linked Ring. The American professionals' displays, even those of their "art department," were densely packed, mostly unframed, and shared exhibition space with apparatus like the camera in the foreground. The English salon presented modestly framed photographs on draped walls with stenciled designs, the pictures given more space and imaginatively grouped.

In order to distinguish art from the technical in the salon, or even further, to do away with the technical altogether, the exhibition had to be commanded by an authoritative body—the jury—that upheld the

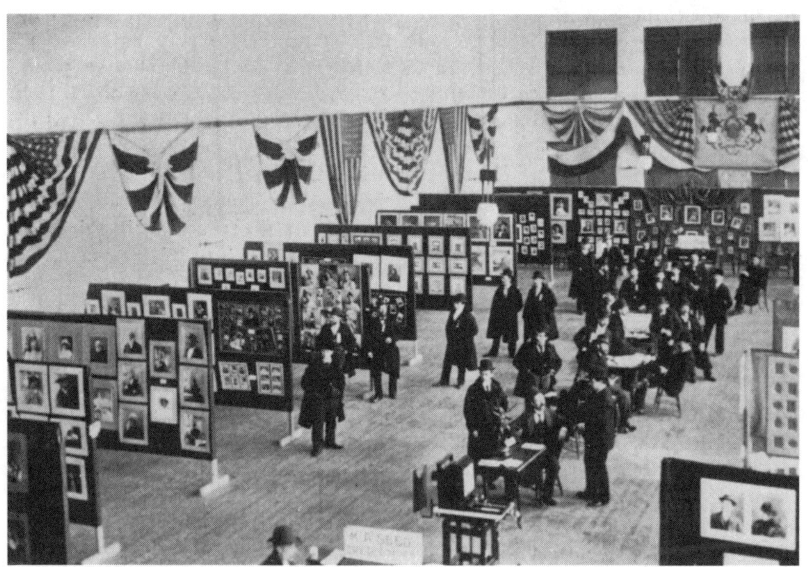

Fig. 45. L. V. Kupper, *View of the Convention Hall—Art Department*, halftone. *Wilson's Photographic Magazine*, March 1897, p. 113. Library Company of Philadelphia.

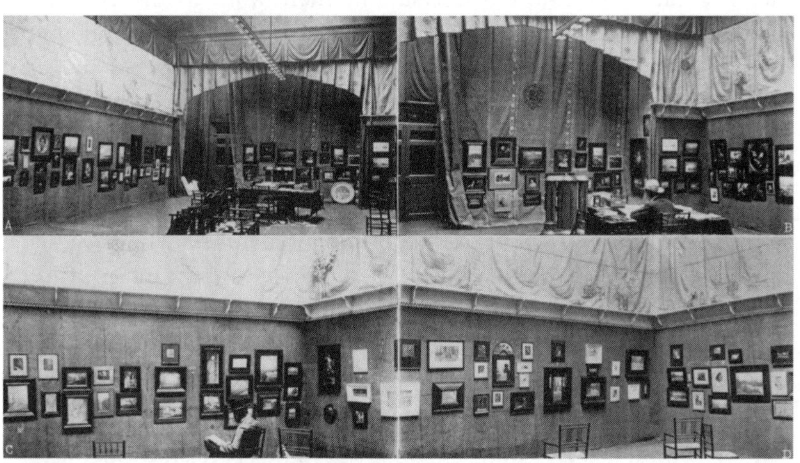

Fig. 46. Photographic Salon (England), 1897, halftone. *Anthony's Photographic Bulletin*, December 1897, p. 179. Library Company of Philadelphia.

high-art ideal. One of the most frequently debated issues of exhibition policy was the appointment of jurors. Those who value technique wanted to be judged by other technicians; those who admired the status and the opinion of the painter wished to be judged by established artists; and toward the end of the century, the progressively elite art photographers opted to be their own judges.

Through the late 1880s the majority of exhibitions catered to commercial interests, tending to reward the sort of technical mastery that most professionals considered integral to quality photography. As more art-minded photographers gained influence, they began to criticize the tendency to appoint photographic technicians to exhibition juries, mandating artistic exhibits where standards were set by artistic merit rather than by technical competence.[57] Attempts to sidestep commercial interests took the tone of competitions like one where American photographers were asked to send prints, signed only with an assumed name, for the *American Amateur Photographer* Artistic Exhibition. The journal then compiled them and sent them on to be judged by George Davison and Henry Peach Robinson.[58] The proper jury was thought to ensure the exclusivity that many elite amateurs deemed essential to the high standards of their art.

Photographers with sufficient prestige managed to agitate the jury system into taking notice of their desire to be evaluated by meritorious panels. Many well-known British photographers, including Davison, Sutcliffe, and Emerson, did not submit their work to the 1894 Joint Exhibition, a phenomenon some reviewers attributed to these photographers' hesitance to be evaluated by an anonymous panel of judges.[59] Stieglitz and his American colleagues quickly picked up on the strategy of boycott as a means of demanding jury members deemed qualified to judge art photography. The Second Annual Members' Exhibition of the Society of Amateur Photographers of New York, which opened in March 1895, lacked work by "most of the prominent members who have made the reputation which the New York society possesses as the most advanced in an artistic sense, in America." Some critics attributed the decision by members like Stieglitz, Rudolf Eickemeyer Jr., and William Post not to submit work for this exhibit to a jury that did not guarantee the correct principles of running the exhibition: while at least one member of the jury seemed capable of representing scientific photography, many believed the artistic side was entirely unrepresented. The names of the judges themselves were not announced until well after the prints were to be received, so, as with the Seventh Joint Exhibition, photographers may have been hesitant to submit work to an unnamed jury.[60]

At the turn of the century, Stieglitz used the boycott to wield his authority on a much higher level. Asked to send a group of American photographs to the Paris Universal Exposition of 1900, Stieglitz declined. Robert Demachy stated that the reason for the boycott by the New York Camera Club and some of the "most distinguished pictorial photographers of the United States" was the regulation that did not allow photographs to be exhibited in the Fine Arts Palace.[61] Stieglitz proposed that a selection of American photographs be judged by the American Art Jury, the same body that approved the American paintings and sculpture that were sent to the exposition. Judged of sufficient quality by the national jury, the photographs would have merited hanging with the other arts. Stieglitz's request was denied, so he refused to solicit and send photographs. The boycott of exhibitions by Stieglitz and his colleagues underscores the escalating authority and prestige of certain photographic circles. That such an act could secure notice is a testament to the international respect commanded by Stieglitz.

By the mid-1890s Americans had a number of progressive foreign prototypes and had made several domestic attempts at shaping an exhibition of "true" art photography. Among the more ambitious adaptations of newer exhibition strategies was the 1896 Washington Salon. Expressly modeled on the London and other European salons, the Washington Salon attempted to create an exhibition, open to Washington club members and invited participants, in which "mere technique did not count, and the password to a place on the walls of which was artistic merit." Probably responding to criticism of recent exhibitions, the committee carefully named three artists (not photographers) to judge artistic merit, along with one professional and one amateur photographer to judge technique. The attempt to equate photography with painting and the photographic salon to the painters' salon was not subtle. The medal awarded to winners in a variety of categories was an equal-armed cross with "Salon" written across the horizontal arm, the sun as an emblem of photography on the upper arm, and a palette with brushes on the lower arm. It was suspended from a ribbon attached to a bar on which "Washington" was inscribed.

Still, the organizers of the Washington Salon were not quite willing to discard all of the generally accepted traditions of the photographic exhibition. While understanding that inclusion on the walls was meant to be sufficient honor, they saw fit to designate two medal awards and a diploma for each exhibitor. In addition, they divided the work into two classes, one judged exclusively on artistic merit and the other reserved for technically remarkable work that was not quite up to standard artistically.

Perhaps the resistance to radical changes in exhibition practice played a role in the nature of the Washington Club, a leisurely amateur society that was a subsidiary of the Capital Bicycle Club, a connection many self-styled "serious" amateurs would have detested.[62]

While the Washington Salon may not have implemented the most progressive of exhibition policies, a noteworthy phenomenon of the event is the attention photography was given by prestigious institutions. The National Museum purchased fifty pictures from the salon to add to its collection of photographs illustrating the history of photographic technology and art.[63] While the association with art institutions and artists was not entirely new, the sponsorship of photography by a major art institution foreshadowed the series of exhibitions most significant to the legitimization of photography as art: The Philadelphia Photographic Salons of 1898 to 1900.[64]

The Philadelphia salons were the joint effort of the Pennsylvania Academy of the Fine Arts and the Photographic Society of Philadelphia. One of the oldest photographic organizations, the society consisted of an increasingly rare alliance of amateurs and professionals. Its association with the highly respected art academy fostered a new enthusiasm among art photographers, prompting writers to admire "the national prestige of the academy in art circles" and proclaim "the advent of a new era in our work" in the "recognition of the purely artistic side of photography by such an institution as the Academy of Fine Arts."[65] With the clout of the academy behind him, these three salons became the forum in which Stieglitz's strategies of exhibition reform were most successfully implemented, establishing in America a more legitimate space for art photography than ever before and successfully pruning the accepted practitioners of photographic art to a select few.

The 1898 Philadelphia Salon, like some of the other photographic salons in America, was consciously modeled on European exhibitions, doing away with "vexatious classifications" and prizes. Each picture stood on its artistic merit, its inclusion in the show was enough recognition. As the catalog stated, "For the first time in this country is presented a photographic exhibition confined exclusively to such pictures, rigidly selected by a jury, whose certificate of acceptance is the only reward."[66] The entry forms and catalog proclaimed, "The purpose of this Exhibition is to show only such pictures produced by photography as may give distinct evidence of individual artistic feeling and execution."[67] The catalog went on to specify that the exhibition would not consider the sort of photograph "which simply reproduces faithfully places and things in themselves interesting . . .

[in which] we think only of the object reproduced admiring perhaps the technical excellence displayed—this is 'only a photograph.'"[68] The technician was to be excluded in favor of the photographer who strove for artistic effect.

The jury appointed to uphold the standards set forth for the 1898 Philadelphia Salon included photographers Robert Redfield and Stieglitz, along with an illustrator, Robert Vonnoh, and two painters, Alice Barber Stephens and William Merritt Chase.[69] Of the more than 1,200 photographs submitted to the jury, 259 were selected, representing the work of a hundred photographers. About one-third of the exhibitors were from Philadelphia, and one-fourth were foreigners. Stieglitz's influence on future salons was foreshadowed in 1898 by the acceptance of his ten submissions, the most any competitor could submit to the jury. Among them were *Scurrying Home, Winter: Fifth Avenue*, and *Decorative Panel*, all of which had previous exhibition success.[70]

Considering Edward L. Wilson's resistance to impressionist and naturalistic trends in photography, the commentary in *Wilson's Photographic Magazine* on the First Philadelphia Photographic Salon of 1898 was surprisingly positive and echoed many critical responses. Wilson's review acknowledged the long apparent need for an American photographic salon based on those of Paris and London, offering the American photographer "distinction and recognition equal to that which they hitherto had to seek over seas." While much of the photography included did not seem to correspond with Wilson's ideal, he recognized the exhibition as "a completely adequate rebuttal to the claim that there is a chasm between the finest photograph and the work of art, and an inspiration to all who are following photography as a method of artistic expression."[71]

As groundbreaking as the First Philadelphia Photographic Salon was in its attempt to focus exclusively on the "artistic," the Second Salon of the following year became even more selective and began to reveal characteristics that, in the Third Salon, would ruffle the feathers of many photographers who did not make the cut in the selection of an ever more elite sphere of art photographers. Perhaps the most momentous change in the exhibition procedure was the composition of the jury. No longer appealing to the prestige of the painter, the jury consisted entirely of well-known photographers: F. Holland Day, Frances Benjamin Johnston, Gertrude Käsebier, Henry Troth, and Clarence H. White.[72] In addition to the all-photographer jury, a major change came in the policy that allowed judges to hang their work in a separate, unjuried complementary exhibition, and international entrants like members of the Linked Ring were invited to exhibit without being subject to judging. Consequently, almost half of the photographs exhibited were not submitted to a jury, while at the same time, only about 20 percent of submitted photographs not exempt from judgment made it to the walls of the salon.[73]

The significance in the changes in the jury and selection process was not lost on the exhibition's reviewers. Philadelphia photographer Charles R. Pancoast called the Second Philadelphia Salon "the first exhibition of pictorial photography in this country where the judges were all photographers of known artistic ability." He viewed the all-artist-photographer jury as a sign of photography's autonomous existence within the realm of the accepted arts, for "picture making by the camera no longer needed the fostering protection and too often the rebuffs of the brush artists. . . . It can stand alone and demand in its own right and on its own merits the recognition of the beautiful."[74] The painter-judge, in Pancoast's mind, was no longer needed to legitimize photography. Still, while they might admire the principles of the exhibition, some writers began to sense an ominous homogeneity in the Second Philadelphia Salon. The reviewer for *Wilson's Photographic Journal*, probably Wilson himself, saw the exhibition as proof of America's devotion to "the pictorial possibilities of photography" yet noted a conspicuous absence of "regular" professional photography that the year before had still been able to assert its artistic investment.[75]

The Third Philadelphia Salon was a showcase for Stieglitz's American circle, the culmination of separatist strategies and exhibition reform. The field of exhibited work was narrowed to 204 photographs. Only 118 were subject to jurying; the rest were presented by judges (Stieglitz, White, Käsebier, Frank Eugene, Eva Lawrence Watson) and four invited foreign contributors (J. Craig Annan, Constant Puyo, Theodor Hofmeister, and Robert Demachy). The exhibition was launched as the exaltation of the exclusive art photographic ideal of the jury, jettisoning that which did not serve the mission of an established elite space for art photography—photographers, theories, and pictures alike. Among the exhibitors were the core members of the Photo-Secession, and the aestheticized soft-focus, textured print predominated.

More conservative photographers were left in dismay: the critic Ellerslie Wallace wondered "whether the idea of art in anything like the true sense had ever been heard or thought of by the great majority of exhibitors." He suggested that photographers look to Ruskin and traditional texts on photography, like Robinson's *Pictorial Effect in Photography*.[76] The photographer James F. Wood criticized a lack of representation of what he considered to be better Philadelphia photographers, and Frederick Gutekunst and John C. Browne, both longtime members of the Photographic Society of Philadelphia, protested trends in the salon and ultimately resigned over them.[77]

The most outspoken critic of the salon was Charles L. Mitchell of the Photographic Society of Philadelphia. Voicing his staunch resistance to the affectations of so-called artistic photographic practice, he complained about the jury and the system of selection for the exhibition, outraged at the high proportion of invited and unjuried photographs. To Mitchell, a harsh critic of invocative practice,

> The key-note of the entire exhibition may be given in the word, imitation. . . . The majority of those whose pictures are exhibited seem to strive to imitate the work of the painter, or of the engraver and etcher. They seem more anxious, however, to represent the defects and peculiarities of their processes than they do to develop their artistic feelings, and, in consequence, their imitations, like all imitations, fall far behind their original. It has always been a mystery to this writer why these prophets of the new school, who, in the public prints and elsewhere, declaim so vehemently for truth in art and proclaim themselves to be the only true artists in photography, should copy so faithfully the defects of their prototypes and give so little of their art.[78]

In Mitchell's eyes, "There has never been given in the United States an exhibition of photographs (so-called) where both photography and photographic art have been more travestied." Mitchell condemned the elitism of what he calls the "Oscar Wilde school of photography," singling out leaders of the trend like White, Keiley, Day, Eugene, and Käsebier, whom he labeled as "high priests of 'fakes,' affectation, eccentricity and egotism."[79]

Photographer and critic Osborne Yellott assailed the judges' definition of artistic feeling as that which happened to appeal to their individual taste, indicating that this individuality could be affectation. "Some of the judges themselves revel in the idea that their work does not meet the commendation of the public. To be different from the masses, to do something which the masses cannot understand, ergo, to be misunderstood by the masses, is to them the final and the only necessary evidence of individuality."[80] He described a deliberate elitist opacity through which these photographers distinguished their art, not unlike that identified (and at times admired) by Sadakichi Hartmann and labeled eccentricity by earlier writers.

Elitist photographic art found its strongest hold yet in the Third Philadelphia Salon, defining itself as a realm apart from the rest of photographic practice. The intensity of resistance in photographic circles seeped into the popular press, testifying that the self-defined artistic elite had indeed distinguished themselves from the indifferent professional, from the pedestrian amateur, and even from many of the earnest advocates of high-art photography.

The sensationalist newspaper the *Philadelphia Item* took a hard stand against the work selected for the 1900 Philadelphia Photographic Salon. In the first in a series of articles mocking the Salon by W. H. Jeffreys, the inquisitive headline "When Is a Photograph Not a Photograph?" was followed by secondary headlines: "Impressionism Has Run Riot in the So-Called 'Third Philadelphia Photographic Salon'"; "Underdeveloped Nightmares"; and "Landscapes That Resemble Nothing on Earth—The Weird Caricatures of Human Faces." Jeffreys proclaimed that "a more marvelous collection of freakish fads in the photographic art has probably never before been collected together." Along with accusations of "freakism," Jeffreys introduced several themes developed in popular criticism that, although much less sophisticated, reflected the criticisms surfacing in the photographic press. Like writers such as Mitchell and Yellott, he located a major fault in the jury's power to pursue a specific agenda and perceived a fraudulent application of photography, contaminated by the excessive incorporation of traditional artistic conventions.[81] Artists and photographers were quoted, offering comments like "freakish fads," "a travesty on real Art," and "the wildest rot that was ever foisted on the public as Art."[82] Reproduced as an example of the photographic outrages at the salon was Mary Devons's *Charcoal Effect* (fig. 18), in which invocative drawing seemed to epitomize the perceived betrayal of the photographic process.

Accusations that "the new school of photography" represented but a fad were common among proponents of the photographic aesthetic. Often they made optimistic predictions like "the chief hope for the new school is in its utter weakness. So much has it gone off track that it will only save itself from utter grief by a thorough recantation."[83] In the short term, these critics were disappointed: naturalism, impressionism, and their progeny ultimately became the styles of photography championed by the elite core of art photographers who established a place for art photography. Nevertheless, the photographic aesthetic was resuscitated within the realm of art photography. When Catharine Weed Barnes stated in 1890 that "in camera work the ideal of to-day becomes the real of to-morrow until it grows so old that it is young again and appears as a new discovery," she seemed to be forecasting the rise and fall of the modes of photography that grew in opposition to the more traditional "photographic" photograph.[84] Indeed, soon after the establishment of a respected sphere for art photography, Stieglitz championed "straight" photography, a modernist celebration of the photographic aesthetic that many seemingly conservative critics so vehemently articulated in the 1880s and 1890s. Rau and Stieglitz, whose takes on photography seemed fundamentally different in the 1890s, eventually served together on the jury for the 1913 annual exhibition sponsored by the John Wanamaker Store, a show that included work by the young Edward Weston.

The exclusivity achieved at the 1900 Philadelphia Salon did not survive into the following year.[85] Elections at the Photographic Society of Philadelphia gave clues that the salon would not continue as it had. With the support of Mitchell, S. Hudson Chapman, who had complained about his rejection from the Third Salon, won his bid for president of the society. Chapman's five-photograph series, *The Sower*, which had been rejected from the Academy of Fine Arts Photographic Salon, received the Allison Cup awarded by the Photographic Society of Philadelphia.[86] The 1901 Salon committee lacked members of the previous three years, George Vaux, Robert Redfield, and John G. Bullock, and instead included Charles I. Berg, Francis Benjamin Johnston, Allen Drew Cook, Dr. Herbert M. Howe, and George W. Hewitt, who was an outspoken critic of the Third Salon.[87]

Despite the continued claim to "exhibit that class of work in which there is distinct evidence of individual artistic feeling and execution," the Fourth Philadelphia Salon was markedly different from those of the previous three years.[88] With the departure of the Stieglitz-controlled jury, the exhibition reverted back to a more conservative aesthetic. These changes were welcomed by many of the photographers and writers who had felt increasingly scorned. One reviewer happily remarked on the absence of work by "the depressionist school" and the small number of works by the jury.[89] As Stieglitz and his colleagues pushed the limits of an elitist art sphere, conservative backpedaling increased the distance between the ranks of photographers.

Having manipulated the salons from 1898 to 1900, Stieglitz discarded the Philadelphia Salon, leaving it to more conservative powers. Having relinquished control, he shunned it by not submitting work to the jury and apparently encouraged his small elite circle to do the same.[90] One reviewer, while generally pleased with the show, understood the significance of Stieglitz's repudiation:

> there must come to some a feeling of regret that a few who have heretofore been prominent in exhibitions of this character are not represented; and with this regret there is also the thought that indications strongly tend to the right to believe that they have not only failed in exhibiting, but have also seriously obstructed the efforts which have been put forth to institute in Philadelphia a Salon which would represent the serious and purposeful work of the typical American School of Photography.[91]

The boycott by Stieglitz and his circle undermined the Philadelphia Society's claim to authority in art photography and thus bolstered their own. There was no Philadelphia Salon in 1902, for it was eclipsed by the new progressive venue, the Photo-Secession exhibition in March 1902 at the National Arts Club in New York. By 1902, Stieglitz realized that a legitimate space for art photography had been created and that usurping control of the Philadelphia Salons had allowed him to assert this "independent course." He notes that his manipulation of the salons, while "ridiculed by press, photographers at large, artists, and even 'artists,' . . . [was] the direct cause of the recognition to-day universally accorded to pictorial photography."[92]

The Photo-Secession and a Space for Art Photography

In 1902 Stieglitz terminated his association with *Camera Notes* and founded *Camera Work*, and on March 5 he established the Photo-Secession, "a revolutionary organization with a select membership, dedicated to destroying the languid condition of American photography."[93] The creation of *Camera Work* and the Photo-Secession was made possible only by the prestige Stieglitz had achieved over the course of a decade that ended in the crescendo of the first three Philadelphia salons.[94] These salons allowed Stieglitz to consolidate power and distill his circle to the point where the Photo-Secession could truly establish itself as a primary, legitimized art photography institution.

The Photo-Secession was fashioned after earlier painters' groups like the Pre-Raphaelite Brotherhood, the Nabis, and the German Secessionists, but as Ulrich F. Keller suggests, the Photo-Secession differed significantly in its basis in social differentiation rather than professional or business

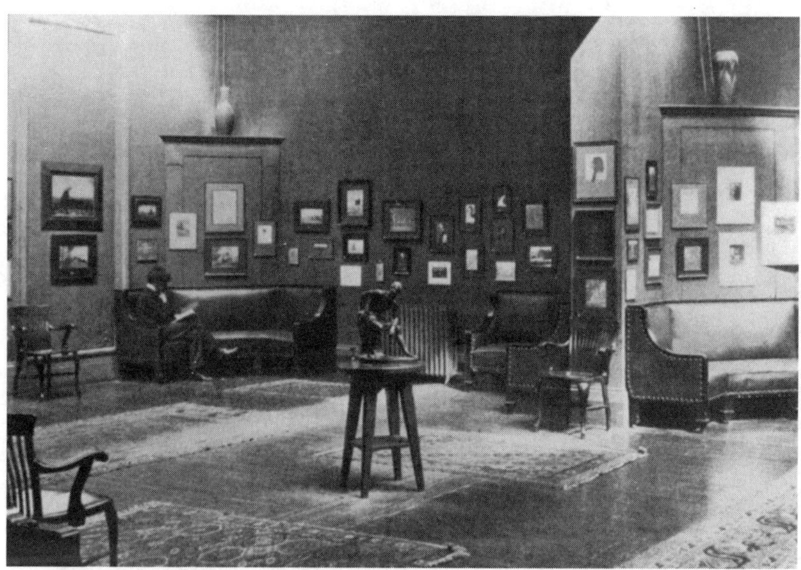

Fig. 47. American Pictorial Photography, National Arts Club, March 5–24, 1902, Yale Collection of American Literature, Beinecke Rare Book and Manuscript Library, Yale University.

recognition.[95] In fact, Sarah Greenough points out the remarkable similarities between work by photographers welcomed by the Photo-Secession and those shunned. She argues convincingly that the Photo-Secession served less to defy the art establishment than to defy other photographers, even other *art* photographers.[96] The Photo-Secession was the culmination of the strategies of differentiation that had begun in the institutional substructure of photography a decade earlier. The institutional legitimization of photography as art, which gained a foothold at the beginning of the twentieth century, continued to build as the century progressed. By the 1929 opening of the Museum of Modern Art, photography was recognized as a facet of the modernist endeavor, and the addition of Beaumont Newhall to the museum's staff in 1935 ensured serious scholarly attention focused on photography and its history.[97]

In addition to the legacy of photographic institutions that emerged in the late nineteenth century, many of the strategies employed by nineteenth-century photographers who sought art status for photography are paralleled in the work of art photographers in the late twentieth century. Just as photographers in the 1880s and 1890s grappled with the challenge of

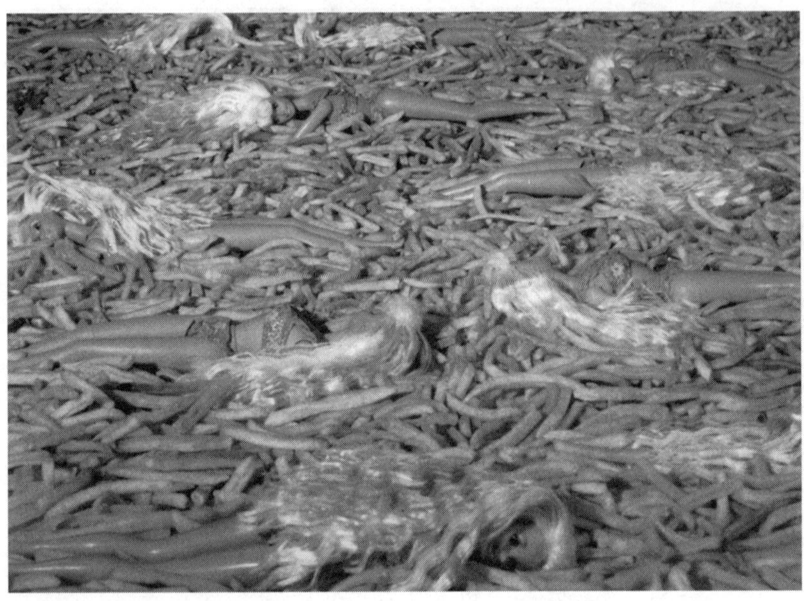

FIG. 48. Sandy Skoglund, *At the Shore,* 1994.

asserting an authorial participation in the seemingly transparent photographic record by denying the apparently inherent capacity of the medium to make an unadulterated document, digital photography has allowed artists to undermine the supposed truth of the photographic record by electronic means.[98] Many recent photographers such as Annette Lemieux and Peter Campus juxtapose the supposed truth of their medium with an evident digital artifice that makes clear the artist's creative role. Other artists incorporate a strategy that parallels nineteenth-century photographers' insistence that the construction of a scene or the selection of a view could be the means of photographic creative investment. With wit and irony typical of the art of the last two decades of the twentieth century, photographic artists like Jeff Wall and Sandy Skoglund build elaborate tableaux and use the recording capacity of the camera to underscore the complex interrelationship of the mediated scene and unmediated image. Vik Muniz marries this artifice with a purposeful reference to other graphic media, echoing the practices of many of his nineteenth-century American predecessors. Using such diverse materials as dirt, chocolate syrup, and thread, Muniz reproduces appropriated images and photographs them. Works like his 1998 *17,500 Yards (Landscape without an Angel, after Hagar and the Angel by Claude Lorrain)* reveal his self-conscious reference to past art in other media

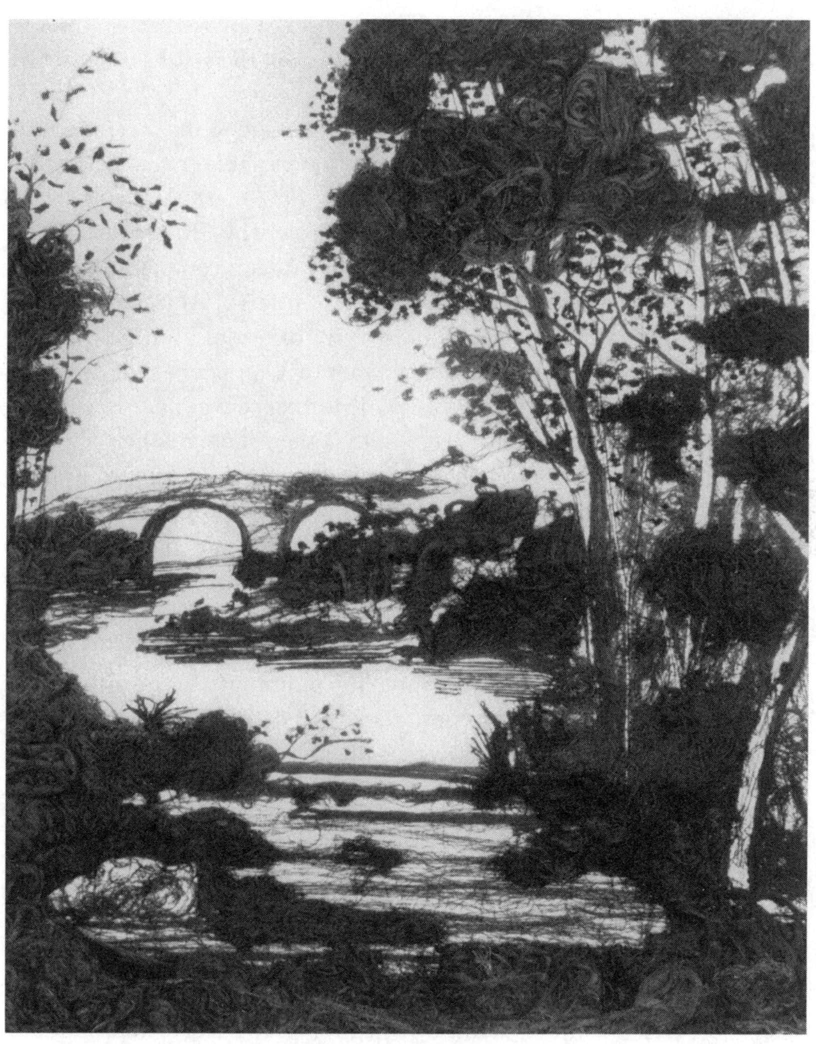

Fig. 49. Vik Muniz, *17,500 Yards (Landscape without an Angel, after Hagar and the Angel by Claude Lorrain)*, 1998.

along with his insistence that the photograph can be used as part of a process of reproduction that demands acknowledgment of the artist's constructive presence.

With the close of the examination I have made of the diverse strategies that were employed in the legitimization of photography as art, it is clear that the establishment of a recognized realm for art photography was not the natural, seamless flowering nurtured solely by Alfred Stieglitz that many historical models have suggested but rather a complex, divergent, often kaleidoscopic barrage of strategies. My study of American journals has demonstrated the richness and diversity of tactics utilized in the legitimization of photography as art in America. On the one hand, photographers looked to academic models, to the formal conventions of painting and the other accepted graphic arts. On the other, photographers explored newer, more subjective notions of the essence of art, looking to impressionism and naturalistic photography. At times, the multiplicity of strategies employed reflected not only an attempt within photography to reconcile the empiricism of science with the romanticism of art but also general misgivings within American society about the growing presence of technology and its threat to eclipse human individuality.

The rapid growth of the photographic community in the wake of the development of the dry plate complicated the definition of artistic practice. This examination has shown that the photographic field became increasingly stratified and fragmented, with writers finding many levels and categories of amateur and professional practice. Revealing a variety of motivating interests, the quest to raise photography to the realm of the fine arts prompted writers and theorists to consider style and photographic technique and to rethink and restructure the institutional bases of photography. In addition, my investigation has brought to light a number of influential personalities in the photographic discourse, theorists who have been obscured by the shadow of Stieglitz. Writers like John Moran, William James Stillman, Catharine Weed Barnes, Xanthus Smith, and, most important, Edward L. Wilson, regain through this study their significance in the history of American photography in the last two decades of the nineteenth century.

Notes

Introduction

1. Photographic historian Sarah Greenough calls "the last two decades [of the nineteenth century] one of the strongest periods of aestheticizing ever seen in the history of photography." Sarah Greenough, "'Of Charming Glens, Graceful Glades, and Frowning Cliffs': The Economic Incentives, Social Inducements, and Aesthetic Issues of American Pictorial Photography, 1880–1902," in *Photography in Nineteenth-Century America*, ed. Martha A. Sandweiss (Fort Worth, Tex.: Amon Carter Museum, 1991), 278.

2. "Individuality in Art: A Conversation with William Hart," *Philadelphia Photographer* (February 1884): 58.

3. "Joseph Pennell on Photography as Art," *Wilson's Photographic Magazine* (January 1898): 42–43. Also published as "Is Photography among the Fine Arts?" *Contemporary Review* 72 (1897): 824–36.

4. This weakness of the medium, which survives in recent critical treatments of photography, centers on what Joel Snyder and Neil Walsh Allen call "automatism," where photography seems to lack any human agency. Joel Snyder and Neil Walsh Allen, "Photography, Vision, and Representation [1975]," in *The Philosophy of the Visual Arts*, ed. Philip Alperson (New York: Oxford University Press, 1992), 289–92.

5. Joel Snyder explains the special attraction of the photograph because it not only looks realistic but also appears "to derive or be caused by the objects they represent. This 'natural connection' has been taken as a reinforcement and even as a guarantee of realistic depiction." Joel Snyder, "Picturing Vision," in *The Language of Images*, ed. W. J. T. Mitchell (Chicago: University of Chicago Press, 1980), 224. Similarly, Jennifer Green-Lewis observes that "built into the idea of photography is the fantasy of

perfect re-presentation, a mirroring of the object which surpasses mimesis." Jennifer Green-Lewis, *Framing the Victorians: Photography and the Culture of Realism* (Ithaca, N.Y.: Cornell University Press, 1996), 25.

6. See, for instance, Edwin Cocking, "The Subjective and Objective of Pictorial Photography," *Photographic Times* (February 1879): 36.

7. While Stillman has not acquired the reputation of other nineteenth-century writers, Elizabeth Lindquist-Cock is among the first recent scholars to underscore Stillman's immense contribution to American literature and criticism. Elizabeth Lindquist-Cock, "Stillman, Ruskin and Rosetti: The Struggle Between Nature and Art," *History of Photography* (January 1979): 2–3.

8. Quoted in "The Exhibition Season," *Photographic Times* (November 1900): 490–91.

9. See Green-Lewis, *Framing the Victorians*, 39–49.

10. Ibid., 9.

11. By 1879, at least three Americans were manufacturing and selling dry plates: Albert Levy in New York, John Carbutt in Philadelphia, and George Eastman in Rochester. Keith Davis, *An American Century of Photography: From Dry-Plate to Digital* (Kansas City, Mo.: Hallmark Cards, 1995), 15.

12. F. C. Beach, "The Society of Amateur Photographers of New York," *American Amateur Photographer* (April 1894): 157.

13. Peter Bacon Hales identifies an agenda as early as the 1860s to harmonize the notion of photography as fine art and the medium's business potential. Peter Bacon Hales, "American Views and the Romance of Modernization," in *Photography in Nineteenth-Century America*, ed. Sandweiss, 208.

14. Hales is the only writer I have encountered who begins to suggest the gravity of Wilson's role in the American discussion of photography as art. See ibid., 208–9, 222–25.

15. Charlotte Adams, "Review of Photographs in Philadelphia Photographer for 1884," *Philadelphia Photographer* (February–April 1885): 86.

16. Green-Lewis points out the vital interchange of journals, books, and photographs between Britain and America that links their "culturally differentiated interest and anxieties." *Framing the Victorians*, 9.

17. For a lucid study of American artists' engagement with the Parisian academic scene, see Annette Blaugrund, ed., *Paris 1889: American Artists at the Universal Exhibition* (Philadelphia: Pennsylvania Academy of the Fine Arts, 1989).

18. "Distinguished Photographers of To-Day: Alfred Stieglitz," *Photographic Times and American Photographer* (December 1, 1893): 689–90.

19. Alfred Stieglitz, "A Plea for Art Photography in America," *Photographic Mosaics, 1892* (1891): 135.

20. Xanthus Smith, "Atmosphere and Effect," *Photographic Times* (February 1895): 68. Educated as a painter, Smith was a key contributor to the discourse on photography as art in America. In the 1880s and 1890s he wrote extensively on photography, but he cut back on his photographic activities by the turn of the century in order to devote more time to painting. See *Russell Smith (1812–1896) Xanthus Smith (1839–1929) Pennsylvania Landscapes 1834–1892* (Boston: Vose Galleries, 1979).

21. Catharine Weed Barnes, "A Camera Trip in Great Britain," *American Amateur Photographer* (January 1893): 1.

22. Alfred Stieglitz, "The Joint Exhibition at Philadelphia," *American Amateur Photographer* (May–June 1893): 201–2. See also "The Joint Exhibition at New York," *American Amateur Photographer* (April 1894): 154. Stieglitz demanded of American photography a worldliness that H. Barbara Weinberg calls "cosmopolitan" in her dis-

cussion of painting of the period. H. Barbara Weinberg, "Cosmopolitan Attitudes," in *Paris 1889*, ed. Blaugrund, 33–51; and H. Barbara Weinberg, "Late-Nineteenth-Century American Painting: Cosmopolitan Concerns and Critical Controversies," *Archives of American Art Journal* (1983): 19–26.

23. "Photography as an Art," *Photographic Mosaics, 1887* (1886): 95–96.

24. Hales considers view photography as a manifestation of a deeper American cultural tendency to reach "into new spaces, organizing, colonizing, exploiting, and transforming them." "American Views," 206.

25. Charlotte Adams, "An Answer to Mr. W. J. Stillman's Opinion of Photo. Art," *Philadelphia Photographer* (July 3, 1886): 386.

26. Green-Lewis elucidates the virtually insatiable nineteenth-century appetite for gathering information and its manifestation in photography. Photography was considered by many of the era as a reliably truthful process of representation that lends itself to positivist observation. *Framing the Victorians*, 2.

27. Marianne Fulton Margolis, "Philadelphia Photographic Salons, 1898–1901," *Image* (September 1978): 6–7. She refers to Joseph T. Keiley, "The American School," *Photograms of '99* (1899): 14.

28. Christopher Phillips offers an insightful analysis of the subtleties of the canonical solidification of Stieglitz as the architect of American art photography. Christopher Phillips, "The Judgment Seat of Photography," in *October: The First Decade, 1976–1986*, ed. Douglas Crimp, Joan Copjec, Rosalind Krauss, and Annette Michelson (Cambridge: MIT Press, 1988).

29. Davis, *An American Century*; Hales, "American Views," 208; Greenough, "'Of Charming Glens,'" 258–81; Sarah Greenough, "Alfred Stieglitz and the Opponents of the Photo-Secession," *New Mexico Studies in the Fine Arts* (1977): 13–19; Ulrich F. Keller, "The Myth of Art Photography: A Sociological Analysis," *History of Photography* (October–December 1984): 249–75; and Ulrich F. Keller, "The Myth of Art Photography: An Iconographic Analysis," *History of Photography* (January–March 1985): 1–38.

30. Mary Warner Marien, *Photography and Its Critics: A Cultural History, 1839–1900* (New York: Cambridge University Press, 1997), chapter 2. Although multifaceted in its approaches to a critical history of nineteenth-century photographic theory, Marien's text focuses most sharply on the middle of the century and on European photographers and writers.

Chapter One

1. A renowned landscape photographer, Moran became a member of the Photographic Society of Philadelphia in 1862 and served as vice president in 1872. He photographed extensively in and around Philadelphia, producing a large body of stereo work as well as editions of large format prints. Moran traveled to Panama as photographer for the Darien Survey under Lt. T. O. Selfridge in 1871, succeeding Timothy O'Sullivan, who held the post the previous year. Moran's expeditionary commissions continued when he was hired as one of a team of photographers who traveled to South Africa and Tasmania in 1874 to photograph the Transit of Venus. Augmenting the technical skill required for expedition and commercial photography, Moran had close ties to the Philadelphia art scene and made a great effort to engage the artistic possibilities of his medium. Moran was associated with the Artist's Fund Society, a group of landscapists who exhibited regularly at the Pennsylvania Academy of the Fine Arts, among them his brother, Thomas, and William Trost Richards. Moran made photographic reproductions of works by major members of the society, which were published as their 1868 annual. Bernard F. Reilly Jr., "The Early Work of John Moran, Landscape Photographer," *American Art Journal* (January 1979): 74–75. Reilly likens

Moran's work to landscape studies of such painters as Church, Durand, and Richards. A short biography of Moran, possibly written by his son, Horace, gives his dates (1831–1903) and states that, in addition to landscape photography Moran studied motion through photography. "John Moran," George Eastman House Online Database, located at http://www.eastman.org; Internet.

2. Unlike many of the writers who follow, Moran did not consider that the character of the photographic record may not have been in accord with artistic truth on a much deeper level than the reproduction of color. As I discuss later, many writers attacked the seeming veracity of the photographic record, finding an empirical account of reality incongruent with artistic truth.

3. John Moran, "The Relation of Photography to the Fine Arts," *Philadelphia Photographer* (1865): 34.

4. Frederic Hart Wilson, "Is Photography Art?" *Photographic Times and American Photographer* (July 9, 1886): 359. Also published in *Anthony's Photographic Bulletin* (August 15–28, 1886): 463–65, 496–97; *Philadelphia Photographer* (July 3, 1886): 392–95; and *Wilson's Photographic Magazine* (October 1893): 437–40. Frederic Hart Wilson was born in Philadelphia in 1864. Nurturing interests in both the classics and sciences, Wilson graduated from Princeton and pursued a career as a journalist. In addition to his fondness for photography, Wilson was a trained painter, studying in the late 1880s under prominent artists, including Adolph William Bouguereau in Paris and James Carroll Beckwith at the Art League of New York. Wilson died in March 1893 in Hygiene, Colorado, where he went to attempt to recuperate from poor health. "Frederic Hart Wilson," *Wilson's Photographic Magazine* (October 1893): 434–37. Wilson's address to the 1886 Photographers' Association of America convention in St. Louis, "Is Photography Art?," was published posthumously in 1893.

5. Catharine Weed Barnes, "The Real and the Ideal," *American Amateur Photographer* (February 1891): 58. Davis is one of a few photographic historians who recognize Barnes's significance in the history of American photography. See *An American Century*, 29.

6. Edward A. Robinson, "Then and Now," *Photographic Times and American Photographer* (April 1883): 178.

7. J. Traill Taylor, "General Notes [Photographer or Artist]," *Photographic Times and American Photographer* (December 1883): 640.

8. J. Traill Taylor, "Photography Not a Fine Art," *Photographic Times and American Photographer* (October 1883): 522.

9. John Moran, "Thoughts on Art, Nature, and Photography," *Philadelphia Photographer* (1875): 179, 180.

10. James Wells Champney, "Composition," *Photographic Times and American Photographer* (January 14–February 4, 1887): 19.

11. Leon Van Loo, "Photography. What Are Its Possibilities in the Art Field Compared with Those of Painting?" *American Amateur Photographer* (June 1895): 267.

12. Many of the photographers who embraced this model of art, particularly those who called for the "photographic aesthetic" discussed in chapter 3, felt quite at home marrying positivist rules of art to the photograph's seeming veracity. In contrast, this trust in a scientific definition of the codes of art was challenged, particularly in the 1890s, by photographers who carried the scientifically based photographic practice beyond positivism and into the realm of the metaphysical.

13. Moran, "Thoughts on Art," 180.

14. A fourth, "On Color," was not included by Wilson in his facsimile edition. Henry Peach Robinson, "Burnet's Essays on Art," *Philadelphia Photographer* (February

18, 1888): 98. In addition to essays, Burnet wrote texts on Rembrandt and Turner, which were reprinted in "Practical Essays on Art. By John Burnet," *Philadelphia Photographer* (June 2, 1888): 333–34.

15. "Burnet's Essays on Art," *Philadelphia Photographer* (December 3, 1887): 731.

16. Ibid. Indeed, Wilson shamelessly plugged the book whenever possible.

17. Andrew Pringle, "Art Education," *Philadelphia Photographer* (July 7, 1888): 391. Also quoted in full in Edward L. Wilson, "Tracing over Old Lines," *Photographic Mosaics, 1889* (1888): 10–14.

18. Enoch Root, "Photography as a Fine Art," *Photographic Times and American Photographer* (July 20, 1888): 341. Also published in *Philadelphia Photographer* (August 4, 1888): 475–78; *American Journal of Photography* (August, 1888): 197–200; *Anthony's Photographic Bulletin* (July 28, 1888): 431–33; and quoted extensively in E. L. Wilson, "Tracing over Old Lines," 15–16.

19. Enoch Root, "Burnet's Art Essays," *Philadelphia Photographer* (February 4, 1888): 88–89.

20. H. P. Robinson, "Burnet's Essays on Art," 97–98.

21. Xanthus Smith, "Art for Photographers," *Philadelphia Photographer* (February 18, 1888): 121.

22. John Burnet, *Practical Essays on Art* (New York: Edward L. Wilson, 1888), 7–10.

23. John Burnet, "Essay on the Education of the Eye, with Reference to Painting," *Philadelphia Photographer* (January–December 1880): 25–28, 43–44.

24. Ibid., 369–70.

25. Burnet, *Practical Essays on Art*, 3–22.

26. Ibid., 79, 81.

27. See David E. Cooper, ed., *A Companion to Aesthetics* (Cambridge, Mass.: Basil Blackwell, 1992), 180.

28. "On Composition in Photography," *Philadelphia Photographer* (December 1884): 365.

29. See, for instance, "Hints to Landscape Photographers," *Photographic Times and American Photographer* (November 5, 1886): 575–76; and Elizabeth Flint Wade, "Artistic Pictures. Suggestions How to Make Them," *American Amateur Photographer* (October 1893): 441.

30. Robert Murray, "A Few Hints to Amateur Landscape Photographers," *Photographic Times* (May 1880): 103–4.

31. See, for instance, W. S. Barlow, "Composition as Applied to Photography," *Photographic Times and American Photographer* (April 10–17, 1885): 190.

32. Xanthus Smith, "Hints on Composition and Selection of Subject," *Photographic Times and American Photographer* (June 3–10, 1887): 302. Also published in *Philadelphia Photographer* (June 18, 1887): 359–61; *American Journal of Photography* (May, 1887): 76–79; and *Anthony's Photographic Bulletin* (May 28–June 11, 1887): 300–1, 337–38.

33. Ibid., 290. To Smith, "picturesque" was a quality that depended on formal features, for "it implies an absence, as far as possible, of flat masses, long continued unbroken lines, stiff curves forming parts of circles, parallel lines and lines intersected by lines cutting them at right angles, all of which destroy the harmony of effect which is agreeable to the cultivated eye." Xanthus Smith, "Composition," *Philadelphia Photographer* (January 16–February 20, 1886): 98.

34. Croughton (1843–1920) studied with Thomas Sidney Cooper of the Royal Academy and was a graduate of the National Art School of England, which was connected with the South Kensington Museum in London. As the son of one of the earliest camera manufacturers in London, he grew up with photography. Croughton

gained prominence as a miniature painter and after moving to the United States in the early 1880s lived in Philadelphia, Richmond, and Rochester. In the employ George Eastman for a few years, Croughton was a retouching demonstrator, teaching artists and photographers techniques for working on bromide paper. He wrote many articles for photography journals and lectured often at photographic conventions. George Hanmer Croughton, "Art and Photography," *Philadelphia Photographer* (January 16–September 4, 1886): 57; "Croughton, George Hanmer," George Eastman House Online Database, located at http://www.eastman.org; Internet.

35. Croughton, "Art and Photography," 193, 194.

36. "Distinguished Photographers of To-Day: Alfred Stieglitz," *Photographic Times and American Photographer* (December 1, 1893): 690.

37. Norman Macbeth, "An Early Taste for Art: Its Training," *Photographic Times and American Photographer* (January 1883): 20–22.

38. Ibid., 20.

39. Philip Gilbert Hamerton, "The Relation between Photography and Painting," in *Thoughts about Art* (Boston: Roberts Brothers, 1871), 122, 143.

40. Jane M. Rabb, *Literature and Photography: Interactions 1840–1990* (Albuquerque: University of New Mexico Press, 1995) 110.

41. Marien, *Photography and Its Critics*, 59, 60.

42. Eugène Véron, *Aesthetics*, trans. W. H. Armstrong (London: Chapman and Hall, 1879), xiii, xxiii, 389.

43. Ibid., 52. The parallels to the perceptual bases of naturalistic and impressionist photography will be addressed in chapter 2. At this point, there is a dependence not on memory or association but on physical stimulus. In fact, Véron's own art ideal was much more allied with the impressionists than with the more academic Burnet.

44. Ibid., i.

45. Richard Shiff, *Cézanne and the End of Impressionism: A Study of the Theory, Technique, and Critical Evaluation of Modern Art* (Chicago: University of Chicago Press, 1984), 24, 29.

46. Jonathan Crary, *Techniques of the Observer: On Vision and Modernity in the Nineteenth Century* (Cambridge: MIT Press, 1990), 76, 83–84. See also Jonathan Crary, "Modernizing Vision," in *Poetics of Space: A Critical Photographic Anthology*, ed. Steve Yates (Albuquerque: University of New Mexico Press, 1995), 85–97.

47. As discussed in the following chapter, many photographers embracing naturalistic and impressionistic theory shared Véron's interest in perception and were willing to discard traditional compositional formulae and/or characteristics that are seemingly inherent to photography.

48. Véron, *Aesthetics*, 33.

49. There was a divergence, however, between subjective experience of the world and the sort of information that the empirical photographic record might provide. Photographers who addressed this divergence are discussed in the following chapter.

50. Véron, *Aesthetics*, 43–51.

51. Ibid., xxiii.

52. Ibid., 53. Véron devoted an entire chapter to the discussion of creative power and genius.

53. Elbridge Kingsley, "Art in Photography," *Photographic Times and American Photographer* (February 18–March 18, 1887): 86.

54. F. C. Lambert, "Genius and Photography," *Photographic Times and American Photographer* (August 15, 1890): 406. The viewer had to be able to *read* the individuality of the artist or the work was meaningless. In the discussion of some of the criticisms of what I term the "antiphotographic," the notion of eccentricity will again arise. To some critics, soft focus and other photographically subversive strategies

lacked legible signification, creating a mimetic indeterminacy that seemed to undermine the expression of the artist's individual intellect.

55. Cocking made a significant qualification to his claim, stating that "in estimating [photography's] value, it should never be subjected to the same method, either of appreciation or criticism—that appertains to the products of fine art." "The Subjective and Objective," 36.

56. Edwin Cocking, "Few Hints about Composition Lines in Photography," *Photographic Times* (March 1880): 56–57. See also Cocking, "The Subjective and Objective," 37.

57. Moran, "The Relation of Photography to the Fine Arts,"33.

58. Linda S. Ferber, "'Determined Realists': The American Association for the Advancement of Truth in Art," in *The New Path: Ruskin and the American Pre-Raphaelites*, ed. Linda S. Ferber and William H. Gerdts (New York: Brooklyn Museum, 1985), 11–13.

59. Enoch Root, "Artistic Spirit in Photography," *Philadelphia Photographer* (January 15, 1887): 35.

60. Hales examines this moralizing celebration of the "pure" record of American landscape in the 1860s comments of Moran, Wilson, and the Reverend H. J. Morton. "American Views," 208–10.

61. Reilly compares Moran's 1870 *Devil's Pool, Cresheim Creek* to William Trost Richard's *Corner of the Woods*. "The Early Work of John Moran," 69–71.

62. "Our Picture [Croughton]," *Philadelphia Photographer* (May 1, 1886): 284–86.

63. John Bartlett (1847–1931) was a member of the Photographic Society of Philadelphia who worked at *Wilson's Photographic Magazine*, the *American Journal of Photography*, and *The Camera*. Despite his applause for its ability to record nature in its unidealized splendor and his suggestions that selection might allow creative investment, Bartlett ultimately turned on photography. Sharing sentiments I identify in the writing of John Moran and William James Stillman at the end of this chapter, Bartlett denied the potential for photography as an equal to traditional arts: "Photography has its limits, and will never vie with art in her own exclusive province of embodying great concepts in nature, or the passions or emotions of the mind." John Bartlett, "Photography in Its Relation to Art," *Photographic Mosaics, 1883* (1884): 111–13. See also John Bartlett, "The Short-Comings of Photography in Relation to Art," *Photographic Times and American Photographer* (February 10–17, 1888): 68. Also published in *American Journal of Photography* (December 1887): 207–11; and *Anthony's Photographic Bulletin* (January 14, 1888): 20–24.

64. Early texts on photography often stressed "nature's exclusive authorship," as in William Henry Fox Talbot's *Pencil of Nature*, where the photographic image was "impressed by Nature's hand"; in Oliver Wendell Holmes writing on photography, where he referred to photography as "a pencil of fire"; and in the title of M. A. Root's *Camera and the Pencil*. Green-Lewis, *Framing the Victorians*, 60, 63.

65. Moran, "Thoughts on Art," 180.

66. Valentine Blanchard was a British photographer who published some essays in America; Wilson is Edward L. Wilson. Ibid.

67. Reilly, "The Early Work of John Moran," 66.

68. Ibid., 74.

69. Smith, "Hints on Composition," 290–91, 302–3.

70. Smith, "Composition" (1886), 50–97.

71. Jerome Stolnitz, "The Aesthetic Attitude [1960]," in *The Philosophy of the Visual Arts*, ed. Alperson, 8–10.

72. Andrew Pringle, "Thoughts on Our Art," *Photographic Times and American Photographer*, January 18–February 22, 1889, 28.

73. Andrew Pringle, "Figures in Landscape Photography," *Photographic Times and American Photographer* (February 24, 1888): 89.

74. Henry Peach Robinson, "Paradoxes of Art, Science and Photography," *Photographic Times and American Photographer* (June 24–July 1, 1892): 340. Also published in *Wilson's Photographic Magazine* (April 16, 1892): 242–45.

75. Edward L. Wilson, "The Progress of Photography during 1892," *Photographic Mosaics, 1892* (1891): 11.

76. Cooper, *A Companion to Aesthetics*, 180, 250–54.

77. See Jonathan Culler, *Structuralist Poetics: Structuralism, Linguistics, and the Study of Literature* (Ithaca, N.Y.: Cornell University Press, 1975).

78. Edward L. Wilson and the editorial staff of the *Philadelphia Photographer* extensively quoted the eighteenth-century philosopher Hugh Blair (1718–1800) from his essay "Rhetoric." To Blair, the reception of beauty was essentially an inherent and universal human ability. Edward L. Wilson, "Taste," *Philadelphia Photographer* (March 1883): 70–73. Also published in *Photographic Mosaics, 1884* (1883): 111–16. Blair's essays were available in a number of American editions.

79. The differentiation between a universal and learned aesthetic appreciation parallels Benedetto Croce's "intuitive" and "logical" knowledge, the first obtained through the imagination and the second through the intellect. Benedetto Croce, "Intuition, Technique and the Classification of the Arts [1922]," in *The Philosophy of the Visual Arts*, ed. Alperson, 40.

80. Edward L. Wilson, "The Advantages of Art Education," *Photographic Times and American Photographer* (March 30, 1888): 145–46.

81. "The Present Aspect of Amateur Photography," *American Amateur Photographer* (July 1889): 5.

82. John Moran, "Reflections on Art," *Philadelphia Photographer* (1875): 294–95.

83. Little biographical data for Moran is available. A short biographical sketch in the East Hampton Free Library, perhaps authored by his son, Horace, notes that "later in life he abandoned photography as a profession and devoted himself again to landscape composition through the medium of oil painting." Quoted in Reilly, "The Early Work of John Moran," 65.

84. Quoted in Ferber, "'Determined Realists,'" 13.

85. In considering the Pre-Raphaelite influence in America, Ferber discusses Stillman's early landscape painting in relation to his photography of the same period. Linda S. Ferber, "'The Clearest Lens': William J. Stillman and American Landscape Painting," in *Poetic Localities: William James Stillman* (New York: Aperture, 1988), 91–103.

86. Elizabeth Linquist-Cock illuminates Stillman's contact with the Pre-Raphaelites and his ambivalent relationship with Ruskin. "Stillman, Ruskin and Rosetti," 3–13.

87. "William J. Stillman," *Photographic Times and American Photographer* (September 1887): 451–53; "W. J. Stillman," *Photographic Times* (August 1901): 377–78. Stillman was a devoted naturalist, particularly fond of squirrels, including his pets, Billy and Hans. William James Stillman, *Billy and Hans, My Squirrel Friends; a True Story* (Portland, Maine: Thomas B. Moser, 1914).

88. William James Stillman, "Photography and Art," *Photographic Times and American Photographer* (January 2, 1885): 1.

89. This is part of a scathing reply to an article in which Charlotte Adams identified Stillman as an "art-critic of the old-fashioned, conservative school," his "weak and illogical" arguments suggesting the art theories of the 1840s and 1850s. Charlotte Adams, "An Answer to Mr. W. J. Stillman's Opinion of Photo. Art," *Philadelphia*

Photographer (July 3, 1886): 386. Stillman asserted that the author, Charlotte Adams, is neither a woman nor an American but rather an English "art" photographer. William James Stillman, "Photography and Art," *Photographic Times and American Photographer* (September 10, 1886): 479. While she may have used a pseudonym, Adams seemed vehemently anti-English, and it is difficult to see where Stillman got the idea that she is an English photographer. She was remarkably pro-American, setting forth one of the strongest claims to a unique national photographic art practice.

90. William James Stillman, "Art and Photography," *Photographic Times* (January 3, 1890): 5.

91. William James Stillman, "The Art in It," *Photographic Times and American Photographer* (March 19–April 2, 1886): 165. Stillman quotes Kenyon Cox from the *New York Nation*. Stillman seems to refer to claims like Frederic Hart Wilson's response to a skeptic who might allege that photography was not art because the photographer could not compose but could only take crude nature as it was. Wilson identified ways in which a photographer chose his or her point of view: "There art began—with the first touch of a man to shape things toward his ideal, be that ideal merely an agreeable composition or a loftiest conception of genius. The higher it is, the more greatly it is art." F. H. Wilson, "Is Photography Art?," 359.

92. William James Stillman, "The Art in Photography," *Photographic Times and American Photographer* (June 21–28, 1889): 308.

93. Stillman, "Art and Photography," 6.

94. Pringle, who opened his piece with the expressed intent of defining a middle ground between those who denied photography's art capacity and those who lauded it unconditionally, allowed the photographer some artist status because "the art of conception is as open to the photographer as so the painter or sculptor." "Thoughts on Our Art," 27. Pringle said that photography cannot reach the "very summit" of art because it can never be sufficiently ideal or imaginative. Nonetheless, it may "climb very far up the hill, and reach a position very honorable, and quite abreast of nine-tenths of the painting we see today." "Art Education," 391.

95. Henry Peach Robinson, "Art in Photography," *Photographic Times and American Photographer* (April 26, 1889): 207–8.

96. William James Stillman, "The Art Side of Photography," Photographic Times and American Photographer (May 3, 1889): 130, 217, 219.

97. Stillman's ties to the traditional arts may have amplified his ambivalence toward claims of photography's art status, for he certainly respected many painters' assessment of photography as merely mechanical. He claimed that he did not mean to discredit photography or the photographer but rather simply wanted to prove that nowhere outside of the discipline of photography was photography considered an art. "Art and Photography," 5. The role of photography as it related to the arts was, in Stillman's mind, linked to the mechanical side of the medium. He shared the opinion of Charles Baudelaire, who stated in 1859 that "photography's real task . . . is in being the servant of science and art, but a very humble servant like typography and stenography which have neither created nor improved literature." Quoted in Deborah Johnson, "Confluence and Influence: Photography and the Japanese Print in 1850," in *Readings in Nineteenth-Century Art*, ed. Janis Tomlinson (Upper Saddle River, N.J.: Prentice Hall, 1996), 86–87. Stillman saw photography as rival to the mechanics of traditional modes of reproduction of art, such as woodcutting or engraving. In fact, he displayed genuine enthusiasm for newly developed methods of photoreproduction that surpassed previous methods of reproduction of works of art. "Photography and Art" (1885), 2.

98. Stillman, "The Art in It," 165–67, 177–78.

Chapter Two

1. Peter C. Bunnell, ed., *A Photographic Vision: Pictorial Photography 1889–1923* (Salt Lake City: Peregrine Smith, 1980), 1.

2. Xanthus Smith, "Photography and Art," *Photographic Times and American Photographer* (April 10, 1885): 184. Also published in *Anthony's Photographic Bulletin* (November 14, 1885): 648–51; and *Philadelphia Photographer* (November, 1885): 371–74.

3. While Smith helps clarify the theorization of the antiphotographic, I will show in the following chapter that he did not endorse many of the subverting practices of impressionist and naturalist photography.

4. In *Camera Notes* and *Camera Work* Stieglitz sought out and reproduced examples from the history of photography that seemed to offer alternatives to these technical developments. The paper negatives of William Henry Fox Talbot and the romantic denial of technical proficiency in Julia Margaret Cameron's portraits can be seen as antecedents to the purposeful manipulation of photographic processes. Even before Stieglitz, George Davison attributed the decline of soft focus in the early days of photography to the masses of mechanical and commercial photographers and looked to Cameron as a precedent for "daring use of focusing." George Davison, "Focusing," *American Amateur Photographer* (December 1894): 538.

5. George Hanmer Croughton, "Artists and Photographers," *American Amateur Photographer* (December 1894): 227.

6. Robinson's letter, titled "Art and Photography," sent to the 1886 edition of *Liesegang's Year Book* reprinted in E. L. Wilson, "The Department of Art," 22.

7. Ironically, Adams used one of the strongest supporters of the photographic aesthetic to describe the effects that would become standards of the antiphotographic. C. Adams, "Review of Photographs in Philadelphia Photographer for 1884," 58.

8. Croughton, "Artists and Photographers," 226–27.

9. Crary, *Techniques*, 70–71.

10. Green-Lewis, *Framing the Victorians*, 79, 89.

11. Davis, *An American Century*, 13.

12. Bunnell, *A Photographic Vision*, 1.

13. "The Joint Exhibition at New York," 155.

14. Bartlett, "The Short-Comings of Photography," 68–69. While his explanation of the mechanics of the process was not entirely accurate, the phenomenon Bartlett describes was an afterimage, the very phenomenon that leads Goethe to a more subjective model of perception. See Crary, *Techniques*.

15. A. J. Treat's discussion of impressionism is emblematic of the complexity of the theoretical bases of impressionism, especially as it relates to photography. Soon after extolling the merits of the "simple purity," he placed further requirements on the image where evidence of authorial mediation returns. A. J. Treat, "Impressionism in Photography," *American Amateur Photographer* (January 1891): 1. Also published in *Wilson's Photographic Magazine* (January 3, 1891): 3–7.

16. Peter Henry Emerson, *Naturalistic Photography for Students of the Art*. The Literature of Photography. (New York: Arno Press, 1889 [1973]), 22. To the editors of *Wilson's Photographic Magazine* and to Emerson himself, the terms "naturalistic" and "impressionistic" could be used interchangeably. Emerson's definition of "naturalism" was quoted as "the true and natural expression of nature by art," a fundamental quality of which the artist was especially perceptive. Peter Henry Emerson, "Naturalistic Photography," *Wilson's Photographic Magazine* (March 1895): 109–10.

17. Snyder and Allen present an efficient synopsis of Emerson's naturalism, where an art image was thought to be identical to the visual impression of a scene. "Photography, Vision, and Representation," 289–90.

18. Alex Eddington, "The Modern School of Photography," *Wilson's Photographic Magazine* (May 1898): 225.

19. See Green-Lewis, *Framing the Victorians,* 332; and Charles Eldredge, *American Imagination and Symbolist Painting* (New York: Grey Art Gallery and Study Center, New York University, 1979). Many photographers' appeals to perception and its subjective and objective qualities parallel the tendencies described in detail by Shiff, who underscores the troubling duality between the subjective and objective impression of nature in his discussion of French impressionist painting. He points out models of impressionist theory that present the painted image as a record of raw perceptual experience and contrasts them to Jules Antoine Castagnary's contemporary assessment of impressionism as an idiosyncratic, subjective response to nature. Shiff finds that, in fact, "for many artists and critics, impressionist painting seems *both* objective and subjective." *Cézanne,* 3–5, 18–19.

20. See Ferber, "'Determined Realists,'" 13.

21. William H. Gerdts, "Through the Glass Brightly: The American Pre-Raphaelites and Their Still Lifes and Nature Studies," in *The New Path,* ed. Ferber and Gerdts, 71.

22. Quoted in ibid., 75.

23. F. C. Lambert, "Our Pictorial Failures," *Photographic Times and American Photographer* (December 1, 1893): 697. As Marien shows, the critical suggestion of purposeful sacrifice of distinct detail dates back to mid century in England and France. *Photography and Its Critics,* 91. See also Green-Lewis, *Framing the Victorians,* 56–59.

24. Alfred Maskell, "On Pictorial Photography; The Old and the New," *Photographic Times* (October 1895): 245–46. Also published in *Anthony's Photographic Bulletin* (September 1895): 293–96.

25. E. Lee Ferguson, "The Unphotographic Photograph," *Photographic Times* (January 1897): 2.

26. "Alfred Stieglitz and His Latest Work," *Photographic Times* (April 1896): 162.

27. "Diffused Images," *Photographic Times and American Photographer* (July 13, 1894): 17–18; Davison, "Focusing," 542. John Henry Dallmeyer invented a doublet lens, used mainly for portraiture, where the combinations of lenses could be slightly separated after focusing, giving a softening effect. For other descriptions of softening focus during exposure and developing, see Max Holzberg, "Mechanical Aids to Artistic Photography," *American Amateur Photographer* (May 1895): 191–98.

28. W. J. Baker, "A Professional View of the P. A. of A. Exhibition." *Wilson's Photographic Magazine* (August 1, 1891): 470.

29. The embrace of these processes led one writer to call Demachy a "father" of the "American School in Photography." Osborne I. Yellott, "Third Philadelphia Photographic Salon," *Photo Era* (December 1900): 167–68.

30. Even as late as 1898, Demachy found America wanting in the exploration of gum bichromate and suggested that leading American workers, among them Stieglitz, Eickemeyer, Farnsworth, and Day, experiment with it. Robert Demachy, "A Few Notes on the Gum Bichromate Process," *Photographic Times* (April 1898): 147.

31. Geraldine Wojno Kiefer, *Alfred Stieglitz: Scientist, Photographer, and Avatar of Modernism, 1880–1913* (New York: Garland, 1991).

32. E. Lee Ferguson, "Philadelphia Photographic Salon," *Photographic Times* (January 1899): 9; and E. Lee Ferguson, "The Second Philadelphia Salon," *Photographic Times* (January 1900): 4.

33. Walter Woodbury, "Some Random Notes on the Philadelphia Salon," *Photographic Times* (January 1900): 7–9. Demachy realized that the process may have been considered unphotographic by some, but he asserted its fidelity to the medium and

noted that new strategies often met with resistance and that "criticism coming from certain quarters can be more flattering than praise," a sentiment that, as I will suggest in chapter 4, many of the self-proclaimed elite shared. Demachy, "A Few Notes," 147–49.

34. Croughton tempered his criticism of "microscopic sharpness," explaining, "do not think I am an advocate of out-of-focus fuzziness. I am opposed to extreme sharpness, where that sharpness is at the sacrifice of truth to nature." George Hanmer Croughton, "Art in Photography," *Photographic Times and American Photographer* (August 7, 1891): 306–8.

35. As he develops his discussion of the nature of objectivity and subjectivity, Shiff often calls upon the photograph as an example of the "observational detail" that to nineteenth-century critics seemed incongruent with subjective experience and its capacity for consideration as "poetically expressive." *Cézanne*, 25.

36. Catharine Weed Barnes, "Artistic Photography," *American Amateur Photographer* (November 1891): 435, 436.

37. Stieglitz also produced some similar portraits that were published in *Camera Notes*.

38. See "On Some Methods of Suppression and Modifications in Pictorial Photography," *Photographic Times and American Photographer* (July 27, 1894): 62.

39. Lambert, "Our Pictorial Failures," 698.

40. Ferguson, "The Unphotographic Photograph," 2.

41. A. J. Treat, "The Artistic Feeling," *Wilson's Photographic Magazine* (December 7, 1889): 726.

42. Treat, "Impressionism in Photography," 5–6.

43. George Davison, "Composition," *Photographic Times* (July–September 1897): 317–18.

44. Quoted in Hugh L. Cameron, "The 'Royal' and Salon Exhibitions," *American Amateur Photographer* (November 1896): 473–74. They were divorcing themselves from both graphic convention and the photographic. Yet the autonomy of the evaluatory criteria of the photograph suggested by this statement was not that championed by the supporters of the "photographic aesthetic" that will be addressed in the following chapter.

45. George Davison, "Impressionism in Photography," *Photographic Times and American Photographer* (January 16–February 15, 1891): 32–33.

46. Ibid., 46, 66.

47. Macbeth, "An Early Taste for Art," 22.

48. William James Stillman, "General Hints for Field Photography," *Photographic Times and American Photographer* (January 1, 1886): 4. See also Frederic Hart Wilson, "Choice of View in Landscape Photography," *Wilson's Photographic Magazine* (April 5, 1890): 216.

49. George A. Sawyer, "Naturalistic Photography," *Photographic Times* (June 1895): 359.

50. Crary, *Techniques*, 86–91.

51. C. Ashleigh Snow, "The Beautiful—How to See It," *Wilson's Photographic Magazine* (July 1896): 294–99.

52. C. Ashleigh Snow, "Painter-Like Pictures, and How to Make Them," *Photographic Mosaics, 1898* (1897): 147–58.

53. F. C. Lambert, "Imagination," *Photographic Times and American Photographer* (December 30, 1892): 674.

54. Davison, "Impressionism in Photography," 32, 55.

55. Ibid., 32–33, 55–57.

56. Ibid., 57, 67.

57. Emerson, *Naturalistic Photography for Students*. Davison's practice drew on Emerson's writing yet broadened the parameters, incorporating overall diffuse focus in addition to differential focus. Responding in his recantation of naturalistic photography to Davison's appropriation of his theory, apparently without sufficient acknowledgment of the source, Emerson, with a noticeable bitterness, welcomed Davison to his "cast-off clothes." Peter Henry Emerson, "Dr. Emerson's Recantation," *Photographic Times and American Photographer* (February 13, 1891): 77. Emerson's book and theory were widely known and often studied. Perhaps the best-documented study of Emerson is Nancy Wynne Newhall, *P. H. Emerson: The Fight for Photography as a Fine Art* (New York: Aperture, 1975).

58. Peter Henry Emerson, "Science and Art," *Wilson's Photographic Magazine* (June 1 1889): 325. Also published in *American Journal of Photography* (May 1889): 170–75; and *Anthony's Photographic Bulletin* (June 13–July 27, 1889): 400–403, 430–32.

59. Marien, *Photography and Its Critics*, 146.

60. Emerson, *Naturalistic Photography for Students*, 97.

61. Peter Henry Emerson, "Photographing, a Pictorial Art," *Philadelphia Photographer* (April 17, 1886): 249. Also published as "Photography as a Pictorial Art," *American Journal of Photography* (April 1886): 3–6.

62. Ibid., 251, 252.

63. Quoted in A. Werner, "Photography in Its Pictorial Aspect," *Wilson's Photographic Magazine* (December 1898): 533.

64. Quoted in Peter Turner and Richard Wood, *P. H. Emerson: Photographer of Norfolk* (Boston: David R. Goodine, 1974), 7–8. Emerson also asserted that physiological processes of perception could be replicated in photography through ratios of intensity of light in the scene translated into the photographic picture, imitating the action of light upon the eye. "Photographing, a Pictorial Art," 252. Emerson's own lengthy experiments disproved photography's ability to record these ratios and prompted him to denounce naturalistic photography.

65. Treat, "Impressionism in Photography," 2, 4.

66. Kingsley, "Art in Photography," 110.

67. Quoted in Turner and Wood, 7–8.

68. Arthur Burchett, "Photography in Relation to Painting," *Anthony's Photographic Bulletin* (September 24, 1892): 351.

69. Shiff addresses symbolist theory in tandem with impressionist theory, pointing out how the two are often intertwined. The symbolism of writers like Maurice Denis and Armand Prudhomme in the mid and late 1890s was an appeal to universal truths. The particular subjectivity of an artist could appeal on a universal level. The object is filtered by the subjective impression yet may still represent an objective truth. *Cézanne*, 36–38.

70. Bunnell, *A Photograph Vision*, 7.

71. Lambert, "Imagination," 673.

72. Davison, "Impressionism in Photography," 43–44.

73. Ibid., 55.

74. Ibid., 33. As Shiff points out, the notion of all objective phenomenon being contingent on the subjectivity of the perceiver is apparent in the principles of Gustave Fechner, Charles Henry, Niels Bohr, and French interpretations of Schopenhauer. Jules Laforgue, like Schopenhauer, whom he admired, saw genius in the union of object and subject. *Cézanne*, 27–28.

75. Kingsley, "Art in Photography," 122, 134.

76. F. C. Lambert, "Imagination and Photography," *Photographic Times* (September 1896): 440.

77. Green-Lewis, *Framing the Victorians*, 20.

78. This subjectivity was evidenced in the "characteristic styles and individuality of certain photographers' work." Davison, "Composition," 365.

79. Smith, "Atmosphere and Effect," 68–69.

80. "Alfred Clements and His Work," *Photographic Times* (October 1895): 219–20.

81. See, for instance, Treat, "Impressionism in Photography," 2; and J. F. Coonley, "The Element of Art in Connection with Photography," *Photographic Times and American Photographer* (April 1884): 185.

82. The idea of individuality as a component of artistic production arose early with reference to art in photography. In an 1884 conversation with the American landscape artist William Hart, reprinted in the *Philadelphia Photographer* from the *Art-Union*, the new publication of the American Art-Union, the artist was encouraged to aim beyond the principles of a master or of a particular "school" and to instead "set out for himself and modify and supplement what he has learned by the impressions he derives individually from Nature. . . . This interpretation must be his own language, and we shall value it in proportion as it possesses strength, directness, truth and beauty." "Individuality in Art," 57. Yet to most readers of photographic journals of the early 1880s, the quest for "individuality" would most likely have been driven by a desire for commercial distinction rather than by the legitimization of their medium. This attitude was evident in an enthusiastic respondent to Hart, who asserted that the high-priced studio work of the commercial photographer "is indelibly stamped with his *individuality*; and that is the cause of his and others' success." John C. Patrick, "An Artist Is Always a Student," *Philadelphia Photographer* (March 1884): 65–66. It would be another decade before "individuality" would be offered up in earnest in the service of art.

83. Frank M. Sutcliffe, "How to Look at Photographs," *Anthony's Photographic Bulletin* (September 10, 1892): 37–39. Also published in *Photographic Times and American Photographer* (September 16, 1892): 477–79.

84. Greenough, "'Of Charming Glens,'" 264.

85. Treat, "Impressionism in Photography," 3.

86. Lambert, "Imagination and Photography," 440.

87. Emerson, "Dr. Emerson's Recantation," 76, 77.

88. Ibid., 78 [line breaks as printed in *Photographic Times and American Photographer*].

89. Peter Henry Emerson, "Naturalistic Photography," *Photographic Times* (February 1896–April 1899).

90. Stieglitz, "The Joint Exhibition," 202.

Chapter Three

1. "An Artist's Thoughts on Photography," *Photographic Times and American Photographer* (July 15, 1887): 357, 358.

2. Ibid.

3. Ibid., 357–58.

4. See Ferber, "'Determined Realists,'" 24–25.

5. In contrast to Emerson's naturalistic photography, Root's "naturalism" was a more generic term referring to the record of nature. E. Root, "Photography as a Fine Art," 342.

6. Bartlett, "Photography in Its Relation to Art," 112–13.

7. Still, Bartlett's realism was not a simple record of nature but rather a selective, suggestive record. "To be of artistic value," explained Bartlett, "a painting or photograph must not be a dull bodying forth of prosaic facts. It will not do to point the cam-

era at everything and expect to touch the feelings of men simply because we show them nature." John Bartlett, "Photography and Realistic Art," *Photographic Mosaics, 1886* (1885): 136, 138–40.

8. Bartlett continued to publish general rules and insights into the artistic and technical issues in photography into the 1890s. See, for instance, John Bartlett, "On Photographing Ice and Snow Scenes," *Wilson's Photographic Magazine* (March 1897): 126–30.

9. Xanthus Smith, "Aesthetics and Photography," *Philadelphia Photographer* (April 17, 1886): 225. Also published in *Photographic Times and American Photographer* (April 23, 1886): 218–20; *American Journal of Photography* (April, 1886): 11–13; and *Anthony's Photographic Bulletin* (April 24, 1886): 239–42. Smith, "Composition" (1886), 100–101. Smith was careful to differentiate between topography and art, insisting that the point of art is not to "map out all clearly and distinctly" but rather to "impress the imagination with a sentiment of beauty . . . by conveying broad truths." Xanthus Smith, "Haze," *Photographic Mosaics, 1900* (1899): 215.

10. Xanthus Smith, "Outdoor Work," *Wilson's Photographic Magazine* (May 1898): 209.

11. C. D. Cheney, "Sharp Vs. Unsharp," *Photographic Times and American Photographer* (September 9, 1892): 460.

12. William James Stillman, "Naturalistic Photography," *Photographic Times and American Photographer* (May 9–23, 1890): 222, 249.

13. E. K. Hough, "About Pictorial Photography," *Photographic Times* (April 1897): 166. See also W. E. Debenham, "The Cult of Indistinctness," *Photographic Times and American Photographer* (August 21, 1891): 420–22. The use of the label "cult" in Debenham's title not only mocked the reliance on these conventions and the "pretensions to artistic superiority" they carry but also suggested an awareness of strategies of separation and demarcation that would take firm root in the 1890s, as discussed in chapter 4.

14. Catharine Weed Barnes, "Figure Studies in the New York Exhibitions," *American Amateur Photographer* (July 1891): 263.

15. Catharine Weed Barnes, "Live and Learn," *American Amateur Photographer* (December 1891): 489.

16. Quoted in "The Exhibition Season," 487–90.

17. This critic, like many other moderates, believed that photography's fullest potential "depends on the happy union of realism and impressionism." Robert Atkinson, "Realism and Impressionism," *American Amateur Photographer* (May 1896): 193–94.

18. Xanthus Smith, "Effect in Art," *Photographic Mosaics, 1894* (1893): 245.

19. Henry Peach Robinson, "The Photographer's Status," *Wilson's Photographic Magazine* (May 1899): 225.

20. George B. Sperry, "The Use and Abuse of Artistic Lighting," *Wilson's Photographic Magazine* (April–July 1899): 145–46, 317, 260–61. Similarly, Walter Woodbury, editor of the *Photographic Times*, asserted that photography did not have to "borrow effects from its sister arts. Its own beauties are all-sufficient." He added that photography needed no "recourse to such imitation." "Some Random Notes," 8.

21. Charles L. Mitchell, "The Third Philadelphia Photographic Salon," *American Amateur Photographer* (December 1900): 560–68. Also published in the *Photo-American* (December 1900): 371–75.

22. Included in the Photographer's Association of America 1891 exhibition in Buffalo, New York, Mitchell's warm gray-black platinum prints of small foreign views were described as of "remarkably fine quality." Baker, "A Professional View," 470. A critic like Stieglitz admired Mitchell's technical perfection but saw his work as

photographs, not up to the high standards of pictures. Stieglitz, "The Joint Exhibition," 207–8.

23. Sadakichi Hartmann, "Frank Eugene. Painter-Photographer," *Photographic Times* (December 1899): 557–60.

24. William James Stillman, "Hints on Out-of-Door Photography," *Photographic Times and American Photographer* (September 25, 1885): 547.

25. William James Stillman, "Photography and Art," *Photographic Times and American Photographer* (September 10, 1886): 480.

26. Stillman, "The Art in Photography," 307.

27. The photographic aesthetic is a fairly fluid concept that defies strict definition. I think of it as an impulse on the part of photographers to theorize an artistic photographic practice that is true to the photographic medium. The notion of what exactly constitutes truth to the medium, as I will show, varies greatly from one photographer to the next.

28. Washington Irving Lincoln Adams, "Pictorial Photography," *Photographic Mosaics, 1890* (1889): 142–43. Adams had a long career in the business of photographic manufacturing. He was a friend of Edward L. Wilson, as well as an important member of the National Photographic Association and editor-in-chief of the *Photographic Times*.

29. Clement Hopkins, "The Photograph and the Painting," *Photographic Times* (March 1898): 116–17. Even in the introduction to the catalog for one of the first art photography exhibitions to broadly revise its award and selection system, the Paris International Exhibition of 1895, Frederic Dillaye rallied around the photographic. He stated in no uncertain terms that "in photographic art there must be no imitation of other art methods, and all the means used must be visibly and purely photographic, and must hold strictly to *the special characteristic* of photography which he lays down is 'a definition, complete, exact and minute, of all objects, a definition unattainable by any other art.'" George Davison, "English Notes: The Recent Paris Exhibition; Critical Notices," *American Amateur Photographer* (June 1895): 257.

30. Stillman, "The Art Side of Photography," 217–18.

31. Stillman, "Art and Photography," 4. The idea of honor in craft reflected a classical and medieval attitude toward the notion of an artist as one among other artisans, contrasted to more modern ideas of the artist set apart by a distinctive creative capacity. See Stolnitz, "The Aesthetic Attitude," 8.

32. Stillman, "The Art in It," 156.

33. Stillman, "Photography and Art," (1886), 480.

34. Ibid.

35. Stillman, "The Art in It," 156–57.

36. Hector Maclean, "Two Chief Photographic Exhibitions of the Year," *Photographic Times* (January–February 1897): 3, 72. Maclean's reference to gender and virility as it relates to artistic style was not a unique analogy. I have addressed this issue in "Sicklied O'er with the Pale Cast of Emasculation: Aberration and Gender in the Critical Resistance to Late-Nineteenth-Century American Art Photography." Paper delivered at the 1999 American Culture Association Annual Conference.

37. Romyn Hitchcock, "Fuzzy Photography a Fad," *Photographic Times* (July 1900): 319–20. The *Photographic Times* actually presented a wide spectrum of views on the production of art photography, from the essays of the foremost English and American theorists to the more conservative critics of pictorialist practice. Integrated in the same volume as Hartmann's monographic articles on some of the most noteworthy pictorialists such as Eickemeyer and Käsebier were standard presentations of compositional formulae and condemnations of the affectations of "fuzzy photography." In a note following the article, the editor explained the inclusion of the article not necessarily as a

reflection of his own opinions but rather as evidence of a widening rift between amateurs who advocated the "new" movement and those who preferred "purely mechanical pictures where composition and choice of subject are the only means of individual expression." In fact, the article prompted a biting response in defense of "fuzziness" as a facet of natural effects. Frederick Felix, "A Critic Who Needs Criticizing," *Photographic Times* (December 1900): 505–7. The editor also observed that each camp was becoming less willing to consider the arguments of the other.

38. George E. Blackman, "Concerning 'High Art' in Photography," *American Amateur Photographer* (December 1891): 470.

39. George Davison, "Pictorial Photography. The London Photographic Salon, 1894," *American Amateur Photographer* (November 1894): 489.

40. Alfred Horsley Hinton, "Individuality—Some Suggestions for the Pictorial Worker," *Photographic Times* (January 1899): 16.

41. The writer used the title "64ists" more than three decades before its time, foreshadowing the ideological affinity between these nineteenth-century photographers and the modernist straight photographers of the 1930s, who called themselves the "Group f/64," referring to the small aperture that allowed a broad depth of field and sharp focus. Werner, "Photography in Its Pictorial Aspect," 533.

42. "Photography Not an Art," *Photographic Times and American Photographer* (August 14, 1885): 468. George Barker, a longtime professional photographer of Niagara Falls, was often praised for the artistic quality of his work. Pointing out that he received a gold medal for landscape photography at the 1886 St. Louis Convention, the commentators in the *Philadelphia Photographer* commended Barker's "industry, care, and taste." In describing the large photos with skies printed in, the formal arrangements were applauded for their "soft masses," "beautiful outlines," "harmonious balance," "a delicacy of tone," and not a "fretting detail." "Mr. Geo. Barker's Views of Niagara Falls and Florida," *Philadelphia Photographer* (August 7, 1886): 475–76.

43. C. Adams, "Review of Photographs in Philadelphia Photographer for 1884," 58–59.

44. Rau may well have had a hand in devising and executing Wilson's *Nubian Landscape*.

45. Davis, *An American Century*, 36.

46. "The Philadelphia Photographic Salon," *Wilson's Photographic Magazine* (December 1898): 530.

47. The editors of the *American Amateur Photographer* became increasingly conservative following the departure of Stieglitz as editor. "The Philadelphia Photographic Salon," *American Amateur Photographer* (December 1898): 553–54. On the other hand, Rau was also singled out as a technically adept photographer who displayed less of the contemporary artistic individuality: "William H. Rau had one print of large size, unframed. It is merely topographical and illustrative of the mechanical excellence of our modern photographic apparatus." Ferguson, "Philadelphia Photographic Salon," 6.

48. "John A. Hodges and His Work," *Photographic Times* (April 1895): 218–20.

49. "Alfred Stieglitz," 166.

50. Ibid., 167.

51. "On the Ground-Glass," *Wilson's Photographic Magazine* (May 1895): 195.

52. "Pictorial Photography," *Wilson's Photographic Magazine* (June 1899): 267.

53. "On the Ground-Glass," *Wilson's Photographic Magazine* (January 1893): 1.

54. Bunnell, *A Photographic Vision*, 2.

55. C. A. Needham, "Picturesque Photography," *Photographic Times and American Photographer* (February–July 1884): 251.

56. Edward L. Wilson, "Photographing the Earth," *Wilson's Photographic Magazine* (May 1894): 203–4.

57. "Alfred Stieglitz," 163–64. Stieglitz received a medal for *Scurrying Home* at the Royal Photographic Society Exhibition, which ran at the same time as London International Photographic Art Exhibition, prompting many critics to speak out against exhibiting the same picture at concurrent shows in the same city. George Davison, "The London Exhibitions," *American Amateur Photographer* (November 1895): 490–92. Hartmann wrote that "'Scurrying Home' is a landmark in the domain of the camera," showing "better than any other American photograph I know the possibilities of artistic photography." Sadakichi Hartmann, "An Art Critic's Estimate of Alfred Stieglitz," *Photographic Times* (June 1898): 260–62.

58. "Alfred Stieglitz," 164. This picture, known earlier as *The Hour of Prayer*, was reproduced as the frontispiece of August 1896 issue of the *Photographic Times*.

59. Emerson's recantation of naturalistic photography was welcomed by Robinson, who saw the reversal as evidence of Emerson's "having failed to prove it in his own works." Henry Peach Robinson, "Individuality in Photography," *Wilson's Photographic Magazine* (August 6, 1892): 468. Also published in *Photographic Times and American Photographer* (September 2, 1892): 452–54; *American Journal of Photography* (September 1892): 390–96; and *Anthony's Photographic Bulletin* (September 10, 1892): 534–37.

60. Henry Peach Robinson, "Roundabout Papers," *Wilson's Photographic Magazine* (September 17–November 19, 1892): 593, 595, 658.

61. H. P. Robinson, "Paradoxes of Art," 331.

62. Henry Peach Robinson, "Dame Nature," *Photographic Times* (May 1895): 307.

63. Alfred Horsley Hinton, "Sharp Focus and Other Matters," *Photographic Times* (January 1897): 34, 35.

64. Ibid., 36–37 [original italics omitted].

65. Alfred Horsley Hinton, "Faking and Control in Principle and Practice," *Photographic Times* (February 1898): 68–70.

66. Alfred Horsley Hinton, "The Objects of which Our Pictures Are Composed," *Photographic Times* (August 1897): 388. For this reason, Hinton was skeptical of the gum bichromate process and was unwilling to accept as much manipulation as a photographer like Demachy would have allowed. Alfred Horsley Hinton, "Methods of Control and Their Influence on the Development of Artistic Photography," *Photographic Times* (September 1897): 441, 442.

67. Hinton, "Faking," 72–73 [original emphasis omitted].

68. Charles Rinaldo King, "The Paris Photographic Salon," *Photographic Times* (August–September 1898): 402.

69. Andrew Pringle, "Mr. Macbeth on Legitimate Photography," *Philadelphia Photographer* (April 16, 1887): 245–46. Pringle did use the phrase "pure photography."

70. Quoted in Edward L. Wilson, "A Few Hints Backward," *Photographic Mosaics, 1888* (1887): 19.

71. Stillman, "The Art Side of Photography," 129.

72. Barnes, "The Real and the Ideal," 60.

73. Yellott, "Third Philadelphia Photographic Salon," 175.

74. George Davison, "To American Photographers," *American Amateur Photographer* (January 1894): 6.

75. Lambert, "Atmosphere and Distance," 601.

76. "The Legitimacy of Handwork in Photography," 323. This is a paraphrase of an address by Alfred Horsley Hinton.

77. Lambert, "Imagination and Photography," 440–41.

78. F. C. Lambert, "Atmosphere and Distance," *Photographic Times and American Photographer* (December 5, 1890): 601.

79. "On the Ground-Glass," *Wilson's Photographic Magazine* (June 1895): 241.

80. "Naturalistic Photography," *Wilson's Photographic Magazine* (March 1895): 110.

81. Henry Peach Robinson, "The English Salon," *Wilson's Photographic Magazine* (November 1894): 518–19. Also published as "Our Aims and End," *Anthony's Photographic Bulletin* (November 1894): 355–57.

82. "Rudolph Eickemeyer, Jr., and His Work," *Photographic Times* (February 1895): 71–72.

83. See Roger Hull, "The Traditional Vision of Rudolf Eickemeyer, Jr.," *History of Photography* (January–March 1986): 45–56.

84. Indeed Hull notes that Eickemeyer found a way to link "materialism and its essential counterpart, spirituality or 'poetry.'" Ibid., 31, 32–35.

85. Sadakichi Hartmann, "Rudolph Eickemeyer, Jr.," *Photographic Times* (April 1900): 161.

86. Sadakichi Hartmann, "Gertrude Käsebier," *Photographic Times* (May 1900): 199.

87. In his appraisal of Eickemeyer's work included in the 1893 Hamburg Exhibition, Dr. Lichtwart, director of the city's art gallery, stated that "Eickemeyer's pictures do not remind me of any ideals in high art as the work of some other exhibitors recall the motives of well known artists." Quoted in "Rudolph Eickemeyer, Jr.," 75.

88. Ibid., 78.

89. In a decision wholeheartedly embraced by Stieglitz, who admired the "delightfully simple and poetic" work, *Sweet Home*, one of twenty-one pictures shown by Eickemeyer, won the President's Medal for the best work by a New York club member in the Seventh Joint Exhibition in 1894. Alfred Stieglitz, "The Seventh Annual Joint Exhibition," *American Amateur Photographer* (May 1894): 215.

90. Hartmann, "Rudolph Eickemeyer, Jr.," 165.

91. Ibid.

92. Xanthus Smith, "Proper Height for the Horizon," *Photographic Mosaics, 1895* (1894): 144–45.

93. Otto Walter Beck, "Critical Notes on the Exhibition of the Salon of the Ohio Photographers," *Wilson's Photographic Magazine* (May 1897): 197. Emerson described "decoration" as harmonious effects, and even after his recantation of photography as an art, he allowed that photography could be decorative. Peter Henry Emerson, "Naturalistic Photography," *American Amateur Photographer* (July 1893): 301.

94. See Weinberg, "Late-Nineteenth-Century American Painting," 21.

95. J. Craig Annan, "Craig Annan on Picture-Making," *American Amateur Photographer* (April 1900): 167.

96. See Keller, "The Myth of Art Photography: A Sociological Analysis," 249–50.

Chapter Four

1. Greenough notes the establishment of photographic schools as a means of enhancing the professionalism of the photographic community. "'Of Charming Glens,'" 261.

2. Charles Ehrmann, "Plea for a Photographic College," *Photographic Times and American Photographer* (February 27, 1885): 99–100.

3. Charlotte Adams, "The Art-Education of Photographers," *Photographic Mosaics, 1887* (1886): 56–57.

4. Beck, "Critical Notes," 197.

5. "Society News. Society of Amateur Photographers of New York," *American Amateur Photographer* (January 1896): 30.

6. Robert T. Tramoh, "Thoughts about Amateurs," *Philadelphia Photographer* (June 1884): 172.

7. B. F. McManus, "Amateur Photographers," *Wilson's Photographic Magazine* (May 17, 1890): 297–98. Also quoted in Edward L. Wilson, "Redeveloping the Year Last Past," *Photographic Mosaics, 1891* (1890): 19–20.

8. Edward L. Wilson, "The Dignity of Photographic Art," *Philadelphia Photographer* (August 1885): 230. Also published in the *Photographic Times and American Photographer* (July 24, 1885): 412; and *Anthony's Photographic Bulletin* (July 25, 1885): 420–23.

9. Charlotte Adams, "Photo-Art among the Studios. New York," *Philadelphia Photographer* (1883): 194–95. The educational possibilities of photography with respect to art were the topic of many nineteenth-century photographic texts. For a fine analysis of these discussions, see Marien, *Photography and Its Critics*, chapter 4.

10. Coonley, "The Element of Art," 187.

11. Sadakichi Hartmann, "The New York Camera Club," *Photographic Times* (February 1900): 61.

12. J. Traill Taylor, "Photographic Matters Connected with America," *Photographic Times and American Photographer* (November 1883): 599.

13. W. H. Burbank, "A League of American Camerists," *American Amateur Photographer* (October 1890): 333.

14. *American Amateur Photographer* (December 1890): xix. In fact, photography and bicycling were often linked pursuits, with clubs engaging in photographic outings on bicycles and specially designed brackets to fix cameras to bicycles. For a discussion of the parallels between cycling and amateur photography, see Jay Ruby, "The Wheelman and the Snapshooter, or, the Industrialization of the Picturesque," in *Shadow and Substance: Essays on the History of Photography in Honor of Heinz K. Henisch*, ed. Kathleen Collins (Bloomfield Hills, Mich.: Amorphous Institute Press, 1990), 261–68.

15. W. H. Burbank, "An Institute of Photography," *American Amateur Photographer* (November 1890): 411.

16. Alice Lee Snelling, ["Anti-Kodak Photographers"], *Wilson's Photographic Magazine* (January 17, 1891): 47–48.

17. John Bull Jr., "Photography in America. (As Viewed by an Englishman.)," *American Amateur Photographer* (April 1895): 144.

18. Frederic Hart Wilson, "Where the Kodaks Come From," *Wilson's Photographic Magazine* (October 19, 1889): 609–10. See also Reese Jenkins, *Images and Enterprise: Technology and the American Photographic Industry, 1839–1925* (Baltimore: Johns Hopkins University Press, 1975).

19. "The Present Aspect of Amateur Photography," 5. "Detective" was a generic term for a small, hand-held camera.

20. "Society News," 30.

21. Beach, "The Society," 160–64.

22. Indeed, Keller is not far off when he attributes to Stieglitz a "main contribution to the history of photography . . . not [in] the production of pictures but [in] the construction of an institutional framework which certified these pictures as 'art.'" "The Myth of Art Photography: A Sociological Analysis," 256, 260.

23. Stieglitz, "The Joint Exhibition," 251.

24. In *Alfred Stieglitz*, Kiefer presents a unique view of Stieglitz, paying special attention to his scientific background and how it effects his work and scientific sensibility.

25. Robert E. M. Bain, "Impressionistic Effects," *Photographic Times* (January 1901): 13–14. See also Hartmann, "An Art Critic's Estimate," 262.

26. George Davison, "American Amateur Photographer Special Prize Competition, 1894," *American Amateur Photographer* (February 1895): 51.

27. "Alfred Stieglitz," 161–62, 164.

28. Ibid., 161, 165. It is important to note that the notion of the artist amateur must not always be taken literally but at times should be considered more a state of mind, a way of thinking about photography. I make this point because several of the photographers included in Stieglitz's elite core group, Eickemeyer and Käsebier, for instance, had professional careers which they pursued in addition to their artistic endeavors.

29. Hartmann, "An Art Critic's Estimate," 257–58.

30. Hartmann, "The New York Camera Club," 61.

31. Richard Hines, "Artistic Photography," *American Amateur Photographer* (July 1898): 294.

32. Hartmann, "The New York Camera Club," 59–60.

33. Thomas Crow, *Modern Art in the Common Culture* (New Haven, Conn.: Yale University Press, 1996), 4.

34. Sadakichi Hartmann, "A Purist," *Photographic Times* (October 1899): 451–52.

35. Hartmann, "Gertrude Käsebier," 196.

36. F. Bennett, "The Amateur," *Wilson's Photographic Magazine* (September 1900): 419.

37. "On the Ground-Glass," *Wilson's Photographic Magazine* (March 1896): 100.

38. "American Photography," *Wilson's Photographic Magazine* (July 1900): 289.

39. Arthur Hewitt, "The Pictorial Movement," *Photographic Times* (November 1900): 481–82.

40. "Some Model Blanks," *Philadelphia Photographer* (February 1884): 60.

41. E. K. Hough, "The Ideal in Art and Its Relation to Photography," *Philadelphia Photographer* (February 5–April 16, 1887): 229.

42. Quoted in "Distinguished Photographers of To-day: H. P. Robinson," *Photographic Times and American Photographer* (April 6, 1894): 216.

43. "Art in the Exhibition in Boston," *Wilson's Photographic Magazine* (December 7, 1889).

44. E. L. Wilson, "Redeveloping the Year," 17, 42.

45. E. L. Wilson, "The Progress of Photography," 15.

46. Beck, "Critical Notes," 196.

47. Stieglitz, "A Plea for Art Photography," 135–37.

48. Ibid., These photographs, which are actually atypical of his work in the 1890s, became the heralded art pictures, held up later as models for secessionist practice.

49. Catharine Weed Barnes, "The Boston Fifth Annual Joint Exhibition," *American Amateur Photographer* (June–July 1892): 300.

50. "Report of the Exhibition Committee," *American Amateur Photographer* (November 1893): 527. As determined as this self-conscious move toward art photography was, even the Joint Exhibition of 1894 still included scientific work such as photographs of bullets in flight, photomicrographs, and surgical photographs.

51. Stieglitz, "The Joint Exhibition," 201. For further references to criticism of the joint exhibitions, see Anne B. Fehr and William Innes Homer, "The Photographic Society of Pennsylvania and the Salon Movement," in *Pictorial Photography in Philadelphia: The Pennsylvania Academy's Salons 1898–1901* (Philadelphia: Pennsylvania Academy of the Fine Arts, 1984), 7–8.

52. Davison, "The London Exhibitions," 485, 491–93.

53. "The Improved Character of Photographic Exhibitions," *American Amateur Photographer* (November 1893): 519. Americans adopted even the terminology of the London Salon. As Joseph T. Keiley explained in *Camera Notes* of 1901, "salon" was chosen because of French use of the term in reference to "fine-art exhibitions of a distinctive and high class character." Quoted in Margolis, "Philadelphia Photographic Salons," 2. Sensing the elitism of exhibition practice, a conservative yet perceptive

writer in the *American Amateur Photographer* differentiated between the salon and the traditional photographic exhibition, conceiving of the salon as a more selective venue where hacks and tradespeople were not encouraged by the chance of an ego- or business-boosting prize. Theodore H. Wright, "The Salon," *American Amateur Photographer* (November 1893): 55–56.

54. George Davison, "The Photographic Salon," *American Amateur Photographer* (November 1893): 495–98.

55. Cameron, "The 'Royal' and Salon Exhibitions," 476–78.

56. Davison, "Focusing," 537–39.

57. George Davison, "English Notes. Exhibitions and Judging," *American Amateur Photographer* (January 1896): 11–12.

58. Each competitor paid ten dollars to cover costs of postage, expenses, and awards. Anonymity was to prevent favoritism, and well-respected judges were to ensure credible criticism. Davison, "American Amateur Photographer," 49–51.

59. "The Joint Exhibition at New York," 153–54.

60. Joseph Obermeyer, "The Second Annual Members' Exhibition of Photographs. Held by the Society of Amateur Photographers of New York," *American Amateur Photographer* (April 1895): 163.

61. Quoted in Alfred Stieglitz, "American Photography at the Paris Exposition," *American Amateur Photographer* (September 1900): 411.

62. "An American Salon," *American Amateur Photographer* (April 1896): 143–51. See also Michelle Anne Delaney, "The 1896 Washington Salon and Art Photography," *American Art Review* (February 1997): 110–15; "Washington Salon and Art Photographic Exhibition of 1896," *Photographic Times* (May 1896): 247–48; and "Washington Art Photographic Salon, 1896," *American Amateur Photographer* (June 1896): 232–37. Similar classifications and awards were used in the 1898 and 1899 salons of the Pittsburgh Amateur Photographers' Society.

63. The works were chosen by G. Brown Goode, director of the National Museum; T. W. Smillie, photographer for the Smithsonian Institution; and Washington artist and architect Robert Stedd. "A National Collection," *American Amateur Photographer* (July 1896).

64. The Pennsylvania Academy of the Fine Arts hosted an exhibition of the Photographic Society of Philadelphia in 1886, yet there were thirty-seven classes in which diplomas were awarded. Fehr and Homer, "The Photographic Society of Pennsylvania," 6. The Seventh Joint Exhibition opened in April 1894 at the galleries of the Society of American Artists, and for years juries included painters. Beach, "The Society," 167. For an insightful overview of the Philadelphia salons and the manifestations of many of the tensions and strategies discussed here, see Margolis, "Philadelphia Photographic Salons," 2–10; and William Inness Homer, ed., *Pictorial Photography in Philadelphia: The Pennsylvania Academy's Salons 1898–1901* (Philadelphia: Pennsylvania Academy of the Fine Arts, 1984).

65. "The Philadelphia Photographic Salon," *American Amateur Photographer* (December 1898): 548–49; Ferguson, "Philadelphia Photographic Salon," 1.

66. "The Philadelphia Photographic Salon," *American Amateur Photographer* (December 1898): 548–49.

67. *Catalogue of the Philadelphia Photographic Salon, October 24 to November 12, 1898* (Philadelphia: Pennsylvania Academy of the Fine Arts and the Photographic Society of Philadelphia, 1898). Phrases like this were adapted from English prototypes. For instance, Davison reported that photographs at the London Exhibition of 1894 were judged according to "artistic effect and to the evidence of personal feeling and individual selection." "Pictorial Photography," 490–91.

68. *Catalogue of the Philadelphia Photographic Salon.*

69. Stieglitz reported that Chase and Vonnoh were too busy to attend the judging session. Alfred Stieglitz, "Painters on Photographic Juries," *American Amateur Photographer* (July 1902): 313. The joint committee in charge of the exhibition included President Edward C. Coates and Secretary Harrison S. Morris from the Pennsylvania Academy of the Fine Arts and George Vaux, John Bullock, and Robert Redfield from the Photographic Society of Philadelphia.

70. Ferguson, "Philadelphia Photographic Salon," 3–8.

71. "The Philadelphia Photographic Salon," *Wilson's Photographic Magazine* (December 1898): 529–31.

72. Stieglitz may not have been a member of the jury, but the presence of Day, Käsebier, and White certainly reflected his values.

73. Charles R. Pancoast, "The Second Photographic Salon at Philadelphia," *American Amateur Photographer* (December 1899): 516–17.

74. See "The Philadelphia Salon," *Wilson's Photographic Magazine* (December 1899): 566.

75. Ibid. The previous year, Stieglitz could find the makings of a "picture" in the work of a commercial photographer like William H. Rau.

76. Ellerslie Wallace, "Artistic Photography in 1900," *Photographic Times* (April 1901): 174–75.

77. "Philadelphia's Most Prominent Photographers Denounce the Academy's Recent Display of Freakish Pictures," *Philadelphia Item* (November 19, 1900): 1; W. H. Jeffreys, "When Is a Photograph Not a Photograph?," *Philadelphia Item* (November 11, 1900): 2.

78. Mitchell, "The Third Philadelphia Photographic Salon," 560–61.

79. Ibid., 560, 567.

80. Yellott, "Third Philadelphia Photographic Salon," 174, 176.

81. Jeffreys, "When Is a Photograph Not a Photograph?" 2.

82. "Philadelphia's Most Prominent Photographers Denounce the Academy's Recent Display of Freakish Pictures," 1; "Leading Photographers Denounce the 'Mutual Admiration Society' at the Academy of Fine Arts! Freak Exhibition Roundly Scored by Experts, Who Know True Art," *Philadelphia Item* (November 22, 1900): 8; Jeffreys "When Is a Photograph Not a Photograph?" 2.

83. "The Philadelphia Salon as It Appeared to an Observer," *Anthony's Photographic Bulletin* (December 1900): 369.

84. Barnes, "The Real and the Ideal," 58.

85. These changes are well outlined in Margolis, "Philadelphia Photographic Salons," 10.

86. "Anti-Impressionists Score Decided Victory!" *Philadelphia Evening Item* (December 14, 1900): 1.

87. Hewitt, "The Pictorial Movement," 481–84.

88. One observer outlined the tensions within the photographic community after the 1900 Philadelphia Salon, suggesting that there were growing binary oppositions between art and utilitarian photography. Mark N. Aronson, "The Old Versus the New School and the 1901 Salon," in *Pictorial Photography in Philadelphia: The Pennsylvania Academy's Salons 1898–1901*, ed. William Inness Homer (Philadelphia: Pennsylvania Academy of the Fine Arts, 1984), 21–26.

89. Charles E. Fairman, "The Fourth Philadelphia Photographic Salon," *American Amateur Photographer* (December 1901): 533–34.

90. Some of the more progressive photographers often associated with Stieglitz did exhibit, including Eickemeyer and Day.

91. Fairman, "The Fourth Philadelphia Photographic Salon," 544.

92. Stieglitz, "Painters on Photographic Juries," 313.

93. Greenough, "Alfred Stieglitz," 14.

94. I differ with Keller, who argues that Stieglitz's attempt to transform organized art photography in America had ended in failure in 1901. Keller sees the Photo-Secession as a new strategy by Stieglitz, regrouping after failure. Keller, "The Myth of Art Photography: A Sociological Analysis," 256.

95. Ibid., 249–75.

96. Greenough, "Alfred Stieglitz," 13–19. Davis outlines the competition between Day and Stieglitz for the central position in American photography, for Day was also elected to the Linked Ring and organized international exhibitions of American work in 1900 and 1901. *An American Century*, 41.

97. An insightful analysis of the emergence of the Museum of Modern Art as the arbiter of photographic history is presented by Phillips, "The Judgment Seat of Photography," 257–93.

98. For a sampling of some of the issues of digital art and the artists addressing them, see Johanna Drucker, ed., "Digital Reflections: The Dialogue of Art and Technology," *Art Journal* (Fall 1997).

Selected Bibliography

Nineteenth- and Early Twentieth-Century Texts

Abel, J. C. "Joseph T. Keiley." *Photographic Times* (June 1900): 262.

Adams, Charlotte. "An Answer to Mr. W. J. Stillman's Opinion of Photo. Art." *Philadelphia Photographer* (July 3, 1886): 386–89.

———. "The Art-Education of Photographers." *Photographic Mosaics, 1887* (1886): 54–60.

———. "Photo-Art among the Studios. New York." *Philadelphia Photographer* (1883): 179–83, 194–98, 236–39, 321–25.

———. "A Review of the Photographic Work in the Phila. Phot." *Philadelphia Photographer* (December 1883): 386–392.

———. "Review of Photographs in *Philadelphia Photographer* for 1884." *Philadelphia Photographer* (February–April 1885): 55–61, 86–89, 103–6.

Adams, Washington Irving Lincoln. "In Nature's Image." *Photographic Times* (January 1899): 22–24.

———. *In Nature's Image: Chapters on Pictorial Photography*. 2nd ed. New York: Baker and Taylor, 1898.

———. "Pictorial Photography." *Photographic Mosaics, 1890* (1889): 141–43.

———, ed. *Sunlight and Shadow: A Book for Photographers Amateur and Professional*. New York: Baker and Taylor, 1898.

"Again—That Question of Art." *American Journal of Photography* (September 1897): 416–20.

Albee, M. H. "An Answer Back to Mr. Bachrach." *Philadelphia Photographer* (January 1883): 5.

———. "Art." *Wilson's Photographic Magazine* (April 5, 1890): 203.
———. "What Ails Photography?" *Philadelphia Photographer* (March 1884): 66–67.
"Alfred Clements and His Work." *Photographic Times* (October 1895): 216–20.
"Alfred Stieglitz and His Latest Work." *Photographic Times* (April 1896): 161–69.
"Amateur Photography." *Anthony's Photographic Bulletin* (September 1896): 290–91.
"American Photography." *Wilson's Photographic Magazine* (July 1900): 289.
"An American Salon." *American Amateur Photographer* (April 1896): 143–51.
Annan, J. Craig. "Craig Annan on Picture-Making." *American Amateur Photographer* (April 1900): 167.
———. "Notes on the Study of the Masters in Painting." *Wilson's Photographic Magazine* (November 1899): 506–8.
———. "Painters Who Have Influenced Me." *Anthony's Photographic Bulletin* (November 1899): 345–48; *Photographic Times* (September 1900): 426–28.
"Art and Art Criticism." *Photographic Times and American Photographer* (July 23, 1892): 379.
"Art in the Exhibition in Boston." *Wilson's Photographic Magazine* (December 7, 1889): 705–17.
The Artist and the Photographer." *Wilson's Photographic Magazine* (November 1897): 525–26.
"Artistic Photography." *Photographic Times* (March 1898): 125–28.
"An Artist's Thoughts on Photography." *Photographic Times and American Photographer* (July 15, 1887): 357–59.
"An Art-Photographic Symposium." *Wilson's Photographic Magazine* (July 1894): 292–98.
"Art Training for Photographers." *Wilson's Photographic Magazine* (June 1898): 262–65.
Atkinson, Robert. "Realism and Impressionism." *American Amateur Photographer* (May 1896): 193–94.
"An Autobiography of This Magazine." *Wilson's Photographic Magazine* (December 1894): 552–58.
Bachrach, D., Jr. "Photographers Versus Artists. A Question That Must Be Settled." *Philadelphia Photographer* (December 1882): 356–58.
Bain, Robert E. M. "Impressionistic Effects." *Photographic Times* (January 1901): 13–15.
Baker, W. J. "A Professional View of the P. A. of A. Exhibition." *Wilson's Photographic Magazine* (August 1, 1891): 468–72.
———. "Art in Photography." *Wilson's Photographic Magazine* (January 2–February 6, 1892): 3–5, 75–77.
Barlow, W. S. "Composition as Applied to Photography." *Photographic Times and American Photographer* (April 10–17, 1885): 190–91, 204–5.
Barnes, Catharine Weed. "An Amateur at the Washington Convention." *American Amateur Photographer* (September 1890): 347–50.
———. "Amateur Photography." *American Amateur Photographer* (August 1893): 358–63.
———. "Amateur Photography in America." *Anthony's Photographic Bulletin* (August 13, 1892): 472–76.

———. "Art in Photography." *American Amateur Photographer* (May 1891): 179–81.
———. "Artistic Photography." *American Amateur Photographer* (November 1891): 434–39.
———. "The Boston Fifth Annual Joint Exhibition." *American Amateur Photographer* (June–July 1892): 259–63, 296–300.
———. "The Buffalo Convention and Its Lessons." *American Amateur Photographer* (October 1891): 393–96.
———. "A Camera Trip in Great Britain." *American Amateur Photographer* (January 1893–September 1894); (1893): frontispiece January 1–9, 47–54, 99–103, 191–97, 239–46; (1894): 203–8, 347–52, 396–403.
———. "Figure Studies in the New York Exhibitions." *American Amateur Photographer* (July 1891): 263.
———. "Illustrating Poems by Photography." *American Amateur Photographer* (July 1890): 260–63.
———. "Illustration of Poems by Photography." *American Amateur Photographer* (August 1891): 300–305.
———. "Live and Learn." *American Amateur Photographer* (December 1891): 488–92.
———. "The Object of Photography." *Photographic Times and American Photographer* (December 2, 1892): 612–14.
———. "Photographic Limits." *Anthony's Photographic Bulletin* (October 22, 1892): 616–19.
———. "The Question of Selection." *American Amateur Photographer* (January 1892): 4–8.
———. "The Real and the Ideal." *American Amateur Photographer* (February 1891): 58–61.
Barnes-Ward, Catharine Weed. "Amateur Photography." *Wilson's Photographic Magazine* (October 1893): 468–69.
Bartlett, John. "Composition." *American Journal of Photography* (November–December 1897): 508–17, 548–57.
———. "Has the Brain a Photographic Function?" *American Journal of Photography* (May 1897): 195–204.
———. "How to Choose a View Suitable for an Artistic Photograph." *American Journal of Photography* (July 1897): 307–10.
———. "On Composition in Landscape." *American Journal of Photography* (November 1887): 187–89.
———. "On Photographing Genre and Still-Life Subjects." *Anthony's Photographic Bulletin* (November 27–December 11, 1886): 690–92; 716–19.
———. "On Photographing Ice and Snow Scenes." *Wilson's Photographic Magazine* (March 1897): 126–30.
———. "On Photographing Still-Life and Genre Subjects." *American Journal of Photography* (November 1886): 3–6.
———. "On the Choice of a Subject Suitable for a Photographic Picture." *American Journal of Photography* (June–July 1897): 255–66; 323–27.
———. "On the Choice of Subject." *American Journal of Photography* (March 1886): 5–7.
———. "Photographic Sophistication." *American Journal of Photography* (June 1900): 270–76.

———. "Photography and Realistic Art." *Photographic Mosaics, 1886* (1885): 136–40.

———. "Photography in Its Relation to Art." *Photographic Mosaics, 1883* (1884): 109–113.

———. "Picture Making." *American Journal of Photography* (March 1887): 38–40.

———. "The Short-comings of Photography in Relation to Art." *Photographic Times and American Photographer* (February 10–17, 1888): 68–69, 78–79.

———. "Still Life Photography." *American Journal of Photography* (June 1886): 3–5.

Beach, F. C. "The Society of Amateur Photographers of New York." *American Amateur Photographer* (April 1894): 157–69.

———. "Some of the Advantages of Amateur Photography." *Anthony's Photographic Bulletin* (January 24, 1885): 43–44.

Beale, Seymour H. "Influence of Mass and Line in Pictorial Photography." *American Amateur Photographer* (April 1897): 174–77.

———. "The Influences of Mass and Line in Pictorial Photography." *Wilson's Photographic Magazine* (March 1897): 121–24.

Beck, Otto Walter. "Critical Notes on the Exhibition of the Salon of the Ohio Photographers." *Wilson's Photographic Magazine* (May 1897): 195–98.

Bennett, F. "The Amateur." *Wilson's Photographic Magazine* (September 1900): 419–20.

Blackman, George E. "Ametropia as an Element of Art Criticism. Especially as Applied to Photography." *American Amateur Photographer* (March 1894): 105–10.

———."Concerning 'High Art' in Photography." *American Amateur Photographer* (December 1891): 470–72.

Blake, Mary Elizabeth. "Let America Be Represented in Art." *Photographic Times and American Photographer* (August 7, 1891): 397.

Browne, John C. *History of the Photographic Society of Philadelphia*. Philadelphia: Photographic Society of Philadelphia, 1884.

Bull, John, Jr. "Photography in America. (As Viewed by an Englishman.)," *American Amateur Photographer* (April 1895): 143–49.

Burbank, W. H. "An Institute of Photography." *American Amateur Photographer* (November 1890): 411–12.

———. "A League of American Camerists." *American Amateur Photographer* (October 1890): 333.

———. "On the Selection of Views." *Photographic Times and American Photographer* (January 4, 1889): 4–5.

———. "Wanted—A Photographic Institute." *Photographic Mosaics, 1891* (1890): 126–29.

Burchett, Arthur. "Photography in Relation to Painting." *Anthony's Photographic Bulletin* (September 24, 1892): 550–53.

Burnet, John. "Essay on the Education of the Eye, with Reference to Painting." *Philadelphia Photographer* (January–December 1880): 25–28, 42–46, 77–81, 118–21, 144–49, 173–75, 204–6, 230–32, 279–81, 308–9, 331–33, 369–71.

———. *Practical Essays on Art*. New York: Edward L. Wilson, 1888.

"Burnet's Art Essays." *Philadelphia Photographer* (March 17, 1888): 185–86.

"Burnet's Essays in England." *Wilson's Photographic Magazine* (February 7, 1891): 89–90.

"Burnet's Essays on Art." *Philadelphia Photographer* (December 3, 1887): 731–32.

Caffin, Charles H. *Photography as Fine Art [1901]*. Hastings-on-the-Hudson, N.Y.: Morgan and Morgan, 1971.

"The Camera and the Pencil." *American Journal of Photography* (August 1888): 194–96.

Cameron, Hugh L. "The 'Royal' and Salon Exhibitions." *American Amateur Photographer* (November 1896): 473–78.

Catalogue of the Fourth Philadelphia Photographic Salon November 18 to December 14, 1901. Philadelphia: Pennsylvania Academy of the Fine Arts and the Photographic Society of Philadelphia, 1901.

Catalogue of the Philadelphia Photographic Salon, October 24 to November 12, 1898. Philadelphia: Pennsylvania Academy of the Fine Arts and the Photographic Society of Philadelphia, 1898.

Champney, James Wells. "An Artist's Opinion of Burnet's Essays on Art." *Photographic Times and American Photographer* (January 6, 1888): 9.

———. "Composition in Photographic Pictures." *Photographic Times and American Photographer* (January 14–February 4, 1887): 19.

Cheney, C. D. "Sharp Vs. Unsharp." *Photographic Times and American Photographer* (September 9, 1892): 460.

———. "Composition in Photographic Pictures." *Photographic Times and American Photographer* (January 14–February 4, 1887): 19–21, 32–33, 45, 61–62.

Clarke, J. F. Mostyn. "Art and Photography." *Philadelphia Photographer* (February 5, 1887): 77–79.

———. "The Present Value of Art in Photography." *Philadelphia Photographer* (April 21, 1888): 247–49.

"Club Types." *American Journal of Photography* (May 1893): 220–23.

Cocking, Edwin. "Few Hints about Composition Lines in Photography." *Photographic Times* (March 1880): 56–57.

———. "The Subjective and Objective of Pictorial Photography." *Photographic Times* (February 1879): 35–37.

"Contentions about Artistic Photography." *Anthony's Photographic Bulletin* (January 1895): 13.

Coonley, J. F. "The Element of Art in Connection with Photography." *Photographic Times and American Photographer* (April 1884): 185–88.

———. "Is Photography Fine Art?" *Photographic Times* (December 1880): 273.

"Correctness and Clearness." *Photographic Times* (December 1879): 276–77.

Craig, James. "The Relation of Photography and Art." *Anthony's Photographic Bulletin* (May 1899): 139–44.

———. "The Relation of Photography to Art." *Wilson's Photographic Magazine* (May 1899): 221–24.

Croce, Benedetto. "Intuition, Technique and the Classification of the Arts [1922]." In *The Philosophy of the Visual Arts*. Ed. Philip Alperson, New York: Oxford University Press, 1992.

Croughton, George Hanmer. "Art and Photography." *Philadelphia Photographer* (January 16–September 4, 1886): 57–58, 193–95, 258–60, 515–17.

———. "Art in Photography." *Photographic Times and American Photographer* (August 7, 1891): 391–93.

———. "Artists and Photographers." *American Journal of Photography* (July 1889): 225–27.

———. "The Art Side of Photography." *Photographic Times and American Photographer* (August 23, 1889): 424–26.

"Croughton, George Hanmer." George Eastman House Online Database, located at http://www.eastman.org; Internet.

Davison, George. "American Amateur Photographer Special Prize Competition, 1894." *American Amateur Photographer* (February 1895): 48–59.

———. "Composition." *Photographic Times* (July–September 1897): 317–20, 365–68, 41–13.

———. "Definition and Diffraction in Photographs." *American Amateur Photographer* (October 1895): 437–42.

———. "English Notes. Exhibitions and Judging." *American Amateur Photographer* (January 1896): 11–12.

———. "English Notes: The Recent Paris Exhibition; Critical Notices." *American Amateur Photographer* (June 1895): 256–58.

———. "Focusing." *American Amateur Photographer* (December 1894): 537–42.

———. "Impressionism in Photography." *Photographic Times and American Photographer* (January 16–February 15, 1891): 32–33, 42–44, 55–57, 66–68, 79–80.

———. "The London Exhibitions." *American Amateur Photographer* (November 1895): 482–93.

———. "The Photographic Salon." *American Amateur Photographer* (November 1893): 495–98.

———. "Pictorial Photography. The London Photographic Salon, 1894." *American Amateur Photographer* (November 1894): 489–95.

———. "To American Photographers." *American Amateur Photographer* (January 1894): 3–7.

———. "Vision and Focusing." *American Amateur Photographer* (June 1894): 251–54.

Debenham, W. E. "The Cult of Indistinctness." *Photographic Times and American Photographer* (August 21, 1891): 420–22.

Demachy, Robert. "A Few Notes on the Gum Bichromate Process." *Photographic Times* (April 1898): 147–50.

"Development of Photography." *Journal of the Franklin Institute* (April 1893): 248.

"Diffused Images." *Photographic Times and American Photographer* (July 13, 1894): 17–18.

"Distinguished Photographers of To-Day: Alfred Stieglitz." *Photographic Times and American Photographer* (December 1, 1893): 689–90.

"Distinguished Photographers of To-Day: H. P. Robinson." *Photographic Times and American Photographer* (April 6, 1894): 213–16.

Dresser, A. R. "On Art in Photography." *Photographic Mosaics, 1895* (1894): 131–35.

Eddington, Alex. "The Modern School of Photography." *Wilson's Photographic Magazine* (May 1898): 225–29.

"The Education of the Eye." *Philadelphia Photographer* (January 1880): 2.

Edwards-Ficken, H. "Picture Making." *Photographic Times and American Photographer* (April 16, 1886): 205–6.

———. "Simplicity." *Photographic Times* (February 1895): 98–99.

Ehrmann, Charles. "The Chautauqua School of Photography." *Anthony's Photographic Bulletin* (December 11, 1886): 720–23.

———. "The Chautauqua School of Photography." *Anthony's Photographic Bulletin* (October 11, 1890): 597–98.

———. "Plea for a Photographic College." *Photographic Times and American Photographer* (February 27, 1885): 99–100.
———. "Schools of Photography." *Photographic Times and American Photographer* (June 10, 1892): 305–6.
Emerson, Max. "Foregrounds in Landscape." *Wilson's Photographic Magazine* (November 1895): 493–96.
Emerson, Peter Henry. "Dr. Emerson's Recantation." *Photographic Times and American Photographer* (February 13, 1891): 76–78.
———. "Naturalistic Photography." *American Amateur Photographer* (July 1893): 301–6.
———. "Naturalistic Photography." *Photographic Times* (February 1896–April 1899); (1896): 66–69, 145–47, 178–80, 218–21, 261–64, 314–16, 376–80, 457–63, 500–4, 550–52; (1897): 38–41, 93–96, 185–88, 272–79, 333–37, 358–63, 413–16, 459–62; (1898): 20–25, 58–61, 121–24, 161–64, 222–24, 263–68, 316–20, 359–62, 411–15, 446–49, 490–96, 536–41; (1899): 43–46, 81–85, 124–29, 167–74.
———. "Naturalistic Photography." *Wilson's Photographic Magazine* (March 1895): 109–10.
———. *Naturalistic Photography for Students of the Art.* The Literature of Photography. New York: Arno Press, 1889 [1973].
———. "Photographing, a Pictorial Art." *Philadelphia Photographer* (April 17, 1886): 249–52.
———. "Photography, A Pictorial Art." *Amateur Photographer* (March 19, 1886): 138–39.
———. "Photography as a Pictorial Art." *American Journal of Photography* (April 1886): 3–6.
———. "Science and Art." *Wilson's Photographic Magazine* (June 1 1889): 323–27.
Emerson, Peter Henry, and T. F. Goodall. "Notes on Perspective Drawing and Vision." *American Journal of Photography* (August 1891): 369–74.
Erichsen, Hugo. "The Medal Question." *American Amateur Photographer* (March 1896): 98.
"The Exhibition Season." *Photographic Times* (November 1900): 487–95.
Fairman, Charles E. "The Fourth Philadelphia Photographic Salon." *American Amateur Photographer* (December 1901): 533–44.
Felix, Frederick. "A Critic Who Needs Criticizing." *Photographic Times* (December 1900): 505–7.
Ferguson, E. Lee. "Philadelphia Photographic Salon." *Photographic Times* (January 1899): 1–9.
———. "The Second Philadelphia Salon." *Photographic Times* (January 1900): 4–6.
———. "The Unphotographic Photograph." *Photographic Times* (January 1897): 1–2.
"The Fifth Annual Joint Exhibition." *Anthony's Photographic Bulletin* (May 28, 1892): 289–91.
"The Fine Arts and Photography." *American Journal of Photography* (April 1899): 190–91.
Fitz, Emma J. "Photography as a Fine Art." *American Amateur Photographer* (December 1894): 543–48.
"Frederic Hart Wilson." *Wilson's Photographic Magazine* (October 1893): 434–37.
"Fuzzitypes." *Anthony's Photographic Bulletin* (July 1900): 193–94.

Gale, James. "Is Photography Art?" *Anthony's Photographic Bulletin* (July 1899): 199.
———. "The Natural in Photography." *American Journal of Photography* (November 1889): 371–74.
Gratacap, L. P. "Impressionistic Photography." *Photographic Times* (December 1898): 530–33.
Hamerton, Philip Gilbert. "The Relation between Photography and Painting." In *Thoughts about Art*. Boston: Roberts Brothers, 1871.
Hartmann, Sadakichi. "An Art Critic's Estimate of Alfred Stieglitz." *Photographic Times* (June 1898): 257–62.
———. "Clarence F. White." *Photographic Times* (January 1900): 18–23.
———. "A Decorative Photographer, F. H. Day." *Photographic Times* (March 1900): 102–6.
———. "A Few Reflections on Amateur and Artistic Photography." *Anthony's Photographic Bulletin* (October 1898): 316–19.
———. "Frank Eugene. Painter-Photographer." *Photographic Times* (December 1899): 555–61.
———. "Gertrude Käsebier." *Photographic Times* (May 1900): 195–99.
———. "The New York Camera Club." *Photographic Times* (February 1900): 59–61.
———. "A Purist." *Photographic Times* (October 1899): 449–55.
———. "Rudolph Eickemeyer, Jr." *Photographic Times* (April 1900): 161–66.
"Has Amateur Photography 'Had Its Day.'" *Wilson's Photographic Magazine* (August 1893): 338.
Hewitt, Arthur. "The Pictorial Movement." *Photographic Times* (November 1900): 481–84.
Hines, Richard. "Artistic Photography." *American Amateur Photographer* (July 1898): 294–302.
Hinton, Alfred Horsley. "Faking and Control in Principle and Practice." *Photographic Times* (February 1898): 67–74.
———. "Individuality—Some Suggestions for the Pictorial Worker." *Photographic Times* (January 1899): 12–19.
———. "Methods of Control, and Their Influence on the Development of Artistic Photography." *Photographic Times* (September 1897): 439–43.
———. "The Objects of which Our Pictures Are Composed." *Photographic Times* (August 1897): 388–90.
———. "Phases of Landscape Photography." *Photographic Times* (December 1901): 561–65.
———. "Sharp Focus and Other Matters." *Photographic Times* (January 1897): 33–38.
"Hints to Landscape Photographers." *Photographic Times and American Photographer* (November 5, 1886): 575–76.
Hitchcock, Romyn. "Fuzzy Photography a Fad." *Photographic Times* (July 1900): 319–20.
Hodges, John A. *Pictorial Landscape Photography*. Chicago: Photo-Beacon, 1901.
Holzberg, Max. "Mechanical Aids to Artistic Photography." *American Amateur Photographer* (May 1895): 191–98.
Hopkins, Clement. "The Photograph and the Painting." *Photographic Times* (March 1898): 116–18.

Hough, E. K. "About Pictorial Photography." *Photographic Times* (April 1897): 166–69.
———. "Burnet's Art Essays and Their Use to Photographers." *Philadelphia Photographer* (January 21, 1888): 33–35.
———. "Business before Art. The Law of the Successful Photographer." *International Annual of Anthony's Photographic Bulletin* (1894): 31–33.
———. "Feeling, the Life of Art." *Philadelphia Photographer* (November 6, 1886): 662.
———. "The Ideal in Art and Its Relation to Photography." *Philadelphia Photographer* (February 5–April 16, 1887): 82–83, 152–53, 229–30.
———. "Now and Then." *Wilson's Photographic Magazine* (January 1893): 17–19.
———. "Our Ideals Govern Us." *International Annual of Anthony's Photographic Bulletin* (1892): 53–57.
———. "A Suggestion for More Art and Better Prices." *Philadelphia Photographer* (December 17, 1887): 750–52.
"Imitation." *American Journal of Photography* (July 1899): 302–4.
"The Improved Character of Photographic Exhibitions." *American Amateur Photographer* (November 1893): 519–20.
"Individuality in Art: A Conversation with William Hart." *Philadelphia Photographer* (February 1884): 57–60.
"In Nature's Image." *Wilson's Photographic Magazine* (November 1898): 509–11.
"Is Photography an Art?" *Anthony's Photographic Bulletin* (March 1898): 65–66.
"John A. Hodges and His Work." *Photographic Times* (April 1895): 218–20.
"The Joint Exhibition at New York." *American Amateur Photographer* (April 1894): 153–56.
"Joseph Pennell on Photography as Art." *Wilson's Photographic Magazine* (January 1898): 42–43.
Keiley, Joseph T. "The Decline and Fall of the Philadelphia Salon." *Camera Notes* (April 1902): 281–88.
———. "The Philadelphia Salon: Its Origin and Influence." *Camera Notes* (January 1899): 116.
———. "The Salon: Its Place, Pictures, Critics and Prospects." *Camera Notes* (January 1901): 196.
———. "The Salon: Its Purpose, Character and Lesson." *Camera Notes* (January 1900): 138.
King, Charles Rinaldo. "The Paris Photographic Salon." *Photographic Times* (August–September 1898): 339–40, 400–402.
Kingsley, Elbridge. "Art in Photography." *Photographic Times and American Photographer* (February 18–March 18, 1887): 86–87, 109–10, 122–23, 134–35.
Kommers, T. J. "The Value of Amateur Photography." *Photographic Times* (May 1899): 224.
Kupper, L. V. "My Aims and Methods in Landscape Work." *Wilson's Photographic Magazine* (April 1896): 150–51.
"La Farge on Art." *American Journal of Photography* (February 1895): 78–81.
Lambert, F. C. "Atmosphere and Distance." *Photographic Times and American Photographer* (December 5, 1890): 601–2.
———. "Concentration." *Anthony's Photographic Bulletin* (August 27, 1892): 488–90.

———. "A Few Hints on Composition." *Photographic Times and American Photographer* (January 1, 1892): 10.
———. "A Few Thoughts on the Nature and Use of Criticism." *Anthony's Photographic Bulletin* (February 13, 1892): 74–78.
———. "Genius and Photography." *Photographic Times and American Photographer* (August 15, 1890): 404–6.
———. "Imagination." *Photographic Times and American Photographer* (December 30, 1892): 673–76.
———. "Imagination and Photography." *Photographic Times* (September 1896): 438–41.
———. "On the Choice of Subject." *International Annual of Anthony's Photographic Bulletin* (1895): 212–13.
———. "Our Pictorial Failures." *Photographic Times and American Photographer* (December 1, 1893): 697–99.
———. "The Photographic Salon of 1897." *Anthony's Photographic Bulletin* (December 1897): 379–83.
———. "Pictorial Composition in Outdoor Work." *Wilson's Photographic Magazine* (March 1901): 120–26.
———. "Preliminary Experiments in Pinhole Photography." *International Annual of Anthony's Photographic Bulletin* (1894): 47–51.
"Landscape." *American Journal of Photography* (June 1899): 268–72.
"The Legitimacy of Handwork in Photography." *Photographic Times and American Photographer* (November 16, 1894): 323–25.
Le Plungeon, Augustus. "Photography Not an Art." *Photographic Times and American Photographer* (August 28, 1885): 495.
Leyde, F. "Professionals and Amateurs and Their Relation to Artistic Photography." *Philadelphia Photographer* (December 1883): 394–96.
Macbeth, Norman. "An Early Taste for Art: Its Training." *Photographic Times and American Photographer* (January 1883): 19–24.
Maclean, Hector. "A Plague of Medals." *American Journal of Photography* (January 1893): 29–30.
———. "Two Chief Photographic Exhibitions of the Year." *Photographic Times* (January–February 1897): 3–10, 69–76.
Madder, Max. "Independence in Photography." *American Amateur Photographer* (September 1895): 391–95.
———. "Photography with a Purpose." *American Amateur Photographer* (October 1895): 442–44.
Maskell, Alfred. "On Pictorial Photography—The Old and the New." *Anthony's Photographic Bulletin* (September 1895): 293–96.
———. "On Pictorial Photography; The Old and the New." *Photographic Times* (October 1895): 245–47.
McManus, B. F. "Amateur Photographers." *Wilson's Photographic Magazine* (May 17, 1890): 296–98.
———. "Art—Its Relation to Photography." *Photographic Times and American Photographer* (June 10, 1892): 307–8.
———. "The Critics Criticized." *Wilson's Photographic Magazine* (June 6, 1891): 335–36.
———. "Picture-Making and How It Should Be Practiced." *Photographic Times and American Photographer* (June 3, 1892): 293–94.

"Miss Catharine Weed Barnes." *Photographic Times and American Photographer* (August 29, 1890): 423.
Mitchell, Charles L. "The Third Philadelphia Photographic Salon." *American Amateur Photographer* (December 1900): 560–68.
Moran, John. "Reflections on Art." *Philadelphia Photographer* (1875): 294–95.
———. "The Relation of Photography to the Fine Arts." *Philadelphia Photographer* (1865): 33–35.
———. "Thoughts on Art, Nature, and Photography." *Philadelphia Photographer* (1875): 179–81.
"Moran, John." George Eastman House Online Database, located at http://www.eastman.org; Internet.
Moritzen, Julius. "A Photographic Salon with a Purpose." *American Amateur Photographer* (March 1898): 98–104.
———. "A Photographic Salon with a Purpose—First Annual Exhibition of the Pittsburg Amateur Photographers' Society." *Anthony's Photographic Bulletin* (April 1898): 121–23.
"Mr. Champney's Views on the Choice of Subject." *Philadelphia Photographer* (January 15, 1887): 59–60.
"Mr. Geo. Barker's Views of Niagara Falls and Florida." *Philadelphia Photographer* (August 7, 1886): 475–76.
Murray, Robert. "A Few Hints to Amateur Landscape Photographers." *Photographic Times* (May 1880): 102–6.
"A National Collection." *American Amateur Photographer* (July 1896): 279–82.
"Naturalistic Photography." *American Journal of Photography* (August 1899): 392–96.
"Naturalistic Photography." *Wilson's Photographic Magazine* (March 1895): 109–11.
"'Naturalistic Photography.' by P. E. Emerson." *The Photographic Times and American Photographer* (April 26, 1889): 214.
Needham, C. A. "Picturesque Photography." *Photographic Times and American Photographer* (February–July 1884): 82–83, 137–39, 195–96, 251–53, 317–18, 369–70.
Nicol, John. "A Plea for the National Recognition of Photography." *Anthony's Photographic Bulletin* (January 1894): 30–32.
Obermeyer, Joseph. "The Second Annual Members' Exhibition of Photographs. Held by the Society of Amateur Photographers of New York." *American Amateur Photographer* (April 1895): 163–65.
"Obituary [Ehrmann]." *Wilson's Photographic Magazine* (December 1894): 560.
"The Old Masters: Their Productions and Our Reproductions." *Anthony's Photographic Bulletin* (September 1899): 261–62.
"On Composition in Photography." *Philadelphia Photographer* (December 1884): 365–67.
"On Some Methods of Suppression and Modifications in Pictorial Photography." *Photographic Times and American Photographer* (July 27, 1894): 61–64.
"On the Ground-Glass." *Wilson's Photographic Magazine* (January 1893): 1–4, 195.
"On the Ground-Glass." *Wilson's Photographic Magazine* (June 1895): 241–42.
"On the Ground-Glass." *Wilson's Photographic Magazine* (May 1895): 195.
"On the Ground-Glass." *Wilson's Photographic Magazine* (March 1896): 98–100.
"Our Picture [Croughton]." *Philadelphia Photographer* (May 1, 1886): 284–86.

"The Outing of the New York Societies." *Anthony's Photographic Bulletin* (September 24, 1887): 545–47.

"Painting and Photography." *American Journal of Photography* (June 1885): 3–4.

Pancoast, Charles R. "A Philadelphian's Review of the Recent New York Seventh Annual Exhibition." *American Amateur Photographer* (October 1894): 472–76.

———. "The Second Photographic Salon at Philadelphia." *American Amateur Photographer* (December 1899): 514–22.

Patrick, John C. "An Artist Is Always a Student." *Philadelphia Photographer* (March 1884): 65–66.

Pennell, Joseph. "Is Photography among the Fine Arts?" *Contemporary Review* (1897): 824–36. Also published in *Living Age* (January 1, 1898): 99–108.

"The Philadelphia Exhibition." *Anthony's Photographic Bulletin* (February 13, 1886): 70–74.

"The Philadelphia Photographic Salon." *American Amateur Photographer* (December 1898): 548–54.

"The Philadelphia Photographic Salon." *American Journal of Photography* (January 1899): 25–28.

"The Philadelphia Photographic Salon." *Wilson's Photographic Magazine* (December 1898): 529–31.

"The Philadelphia Photographic Salon." *Wilson's Photographic Magazine* (December 1901): 488.

"The Philadelphia Salon." *Wilson's Photographic Magazine* (December 1899): 565–66.

"The Philadelphia Salon as It Appeared to an Observer." *Anthony's Photographic Bulletin* (December 1900): 368–69.

"Philosophy of Art." *American Journal of Photography* (August 1893): 348–49.

"Photographers' and Artists' Mutual Benefit Association." *Anthony's Photographic Bulletin* (July 27, 1889): 439.

"Photographic Exhibitions." *Anthony's Photographic Bulletin* (April 12, 1890): 193–95.

"Photographic Impressionism." *Wilson's Photographic Magazine* (April 1896): 168–70.

"The Photographic Society of Philadelphia [awards at joint exhibition]." *Anthony's Photographic Bulletin* (May 13, 1893): 284–85.

"A Photographic Tour." *American Journal of Photography* (July 1893): 335.

"Photography and Art Criticism." *American Journal of Photography* (August 1886): 1–2.

"Photography as an Art." *Photographic Mosaics, 1887* (1886): 93–98.

"Photography as an Educator." *Anthony's Photographic Bulletin* (July 8, 1893): 385–87.

"Photography Not an Art." *Photographic Times and American Photographer* (August 14, 1885): 468.

"Photography, Past Present and Future." *American Amateur Photographer* (September 1900): 404–5.

"Photography: Should It Be Classed among the Fine Arts?" *Photographic Times* (July 1880): 148–49.

"Photography-The Science and the Art." *American Journal of Photography* (June 1890): 173–74.

"Pictorial Photography." *American Journal of Photography* (January 1900): 34–38.
"Pictorial Photography." *Wilson's Photographic Magazine* (June 1899): 267–68.
"The Pittsburgh Salon." *American Amateur Photographer* (March 1899): 96–106.
"A Plea for Imperfection." *Wilson's Photographic Magazine* (May 1898): 224–25.
"Practical Essays on Art. By John Burnet." *Philadelphia Photographer* (June 2, 1888): 333–34.
"The Present Aspect of Amateur Photography." *American Amateur Photographer* (July 1889): 5.
Price, Lake. "Art Culture in Photography." *American Journal of Photography* (January 1889): 17–20.
Princep, Valentine. "The Influence of Photography on Art." *Anthony's Photographic Bulletin* (September 1898): 272–74.
Pringle, Andrew. "Art Education." *Philadelphia Photographer* (July 7, 1888): 390–91.
———. "Figures in Landscape Photography." *Photographic Times and American Photographer* (February 24, 1888): 88–90.
———. "Mr. Macbeth on Legitimate Photography." *Philadelphia Photographer* (April 16, 1887): 245–46.
———. "Thoughts on Our Art." *Photographic Times and American Photographer* (January 18–February 22, 1889): 27–28, 91–92.
"Professional Versus Amateur." *Anthony's Photographic Bulletin* (November 1899): 325–26.
Punnett, Milton B. "A School of Photography." *American Journal of Photography* (January 1895): 3–5. Also published in *International Annual of Anthony's Photographic Bulletin* (1894): 221–22; and *Photographic Times* (February 1898): 65–67.
Randall, Herbert. "The Application of Art Principles." *Wilson's Photographic Magazine* (July 1896): 329–30.
———. "The Artist." *Photographic Mosaics, 1900* (1899): 142–43.
———. "A Plea for High Art in Photography." *Wilson's Photographic Magazine* (May 1896): 219–20.
Rau, Carl. "Art and Photography." *Photographic Times* (May 1898): 204–5.
———. "Correct Delineation." *Photographic Times* (January 1898): 12–13.
Rau, William H. "How I Photograph Railroad-Scenery." *Photo-Era* (June 1916): 261–66.
———. "A Journey through Arabia Petra with the Camera." *American Journal of Photography* (June–August 1887): 94–96, 118–21, 137–40.
———. "Photographic Experiences in the East." *Philadelphia Photographer* (1882–83); (1882): 149–51, 181–85, 198–02, 243–46, 342–44; (1883): 24–27, 57–59, 88–90, 123–25, 221–22, 371–74.
———. "Photographing a World's Fair." *Photographic Times* (December 1905): 539–45.
———. "Photographing the Transit of Venus in 1874." *American Journal of Photography* (October 1899): 452–59.
———. "Railroad Photography." *American Journal of Photography* (April 1897): 169–76.
———. "A Trip with the Roll Holder through Belgium, Germany and Switzerland." *American Journal of Photography* (July 1886): 10–14.
———. "With the 'Dry' in New Mexico." *Philadelphia Photographer* (December 1881): 363–64.

"Report of the Exhibition Committee." *American Amateur Photographer* (November 1893): 526–28.
Robinson, Edward A. "Then and Now." *Photographic Times and American Photographer* (April 1883): 177–79.
Robinson, Henry Peach. "Aim High." *Photographic Times* (September 1896): 425–26.
———. "The Application of Art to Photography." *Anthony's Photographic Bulletin* (February 13, March 25, June 25, July 23, August 13, 1892): 78–81, 168–72, 368–71, 429–32, 457–60.
———. "Art in Photography." *Photographic Times and American Photographer* (April 26, 1889): 207–208.
———. "Burnet's Essays on Art." *Philadelphia Photographer* (February 18, 1888): 97–99.
———. "Dame Nature." *Photographic Times* (May 1895): 307.
———. "Definition." *Wilson's Photographic Magazine* (October 19, 1889): 614–16.
———. "Digressions. The Picturesque and the Beautiful." *Photographic Times* (January 1897): 41–43.
———. "The English Salon." *Wilson's Photographic Magazine* (November 1894): 518–21.
———. "Foregrounds." *Photographic Times* (July 1895): 1–3.
———. "The Genesis of a Picture." *Philadelphia Photographer* (August 1884): 233–36.
———. "If You Want to Make Pictures." *Photographic Mosaics, 1892* (1891): 125–27.
———. "Individuality in Photography." *Wilson's Photographic Magazine* (August 6, 1892): 468–70.
———. *Letters on Landscape Photography. Scovill's Photographic Series, 27*. New York: Scovill, 1888. Reprint, New York: Arno Press, 1973.
———. "Letters on Landscape, Addressed to an American Friend." *Photographic Times and American Photographer* (June 17–December 30, 1887): 310–12, 345–47, 394–96, 441–42, 454–55, 492–94, 538–40, 600–601, 641–43, 665–68.
———. "Naturalism and Photography." *Philadelphia Photographer* (November 20, 1886): 693–94.
———. "The New Movement in England." *Anthony's Photographic Bulletin* (January 1894): 8–10.
———. "Our Aims and End." *Anthony's Photographic Bulletin* (November 1894): 355–37.
———. "Paradoxes of Art, Science and Photography." *Photographic Times and American Photographer* (June 24–July 1, 1892): 331–32, 339–41.
———. "The Photographer's Status." *Wilson's Photographic Magazine* (May 1899): 224–25.
———. "Roundabout Papers." *Wilson's Photographic Magazine* (September 17–November 19, 1892): 549–51, 593–95, 658–60.
———. "The Study of Nature." *Anthony's Photographic Bulletin* (December 12, 1891): 721–23.
———. "The Transition Period." *Wilson's Photographic Magazine* (November 7, 1891): 641–44.
———. "Who Should Have the Honor?" *Anthony's Photographic Bulletin* (December 26, 1885): 743–45.

Root, Enoch. "Artistic Spirit in Photography." *Philadelphia Photographer* (January 15, 1887): 33–35.

———. "Burnet's Art Essays." *Philadelphia Photographer* (February 4, 1888): 88–89.

———. "Photography as a Fine Art." *Philadelphia Photographer* (August 4, 1888): 475–78.

———. "Photography as a Fine Art." *Photographic Times and American Photographer* (July 20, 1888): 341–43.

Root, Marcus Aurelius. *The Camera and the Pencil.* Philadelphia: J. B. Lippincott, 1864. Reprint, Pawlet, Vt.: Helios, 1971.

"Rudolph Eickemeyer, Jr., and His Work." *Photographic Times* (February 1895): 71–78.

Ruskin, John. *Modern Painters.* Vol. 5 of *The Works of John Ruskin.* London: George Allen, 1904.

Ryder, J. F. "Palette vs. Camera." *Photographic Mosaics, 1900* (1899): 261–64.

"Salonistic." *American Journal of Photography* (September 1899): 425–29.

Sawyer, George A. "Naturalistic Photography." *Photographic Times* (June 1895): 358–59.

"Seeing Natural Scenery with Photographic Effect." *Photographic Times and American Photographer* (October 9, 1885): 573–74.

The Sixth Joint Annual Exhibition of the Boston Camera Club, the New York Society of Amateur Photographers and the Photographic Society of Philadelphia. Philadelphia, n.p.: 1893.

"The Sixth Joint Exhibition." *American Journal of Photography* (May 1893): 212–19.

Smith, Xanthus. "Advice to Landscape Photographers." *American Journal of Photography* (July 1892): 315–19.

———. "Aerial Perspective." *American Journal of Photography* (January 1893): 7–10.

———. "Aesthetics and Photography." *Philadelphia Photographer* (April 17, 1886): 225–27.

———. "Art for Photographers." *Philadelphia Photographer* (February 18, 1888): 120–21.

———. "Artistic Work on Negatives." *American Journal of Photography* (January 1894): 15–18.

———. "Atmosphere and Effect." *Photographic Times* (February 1895): 68–70.

———. "Careless Versus Careful Work." *American Journal of Photography* (March 1893): 123–27.

———. "Choice of Subject." *Photographic Times* (November 1895): 284–85.

———. "Composition." *American Journal of Photography* (March 1888): 51–53.

———. "Composition." *Philadelphia Photographer* (January 16–February 20, 1886): 50–53, 97–101.

———. "Cutting Prices." *American Journal of Photography* (November 1890): 309–11.

———. "The Danger of Cheapening Art." *American Journal of Photography* (October 1892): 441–44.

———. "Effect in Art." *Photographic Mosaics, 1894* (1893): 241–45.

———. "The Fascinations of Photography." *American Journal of Photography* (January 1886): 4–6.

———. "Focusing." *American Journal of Photography* (February 1891): 59–61.
———. "The Growing Importance of the Photographic Art." *Philadelphia Photographer* (June 4, 1887): 332–35.
———. "Haze." *Photographic Mosaics, 1900* (1899): 214–17.
———. "The Higher Refinements in Development." *American Journal of Photography* (November 1892): 493–95.
———. "Hints on Composition and Selection of Subject." *Photographic Times and American Photographer* (June 3–10, 1887): 290–91, 302–3.
———. "Hints to Amateurs." *Photographic Mosaics, 1885* (1884): 99–102.
———. "Illustration Better than Precept." *Photographic Mosaics, 1898* (1897): 228–31.
———. "Impressionism in Art." *American Journal of Photography* (May 1892): 201–5.
———. "Keep up Your Prices." *American Journal of Photography* (May 1894): 206–8.
———. "Landscape Art." *American Journal of Photography* (March 1891): 106–8.
———. "A Neglected Art." *American Journal of Photography* (June 1893): 255–60.
———. "Outdoor Work." *Wilson's Photographic Magazine* (May 1898): 209–13.
———. "Photography a Fine Art." *Photographic Mosaics, 1886* (1885): 95–98.
———. "Photography and Art." *Photographic Times and American Photographer* (April 10, 1885): 184.
———. "Poetry in Landscape." *American Journal of Photography* (January 1887): frontispiece, 1–2.
———. "Proper Height for the Horizon." *Photographic Mosaics, 1895* (1894): 143–46.
———. "'Realistic Photography'." *American Journal of Photography* (November 1891): 494–95.
———. "Rembrandt Lighting." *American Journal of Photography* (July 1894): 296–300.
———. "'Self-Praise No Recommendation'." *American Journal of Photography* (July 1893): 324–27.
———. "Skies in Landscapes." *American Journal of Photography* (May 1891): 193–95.
Snelling, Alice Lee. ["Anti-Kodak Photographers."] *Wilson's Photographic Magazine* (January 17, 1891): 47–48.
Snow, C. Ashleigh. "The Beautiful—How to See It." *Wilson's Photographic Magazine* (July 1896): 294–99.
———. "Painter-Like Pictures, and How to Make Them." *Photographic Mosaics, 1898* (1897): 147–58.
———. "Picture-Making." *Anthony's Photographic Bulletin* (February 1897): 45–46.
———. "Pictures by Photography." *Wilson's Photographic Journal* (June 1897): 259–61.
"Society News. Society of Amateur Photographers of New York." *American Amateur Photographer* (January 1896): 30.
"Some Model Blanks." *Philadelphia Photographer* (February 1884): 60.
"Some Views on Photography. By a Painter." *American Amateur Photographer* (January 1896): 31–35.
Sperry, George B. "Art or Technique." *Photographic Mosaics, 1891* (1890): 253–55.
———. "The Dignity of the Profession." *Photographic Mosaics, 1899* (1898): 159–65.

———. "The Education of the Public." *Wilson's Photographic Magazine* (October 1898): 433–34.
———. "A New Era." *Photographic Mosaics, 1896* (1895): 135–37.
———. "The Use and Abuse of Artistic Lighting." *Wilson's Photographic Magazine* (April–July 1899): 145–47, 257–61, 316–18.
Stieglitz, Alfred. "The American Photographic Salon." *American Annual of Photography and Photographic Times Almanac* (1896): 27.
———. "American Photography at the Paris Exposition." *American Amateur Photographer* (September 1900): 411–14.
———. "The Joint Exhibition at Philadelphia." *American Amateur Photographer* (May–June 1893): 201–8, 249–54.
———. "Painters on Photographic Juries." *American Amateur Photographer* (July 1902): 311–34.
———. "Pictorial Photography in the United States." *Photograms of the Year* (1896): 43–44.
———. "A Plea for a Photographic Art Exhibition." *American Annual of Photography and Photographic Times Almanac* (1895): 27.
———. "A Plea for Art Photography in America." *Photographic Mosaics, 1892* (1891): 135–37.
———. "The Seventh Annual Joint Exhibition." *American Amateur Photographer* (May 1894): 209–19.
Stillman, William James. *The Acropolis of Athens; Illustrated Picturesquely and Architecturally in Photography*. London: F. S. Ellis, 1870.
———. "Advice to Amateurs Travelling." *British Journal Photographic Almanac* (1879): 79–82.
———. "The Aesthetic Side of Photography." *Photographic Times and American Photographer* (May 24, 1889): 256–57.
———. "Ancient and Modern Art. A Word to Mr. Edwards-Ficken." *Photographic Times and American Photographer* (September 12, 1890): 454–56.
———. "Art and Photography." *Photographic Times* (January 3, 1890): 4–7.
———. "The Art in It." *Photographic Times and American Photographer* (March 19–April 2, 1886): 156–57, 165–67, 177–78.
———. "The Art in Photography." *Photographic Times and American Photographer* (June 21–28, 1889): 306–9, 316–18.
———. "Artistic Photography." *British Journal Photographic Almanac* (1872): 106–10.
———. "The Art Side of Photography." *Photographic Times and American Photographer* (May 3, 1889): 217–20.
———. *Billy and Hans, My Squirrel Friends; a True Story*. Portland, Maine: Thomas B. Moser, 1914.
———. "Country Correspondence-Adirondack Woods, Sept. 13th." *The Crayon* (October 1859): 321–22.
———. "General Hints for Field Photography." *Photographic Times and American Photographer* (January 1, 1886): 3–5.
———. "Hints on Out-of-Door Photography." *Photographic Times and American Photographer* (September 25, 1885): 546–47.
———. "Naturalistic Photography." *Photographic Times and American Photographer* (May 9–23, 1890): 222–24, 236–37, 247–51.
———. "The Nature and Use of Beauty." *The Crayon* (January–July 1856): 1–4, 33–36, 65–67, 97–99, 129–32, 161–62, 193–95.

———. *Photographic Studies by William James Stillman. Part 1. The Forest. Adirondack Woods*. Boston: J. W. Black, 1860.
———. "Photography." *The Crayon* (March 14, 1855): 170.
———. "Photography and Art." *Photographic Times and American Photographer* (January 2, 1885): 1–2.
———. "Photography and Art." *Photographic Times and American Photographer* (September 10, 1886): 479–80.
———., ed. *Poetic Localities of Cambridge*. Boston: James R. Osgood, 1876.
"The Story of the Photographic Times." *Photographic Times and American Photographer* (December 15, 1893): 725–28.
"Studies by Frank M. Sutcliffe." *Wilson's Photographic Magazine* (July 1893): 299–302.
"Style and Individuality." *American Journal of Photography* (May 1899): 197–200.
"A Summer Art School." *Wilson's Photographic Magazine* (August 1893): 382.
"Sunlight and Shadow." *Wilson's Photographic Magazine* (November 1897): 502–5.
Sutcliffe, Frank M. "How to Look at Photographs." *Anthony's Photographic Bulletin* (September 10, 1892): 537–39.
Swift, W. B. "The Chance Picture at the Photographic Salon of 1899." *Wilson's Photographic Magazine* (March 1900): 102–3. Also published as "A Chance Picture in the Photographic Salon." *American Journal of Photography* (February 1900): 69–71.
———. "Henry Peach Robinson." *Photographic Times* (May 1901): 193–95.
———. "What the Landscape-Worker Should Look for Before He Sets Up His Instrument." *Wilson's Photographic Magazine* (March 1897): 106–7.
———. "A Word about Ideals in Picture-Making and the Value of Art Study." *Photographic Mosaics, 1898* (1897): 172–77.
Taylor, J. Traill. "Artificial Atmosphere and Its Uses." *Photographic Times and American Photographer* (April 1884): 171–72.
———. "General Notes [Photographer or Artist]." *Photographic Times and American Photographer* (December 1883): 640.
———. "How to Take Artistic Landscapes." *Photographic Times and American Photographer* (June 1883): 245–46.
———. "The Influence of Amateurs." *Photographic Times and American Photographer* (June 1883): 279–80.
———. "Photographic Matters Connected with America." *Photographic Times and American Photographer* (November 1883): 598–602.
———. "Photography Not a Fine Art." *Photographic Times and American Photographer* (October 1883): 521–22.
Tramoh, Robert T. "Thoughts about Amateurs." *Philadelphia Photographer* (June 1884): 172–73.
Treat, A. J. "The Application of Certain Elements of the Beautiful to the Work of the Camera." *Photographic Mosaics, 1892* (1891): 144–47.
———. "The Artistic Feeling." *Wilson's Photographic Magazine* (December 7, 1889): 725–28.
———. "Burnet on the Pacific Coast." *Philadelphia Photographer* (March 3, 1888): 140.
———. "Fine Art and Photography." *Philadelphia Photographer* (December 17, 1887): 743–45.

———. "Impressionism in Photography." *American Amateur Photographer* (January 1891): 1–7.
———. "Some Art Principles Applied to Photography." *Philadelphia Photographer* (April 7–May 19, 1888): 195–200, 274–76, 290–98.
"Unfrequented Paths for New York Artists." *Photographic Times and American Photographer* (August 28, 1885): 493–94.
"The Uses of Photography in the Railway World." *Photographic Times and American Photographer* (April 10, 1885): 191.
Van Loo, Leon. "Photography. What Are Its Possibilities in the Art Field Compared with Those of Painting?" *American Amateur Photographer* (June 1895): 267–70.
Véron, Eugène. *Aesthetics*. Trans. W. H. Armstrong. London: Chapman and Hall, 1879.
Wade, Elizabeth Flint. "Artistic Pictures. Suggestions How to Make Them." *American Amateur Photographer* (October 1893): 441–47.
Wallace, Ellerslie. "Artistic Photography in 1900." *Photographic Times* (April 1901): 174–75.
———. "Focusing in Landscape Photography." *American Journal of Photography* (April 1890): 101–2.
———. "Photographic Critics." *American Journal of Photography* (April 1888): 75–76.
———. "Photography, Art, and Business." *American Journal of Photography* (February 1885): 1–3.
———. "Selection of Out-Door Subjects." *Photographic Mosaics, 1884* (1883): 48–51.
Wardlaw, S. D. "Amateurs Kill the Business." *Anthony's Photographic Bulletin* (April 11, 1885): 205–6.
"Washington Art Photographic Salon, 1896." *American Amateur Photographer* (June 1896): 232–37.
"Washington Irving Adams." *Wilson's Photographic Magazine* (April 1894): 148–51.
"Washington Salon and Art Photographic Exhibition of 1896." *Photographic Times* (May 1896): 247–48.
Welford, Walter D. "Artistic Photography and Wholesale Development." *Photographic Times* (December 1896): 578–80.
———. "Individuality Vs. Standards." *Photographic Times* (December 1898): 570–72.
———. "Photographic Namby-Pambyism." *American Journal of Photography* (April 1892): 164–66.
———. "Thoughts on Photographic Societies." *American Journal of Photography* (December 1895): 556–61; (1896): 29.
Werner, A. "Photography in Its Pictorial Aspect." *Wilson's Photographic Magazine* (December 1898): 531–35.
"What is Art?" *Photographic Mosaics, 1885* (1884): 124–25.
White, T. Lloyd. "Camera and Brush." *American Journal of Photography* (June 1900): 287–88.
Whittet, Robert. "Art in Photography and the Choice of Titles." *Photographic Times* (February 1896): 73–75.

"William Henry Jackson-Landscape Photographer." *Wilson's Photographic Magazine* (May 1893): 228–31.
"William J. Stillman." *Photographic Times and American Photographer* (September 1887): 451–453.
Wilson, Edward L. "The Advantages of Art Education." *Photographic Times and American Photographer* (March 30, 1888): 145–46.
———. "Art-Training and Photographic Art." *Philadelphia Photographer* (March 1881): 71–73.
———. "'The Beautiful and Agreeable' in Art." *Philadelphia Photographer* (December 17, 1887: 738–40.
———. "Considerations on the Present Status of Photography." *Philadelphia Photographer* (February 1882): 42–45.
———. "The Department of Art." *Philadelphia Photographer* (January 2–October 2, 1886): 21–23, 131–35, 289–92, 354–56, 579–83.
———. "The Dignity of Photographic Art." *Philadelphia Photographer* (August 1885): 229–31.
———. "Echoes from the Orient." *Philadelphia Photographer* (March–December 1882): 65–69, 98–101, 131–35, 161–65, 193–98, 225–29, 358–61; (January–October 1883): 18–22, 50–53, 76–78, 150–53, 168–71, 199–200, 243–45, 329–31.
———. "Expression in Outdoor Work." *Wilson's Photographic Magazine* (November 1894): 499–502.
———. "A Few Hints Backward." *Photographic Mosaics, 1888* (1887): 9–42.
———. "Is Photography Art?" *Philadelphia Photographer* (December 1883): 393–94.
———. "A Photographic Institute and Home for America." *Wilson's Photographic Magazine* (November 1, 1890): 667–68.
———. "Photographing the Earth." *Wilson's Photographic Magazine* (May 1894): 202–8.
———. "The Progress of Photography during 1892." *Photographic Mosaics, 1892* (1891): 9–124.
———. "Redeveloping the Year Last Past." *Photographic Mosaics, 1891* (1890): 9–112.
———. "Taste." *Philadelphia Photographer* (March 1883): 70–73.
———. "Tracing over Old Lines," *Photographic Mosaics, 1889* (1888): 9–26.
———. "A Tribute to the Memory of Washington Irving Adams." *Wilson's Photographic Magazine* (February 1896): 63–65.
———. "Variety, Individuality, and Invention." *American Journal of Photography* (May 1893): 228–30.
Wilson, Frederic Hart. "Choice of View in Landscape Photography." *Wilson's Photographic Magazine* (April 5, 1890): 214–16.
———. "Is Photography Art?" *Photographic Times and American Photographer* (July 9, 1886): 359–61.
———. "Photograph or Picture?" *Photographic Times and American Photographer* (June 7–14, 1889): 281–83, 293–94.
———. "A Plea for Imperfection." *Wilson's Photographic Magazine* (June 6, 1891): 336–37.
———. "Where the Kodaks Come From." *Wilson's Photographic Magazine* (October 19, 1889): 609–10.
"W. J. Stillman." *Photographic Times* (August 1901): 377–78.

Woodbury, Walter. "The American Institute Photographic Salon, 1899." *Photographic Times* (January 1900): 26–28.

———. "Some Random Notes on the Philadelphia Salon." *Photographic Times* (January 1900): 7–9.

Wright, Theodore H. "The Salon." *American Amateur Photographer* (November 1893): 55–56.

Yellott, Osborne I. "Practical Pinhole Photography." *Photographic Times* (February 1900): 49–54.

———. "The Rule or Ruin School of Photography." *Photo Era* (November 1901): 164.

———. "Third Philadelphia Photographic Salon." *Photo Era* (December 1900): 165–77.

Recent Scholarship

Andrews, Ralph. *Photographers of the Frontier West . . . 1875–1915*. Seattle: Superior, 1965.

Arnheim, Rudolf. "On the Nature of Photography." *Critical Inquiry* (September 1974): 149–61.

Aronson, Mark N. "The Old Versus the New School and the 1901 Salon." In *Pictorial Photography in Philadelphia: The Pennsylvania Academy's Salons 1898–1901*. Ed. William Inness Homer (Philadelphia: Pennsylvania Academy of the Fine Arts, 1984).

Barrow, Thomas F., Shelly Armitage, and William E. Tydeman, eds. *Reading into Photography: Selected Essays, 1959–1980*. Albuquerque: University of New Mexico Press, 1982.

Barthes, Roland. *Camera Lucida: Reflections on Photography*. Trans. Richard Howard. New York: Hill and Wang, 1981.

Bartlett, Richard A. *Great Surveys of the American West*. Norman: University of Oklahoma Press, 1962.

Bastoni, Gerald. "William Herman Rau." In *Reflections on 19th Century Pennsylvania Landscape Photography*. Bethlehem, Penn.: Lehigh University Art Galleries, 1986.

Benjamin, Walter. "The Work of Art in the Age of Mechanical Reproduction." In *Illuminations*. Trans. Harry Zohn. New York: Schocken Books, 1969.

Blaugrund, Annette, ed. *Paris 1889: American Artists at the Universal Exhibition*. Philadelphia: Pennsylvania Academy of the Fine Arts, 1989.

Bolton, Richard. *The Contest of Meaning: Critical Histories of Photography*. Cambridge: MIT Press, 1989.

Brecheen-Kirkton, R. Kent. "The Mind's Eye: A History of the Discourse on American Photography, 1902–1960." Ph.D. diss., University of Iowa, 1988.

Brey, William. "On the Rails with William H. Rau." *Photographica* (September 1988): 3–5.

———. "William H. Rau's Photographic Experiences in the East." *Stereo World* (May–June 1984): 4–11.

Brey, William, and Marie Brey. *Philadelphia Photographers 1840–1900*. Cherry Hill, N.J.: Willowdale Press, 1992.

Brown, Julie K. *Contesting Images: Photography at the World's Columbian Exposition*. Tucson: University of Arizona Press, 1994.

Browne, Turner, and Elaine Partnow. *Macmillan Biographical Encyclopedia of Photographic Artists and Innovators*. New York: Macmillan, 1983.

Buerger, Janet E. *The Last Decade: The Emergence of Art Photography in the 1890s.* Rochester: International Museum of Photography at George Eastman House, 1984.

Bunnell, Peter C. *Degrees of Guidance: Essays on Twentieth-Century American Photography.* Cambridge: Cambridge University Press, 1993.

———, ed. *A Photographic Vision: Pictorial Photography 1889–1923.* Salt Lake City: Peregrine Smith, 1980.

Burns, Sarah. *Inventing the Modern Artist: Art and Culture in Gilded Age America.* New Haven, Conn.: Yale University Press, 1996.

Collins, Kathleen, ed. *Shadow and Substance: Essays on the History of Photography in Honor of Heinz K. Henisch.* Bloomfield Hills, Mich.: Amorphous Institute Press, 1990.

Cooper, David E., ed. *A Companion to Aesthetics.* Cambridge, Mass.: Basil Blackwell, 1992.

Cotkin, George. *Reluctant Modernism: American Thought and Culture, 1880–1900.* New York: Twayne, 1992.

Crary, Jonathan. "Modernizing Vision." In *Poetics of Space: A Critical Photographic Anthology.* Ed. Steve Yates. Albuquerque: University of New Mexico Press, 1995.

———. *Techniques of the Observer: On Vision and Modernity in the Nineteenth Century.* Cambridge: MIT Press, 1990.

Crow, Thomas. *Modern Art in the Common Culture.* New Haven, Conn.: Yale University Press, 1996.

Culler, Jonathan. *Structuralist Poetics: Structuralism, Linguistics, and the Study of Literature.* Ithaca, N.Y.: Cornell University Press, 1975.

Davis, Keith. *An American Century of Photography: From Dry-Plate to Digital.* Kansas City, Mo.: Hallmark Cards, 1995.

Delaney, Michelle Anne. "The 1896 Washington Salon and Art Photography." *American Art Review* (February 1997): 110–15.

Donovan, Kevin A. *Culture and Record: Nineteenth-Century Photographers from the University of New Mexico Art Museum.* Madison: Elvehjem Museum of Art, University of Wisconsin, 1984.

Doty, Robert. *Photography in America.* New York: Whitney Museum of American Art, 1974.

Drucker, Johanna, ed. "Digital Reflections: The Dialogue of Art and Technology." *Art Journal* (fall 1997).

Earle, Edward W., ed. *Points of View: The Stereograph in America-A Cultural History.* Rochester, N.Y.: Visual Studies Workshop Press, 1979.

Edwards, Gary. *International Guide to Nineteenth-Century Photographers and Their Works, Based on Catalogues of Auction Houses and Dealers.* Boston: G. K. Hall, 1988.

Edwards, Gary, and Jo Tartt Jr. *Eastern Wilderness, Photographs 1850–1900.* Washington, D.C.: Tartt Gallery, 1990.

Ehrenkranz, Anne. *Poetic Localities: William James Stillman.* New York: Aperture, 1988.

Eisinger, Joel. "The Renaissance of American Photographic Criticism." Ph.D. diss., Indiana University, 1988.

Eldredge, Charles. *American Imagination and Symbolist Painting.* New York: Grey Art Gallery and Study Center, New York University, 1979.

Fehr, Anne B., and William Innes Homer. "The Photographic Society of Pennsylvania and the Salon Movement." In *Pictorial Photography in*

Philadelphia: The Pennsylvania Academy's Salons 1898–1901. Philadelphia: Pennsylvania Academy of the Fine Arts, 1984.

Ferber, Linda S. "'The Clearest Lens': William J. Stillman and American Landscape Painting." In *Poetic Localities: William James Stillman*. New York: Aperture, 1988.

———. "'Determined Realists': The American Association for the Advancement of Truth in Art." In *The New Path: Ruskin and the American Pre-Raphaelites*. Ed. Linda S. Ferber and William H. Gerdts. New York: Brooklyn Museum, 1985.

Ferber, Linda S., and William H. Gerdts, eds. *The New Path: Ruskin and the American Pre-Raphaelites*. New York: Brooklyn Museum, 1985.

Ferrante, Anne. "Early Photographic Images of the Smiths: A Family of Artists." *Archives of American Art Journal* (1981): 18–23.

Finkel, Kenneth. *Nineteenth Century Photography in Philadelphia: 250 Historic Prints from the Library Company of Philadelphia*. New York: Dover, 1980.

Foresta, Merry. *American Photographs: The First Century*. Washington, D.C.: National Museum of American Art, Smithsonian Institution, 1996.

Galassi, Peter. *American Photography 1890–1965 from the Museum of Modern Art New York*. New York: Museum of Modern Art, 1995.

———. *Before Photography: Painting and the Invention of Photography*. New York: Museum of Modern Art, 1981.

———. *Photo-Secession*. Washington, D.C.: Lunn Gallery, Graphics International, 1977.

Gerdts, William H. "Through the Glass Brightly: The American Pre-Raphaelites and Their Still Lifes and Nature Studies." In *The New Path: Ruskin and the American Pre-Raphaelites*. Ed. Linda S. Ferber and William H. Gerdts. New York: Brooklyn Museum, 1985.

Gernsheim, Helmut, and Alison Gernsheim. *The History of Photography from the Earliest Use of the Camera Obscura in the Eleventh Century up to 1914*. London: Oxford University Press, 1955.

Goldberg, Vicki, ed. *Photography in Print*. Albuquerque: University of New Mexico Press, 1988.

Greene, Jonathan. *Camera Work: A Critical Anthology*. New York: Aperture, 1973.

Greenhill, Gillian Barrie. "The Outsiders: The Salon Club of America and the Popularization of Pictorial Photography." Ph.D. diss., Pennsylvania State University, 1986.

Green-Lewis, Jennifer. *Framing the Victorians: Photography and the Culture of Realism*. Ithaca, N.Y.: Cornell University Press, 1996.

Greenough, Sarah. "Alfred Stieglitz and the Opponents of the Photo-Secession." *New Mexico Studies in the Fine Arts* (1977): 13–19.

———. "'Of Charming Glens, Graceful Glades, and Frowning Cliffs': The Economic Incentives, Social Inducements, and Aesthetic Issues of American Pictorial Photography, 1880–1902." In *Photography in Nineteenth-Century America*. Ed. Martha A. Sandweiss. Fort Worth, Tex.: Amon Carter Museum, 1991.

Guimond, James. *American Photography and the American Dream*. Chapel Hill: University of North Carolina Press, 1991.

Hales, Peter Bacon. "American Views and the Romance of Modernization." In *Photography in Nineteenth-Century America*. Ed. Martha A. Sandweiss. Fort Worth, Tex.: Amon Carter Museum, 1991.

———. *Silver Cities: The Photography of American Urbanization, 1839–1915.* Philadelphia: Temple University Press, 1984.

———. *William Henry Jackson and the Transformation of American Landscape.* Philadelphia: Temple University Press, 1988.

Hambourg, Maria Morris. *The Waking Dream: Photography's First Century, Selections from the Gilman Paper Company Collection.* New York: Metropolitan Museum of Art, 1993.

Harker, Margaret. *The Linked Ring: The Secession Movement in Photography in Britain, 1892–1910.* London: William Heinemann, 1979.

Hemingway, Andrew. *Landscape Imagery and Urban Culture in Early Nineteenth-Century Britain.* Cambridge: University of Cambridge Press, 1992.

History of Photography: Bibliography and Reel Guide to the Microfilm Collection. Woodbridge, Conn.: Research Publication, 1982.

Homer, William Innes. *Alfred Stieglitz and the Photo-Secession.* New York: New York Graphic Society, 1983.

———, ed. *Pictorial Photography in Philadelphia: The Pennsylvania Academy's Salons 1898–1901.* Philadelphia: Pennsylvania Academy of the Fine Arts, 1984.

Hoyle, Pamela. *The Boston Ambiance: An Exhibition of Nineteenth-Century Photographs.* Boston, n.p.: 1981.

Hull, Roger. "Rudolf Eickemeyer, Jr., and the Politics of Photography." *New Mexico Studies in the Fine Arts* (1977): 20–25.

———. "The Traditional Vision of Rudolf Eickemeyer, Jr." *History of Photography* (January–March 1986): 31–62.

Isaacs, Charles. *The Strange and the Sublime: American Photography 1850–1920.* Bethlehem, Penn.: Kemerer Museum of Decorative Arts, 1989.

Jenkins, Reese. *Images and Enterprise: Technology and the American Photographic Industry, 1839–1925.* Baltimore: Johns Hopkins University Press, 1975.

Johnson, Brooks. *Nineteenth-Century Mammoth Plates of the American West.* Norfolk, Va.: Chrysler Museum, 1979.

Johnson, Deborah. "Confluence and Influence: Photography and the Japanese Print in 1850." In *Readings in Nineteenth-Century Art.* Ed. Janis Tomlinson. Upper Saddle River, N.J.: Prentice Hall, 1996.

Johnson, William. *Nineteenth-Century Photography: An Annotated Bibliography, 1839–1879.* Boston: G. K. Hall, 1990.

Jussim, Estelle, and Elizabeth Lindquist-Cock. *Landscape as Photograph.* New Haven, Conn.: Yale University Press, 1985.

Keller, Ulrich F. "The Myth of Art Photography: An Iconographic Analysis." *History of Photography* (January–March 1985): 1–38.

———. "The Myth of Art Photography: A Sociological Analysis." *History of Photography* (October–December 1984): 249–75.

Kiefer, Geraldine Wojno. *Alfred Stieglitz: Scientist, Photographer, and Avatar of Modernism, 1880–1913.* New York: Garland, 1991.

Krauss, Rosalind E. "Photography's Discursive Spaces: Landscape/View." In *The Originality of the Avant-Garde and Other Modernist Myths.* Cambridge: MIT Press, 1985.

Lawton, Harry W., and George Knox, eds. *The Valiant Knights of Daguerre: Selected Critical Essays on Photography and Profiles of Photographic Pioneers.* Berkeley: University of California Press, 1978.

Lears, Jackson. *No Place of Grace: Antimodernism and the Transformation of American Culture, 1880–1920.* New York: Pantheon, 1981.

Levine, Lawrence W. *Highbrow/Lowbrow: The Emergence of Cultural Hierarchy in America*. Cambridge: Harvard University Press, 1988.

The Life and Times of Sadakichi Hartmann, 1867–1944. Riverside: University of California, 1970.

Lindquist-Cock, Elizabeth. *The Influence of Photography on American Landscape Painting, 1839–1880*. New York: Garland, 1978.

———. "Stillman, Ruskin and Rosetti: The Struggle Between Nature and Art." *History of Photography* (January 1979): 1–14.

Maddox, Jerald C. "Creative Photography 1869–1969." In *A Century of Photographs, 1846–1946*. Ed. Renata V. Shaw. Washington, D.C.: Library of Congress, 1980.

Madigan, Mary Jean. *The Photography of Rudolf Eickemeyer, Jr*. Yonkers, N.Y.: Hudson River Museum, 1972.

Margolis, Marianne Fulton. "Philadelphia Photographic Salons 1898–1901." *Image* (September 1978): 2–10.

Marien, Mary Warner. *Photography and Its Critics: A Cultural History, 1839–1900*. New York: Cambridge University Press, 1997.

Marx, Leo. *The Machine in the Garden*. New York: Oxford University Press, 1966.

Neaf, Weston, and James N. Wood. *Era of Exploration: The Rise of Landscape Photography in the American West, 1860–1885*. Buffalo and New York: Albright-Knox Art Gallery and Metropolitan Museum of Art, 1975.

Newhall, Beaumont. *The History of Photography from 1839 to the Present Day*. New York: Museum of Modern Art, 1964.

Newhall, Nancy Wynne. *P. H. Emerson: The Fight for Photography as a Fine Art*. New York: Aperture, 1975.

Novak, Barbara. "Landscape Permuted: From Painting to Photography." *Artforum* (1975): 40–45.

Orvell, Miles. "Almost Nature: The Typology of Late Nineteenth-Century American Photography." In *Multiple Views: Logan Grant Essays on Photography*. Ed. Daniel P. Younger. Albuquerque: University of New Mexico, 1991.

Ostroff, Eugene. *Western Views and Eastern Visions*. Washington, D.C.: Smithsonian Institution, 1981.

Panzer, Mary. *In My Studio: Rudolf Eickemeyer, Jr. and the Art of the Camera 1885–1930*. Yonkers, N.Y.: Hudson River Museum, 1986.

———. *Philadelphia Naturalistic Photography 1865–1906*. New Haven, Conn.: Yale University Art Gallery, 1982.

———. "William H. Rau and the Archives of Photographic History." *Afterimage* (1988): 9–11.

Perloff, Stephen. William H. Rau: *Lehigh Valley Railroad Photographs, 1899*. Bethlehem, Penn.: Lehigh University Art Galleries, 1989.

Phillips, Christopher. "The Judgment Seat of Photography." In *October: The First Decade, 1976–1986*. Ed. Douglas Crimp, Joan Copjec, Rosalind Krauss, and Annette Michelson. Cambridge: MIT Press, 1988.

Poulson, Elizabeth. "Catharine Weed Barnes Ward: Another Forgotten Victorian Photographer." History of Photography Monograph Series. Tempe: Arizona State University, 1984.

Rabb, Jane M., ed. *Literature and Photography: Interactions 1840–1990*. Albuquerque: University of New Mexico Press, 1995.

Reilly, Bernard F., Jr. "The Early Work of John Moran, Landscape Photographer." *American Art Journal* (January 1979): 65–75.

Roark, Carol E., Paula Ann Stewart, and Mary Kennedy McCabe. *Catalogue of the Amon Carter Photography Collections.* Fort Worth, Tex.: Amon Carter Museum, 1993.

Roosens, Laurent, and Luc Salu. *History of Photography: A Bibliography of Books.* London: Mansell, 1989.

Ruby, Jay. "Images of Rural America: View Photographs and Picture Postcards." *History of Photography* (October–December 1988): 327–42.

———. "The Wheelman and the Snapshooter, or, the Industrialization of the Picturesque." In *Shadow and Substance: Essays on the History of Photography in Honor of Heinz K. Henisch.* Ed. Kathleen Collins. Bloomfield Hills, Mich.: Amorphous Institute Press, 1990.

Russell Smith (1812–1896) Xanthus Smith (1839–1929) Pennsylvania Landscapes 1834–1892. Boston: Vose Galleries, 1979.

Sandweiss, Martha A. *Masterworks of American Photography: The Amon Carter Museum Collection.* Birmingham: Oxmoor House, 1982.

———, ed. *Photography in Nineteenth-Century America.* Fort Worth, Tex.: Amon Carter Museum, 1991.

Schloss, Carol. *In Visible Light, Photography and the American Writer: 1840–1940.* Oxford: Oxford University Press, 1987.

Searle, Edward E., ed. *Points of View: The Stereograph in America—A Cultural History.* Rochester, N.Y.: Visual Studies Workshop Press, 1979.

Sennett, Robert S. *The Nineteenth-Century Photographic Press: A Study Guide.* New York: Garland, 1987.

———. *Photography and Photographers to 1900: An Annotated Bibliography.* New York: Garland, 1985.

Shiff, Richard. *Cézanne and the End of Impressionism: A Study of the Theory, Technique, and Critical Evaluation of Modern Art.* Chicago: University of Chicago Press, 1984.

Smith, Henry Nash. *The Virgin Land: The American West as Myth and Symbol.* New York: Vintage, 1950.

Snyder, Joel. "Aesthetics and Documentation: Remarks Concerning Critical Approaches to the Photographs of Timothy H. O'Sullivan." In *Perspectives on Photography: Essays in Honor of Beaumont Newhall.* Ed. Peter Walsh and Thomas F. Barrow. Albuquerque: University of New Mexico Press, 1986.

———. "Picturing Vision." In *The Language of Images.* Ed. W. J. T. Mitchell. Chicago: University of Chicago Press, 1980.

———. "Territorial Photography." In *Landscape and Power.* Ed. W. J. T. Mitchell. Chicago: University of Chicago Press, 1994.

Snyder, Joel, and Doug Munson. *The Documentary Photograph as a Work of Art: American Photographs, 1860–1876.* Chicago: David and Alfred Smart Gallery, University of Chicago, 1976.

Snyder, Joel, and Neil Walsh Allen. "Photography, Vision, and Representation [1975]." In *The Philosophy of the Visual Arts.* Ed. Philip Alperson. New York: Oxford University Press, 1992.

Solomon-Godeau, Abigail. *Photography at the Dock: Essays on Photographic History, Institutions, and Practices.* Minneapolis: University of Minnesota Press, 1991.

Sternberger, Paul. "Sicklied O'er with the Pale Cast of Emasculation: Aberration and

Gender in the Critical Resistance to Late-Nineteenth-Century American Art Photography." Paper delivered at the 1999 American Culture Association Annual Conference.

Stilgoe, John R. *The Metropolitan Corridor: Railroads and the American Scene.* New Haven, Conn.: Yale University Press, 1983.

Stolnitz, Jerome. "The Aesthetic Attitude [1960]." In *The Philosophy of the Visual Arts.* Ed. Philip Alperson. New York: Oxford University Press, 1992.

Strange, Maren. *Symbols of Ideal Life: Social Documentary Photography in America, 1890–1950.* Cambridge: Cambridge University Press, 1989.

Szarkowski, John. *American Landscape.* New York: Museum of Modern Art, 1981.

———. *The Photographer and the American Landscape.* New York: Museum of Modern Art, 1963.

———. *Photography Until Now.* New York: Museum of Modern Art, 1989.

Taft, Robert. *Photography and the American Scene: A Social History, 1839–1889.* New York: Dover, 1938.

Tagg, John. *The Burden of Representation: Essays on Photographies and Histories.* Amherst: University of Massachusetts Press, 1988.

Thomas, Alan. *Time in a Frame: Photography and the Nineteenth-Century Mind.* New York: Schocken, 1977.

Trachtenberg, Alan. *Democratic Vistas: 1860–1880.* New York: Brazillier, 1970.

———. *Reading American Photographs: Images as History, Matthew Brady to Walker Evans.* New York: Hill and Wang, Noonday Press, 1990.

Travis, David. *Photography Rediscovered: American Photographs, 1900–1930.* New York: Whitney Museum of American Art, 1979.

Turner, Peter, and Richard Wood. *P. H. Emerson: Photographer of Norfolk.* Boston: David R. Goodine, 1974.

Underwood, Sandra Lee. "Charles H. Caffin: A Voice for Modernism." Ph.D. diss., Indiana University, 1981.

Varnedoe, Kirk. "The Artifice of Candor: Impressionism and Photography Reconsidered." *Art in America* (January 1980): 66–78.

Walther, Susan Danly, ed. *The Railroad in the American Landscape 1850–1950.* Wellesley, Mass.: Wellesley University Press, 1981.

Weinberg, H. Barbara. "Cosmopolitan Attitudes: The Coming of Age of American Art." In *Paris 1889: American Artists at the Universal Exhibition.* Ed. Annette Blaugrund. Philadelphia: Pennsylvania Academy of the Fine Arts, 1989.

———. "Late-Nineteenth-Century American Painting: Cosmopolitan Concerns and Critical Controversies." *Archives of American Art Journal* (1983): 19–26.

Welling, William. *Collectors' Guide to Nineteenth-Century Photographs.* New York: Macmillan, 1976.

———. *Photography in America: The Formative Years, 1839–1900.* New York: Thomas Y. Crowell, 1978.

Wolf, Daniel, ed. *The American Space: Meaning in Nineteenth-Century Landscape Photography.* Middletown, Conn.: Wesleyan University Press, 1983.

Yates, Steve, ed. *Poetics of Space: A Critical Photographic Anthology.* Albuquerque: University of New Mexico Press, 1995.

Younger, Daniel P., ed. *Multiple Views: Logan Grant Essays on Photography.* Albuquerque: University of New Mexico Press, 1991.

INDEX